Basic Quality
Improvement

Basic Quality Improvement

Susan M. Garrity

REGENTS/PRENTICE HALL
Englewood Cliffs, New Jersey 07632

Library of Congress Cataloging-in-Publication Data

Garrity, Susan.
  Basic quality improvement / Susan Garrity.
    p. cm.
  Includes index.
  ISBN 0-13-480906-8
  1. Quality control. 2. Process control—Statistical methods.
I. Title.
TS156.G39 1993
658.5'62—dc20   92-31852
                                    CIP

Acquisitions Editor: Ed Francis
Editorial/production Supervision: WordCrafters Editorial Services, Inc.
Interior Design: Patrick Walsh
Cover Design: Mary Ann Frasco
Prepress Buyer: Ilene Levy
Manufacturing Buyer: Ed O'Dougherty

 ©1993 by REGENTS/PRENTICE HALL
A Division of Simon & Schuster
Englewood Cliffs, New Jersey 07632

Printed in the United States of America

10   9   8   7   6   5   4   3   2   1

ISBN 0-13-480906-8 01

Prentice-Hall International (UK) Limited, *London*
Prentice-Hall of Australia Pty. Limited, *Sydney*
Prentice-Hall Canada Inc., *Toronto*
Prentice-Hall Hispanoamericana, S.A., *Mexico*
Prentice-Hall of India Private Limited, *New Delhi*
Prentice-Hall of Japan, Inc., *Tokyo*
Simon & Schuster Asia Pte. Ltd., *Singapore*
Editora Prentice-Hall do Brasil, Ltda., *Rio de Janeiro*

Quality is never an accident.
It is always the result of
high intention, sincere effort,
intelligent direction, and skillful execution.
It represents the wise choice
from many alternatives.

Willa A. Foster

Contents

Preface

For years, America was known as the land of plenty. Many great ideas were born in the United States and countless people in history made possible the seemingly impossible. Through this pioneering and industrious spirit, the United States emerged as the leader in providing goods and services throughout the world.

Today, however, the rules have changed. Competitors from virtually every nation around the world now offer a vast array of products and services in today's global market. Given this situation, customers have many options available to them, and they hold the power to choose which products and services they are willing to buy. Recent estimates indicate that 28 cents of every dollar is now spent on goods made outside of the United States, and 70 cents of every dollar is competing with international markets. Across the globe, organizations are committed to satisfying customer requirements in order to gain market share. Increasing pressures from global competitors are driving the need to supply high-quality goods and services to customers at competitive prices. Emerging global competition is forcing rapid and massive changes in organizations throughout the world.

To compete in today's global market, every industry—domestic and international—must provide world-class quality products and services that satisfy the customer at a competitive price. Quality improvement is the key to success and survival in today's rapidly changing world.

Quality improvement begins with an in-depth understanding of customers and processes. This book outlines the important measurement tools and methods required to improve process quality. Continuous quality improvement is the only path to increased customer satisfaction, market share, profits, and success in today's rapidly changing global economy.

Chapter 1

An Introduction

In Chapter 1 we outline the historical events that have led up to our current economic position. The chapter contains three units. In Unit 1A we explain the evolution of certain processes and techniques used to produce products and services. Unit 1B illustrates the relationship between these practices and our competitive position. In Unit 1C we introduce the solutions required to offset declining market share and examine the benefits of using new methods to improve quality. This information provides the framework required for quality improvement.

INSTRUCTIONAL OBJECTIVES

When you have completed this chapter, you will be able to:

- Identify three reasons for the emphasis placed on quantity versus quality.
- List two major drawbacks of mass inspection.
- Identify how cost increases through mass inspection.
- Define the relationship between cost and market share.
- Describe the trend of productivity and world market share.
- List two changes required for quality improvement.

LEARNING ACTIVITIES

_____1A: Where It All Began
_____1B: The Expense of Not Doing Things Right
_____1C: Building a Stronger Offense

1A: WHERE IT ALL BEGAN

After World War II ended, memories of the Great Depression faded quickly. The United States had established itself as the world's strongest and wealthiest nation. Even into the 1960s, the United States was producing more than 25% of the goods in the world and supplying 98% of the goods at home. It was an age when nothing seemed impossible. During these tremendously prosperous times, our economic growth and increasingly higher standards of living seemed endless. American factories were operating at or near full capacity. Demand for services was high. Jobs were plentiful and prosperity was an economic reality. The U.S. standard of living was unparalleled in growth. Through the years, personal income and the demand for products and services continued to grow at an increasing pace. To make matters even better, there was no serious threat of competition. We in the United States came to believe that economic growth had no limits and that our wealth was endless.

As each year passed, every sector of society sought to achieve higher standards:

- Stockholders wanted greater returns on their investments. This, in turn, forced business to concentrate on maximizing profits.
- Business leaders wanted more production to increase revenues.
- Managers wanted more production to satisfy their bosses.
- Workers wanted more money to build a better life for themselves and their families.

Each group concentrated on its own basic goals. But one of the most critical elements of business was lost along the way: *providing high-quality products and services that satisfied the needs of customers.* Given the tremendous demand for products and services, everything produced and delivered was sold. The only way to achieve higher standards, across the board, was to produce more products and deliver more services. To accomplish this, companies hired people, purchased the materials and machinery required, and developed methods and measurements to produce products and provide services. Once products and methods to deliver services were developed, periodic inspections were made to ensure that acceptable quality standards were met. Products and services that met these standards were accepted and those that did not were rejected. Rejected products and services were either reworked or scrapped.

Figure 1-1 represents the model that has been used historically to produce goods and services. This model evolved from the excessive demand for products and services. Although this model has been widely used, it has many drawbacks. Products and services produced in this manner do not take into account the importance of people, quality, safety, environment, or pride in workmanship. This model also generates tremendous waste and lost opportunities.

The waste that occurs in this process becomes evident during the *inspection* phase. It costs just as much to produce or provide bad products and services as it does to produce good ones. In addition, each rejected product or service requires additional personnel, machinery, materials, equipment, and methods. This represents a tremendous waste of the company's resources. On average, approximately 25 to 30% of sales revenues is spent on finding and fixing defects and errors. This

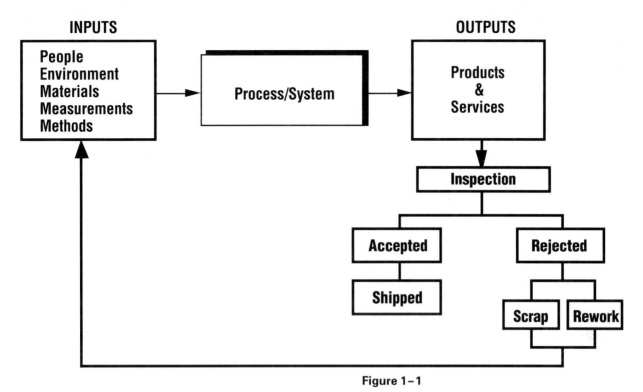

Figure 1–1

model also fails to take into account customer satisfaction. If inferior products or services are delivered to customers, dissatisfaction occurs. Once customers are dissatisfied, it is unlikely that they will want to purchase products and services from the organization again. This represents lost opportunities.

In addition to these drawbacks, mass inspection methods are not foolproof. Two of the drawbacks associated with mass inspection methods are:

1. Mass inspection is not 100% effective.
2. Mass inspection only identifies problems—it does not fix them.

Drawback 1: Mass Inspection Is Not 100% Effective. In theory, mass inspection is designed to detect all defects. In reality, this is not humanly possible or likely to occur. Many variables cannot be controlled. Some of the variables that affect the effectiveness of mass inspection are:

- Fatigue level of the inspector
- Physical and mental health of the inspector
- Boredom associated with routine inspection
- Pressure to maintain a certain level or quota of products and services
- Accuracy of measurement devices and gages
- Certain defects are difficult or impossible to detect
- Skills and expertise of each inspector varies

Based on the many uncontrollable variables that affect mass inspection, it *is not* 100% effective. The following exercise is designed to illustrate this.

Exercise: Read the following paragraph and count all the "F"'s in the paragraph. Indicate your answer in the space provided below.

THE FARMER FOUND THAT HIS FIELD OF ALFALFA HAD A CERTAIN TYPE OF FUNGUS ON IT. THE FUNGUS WAS PART OF A FAMILY OF PARASITICAL MICROBES. THE ONLY ANSWER THAT THE FARMER HAD FOUND TO FIGHT THE FEISTY FUNGUS WAS TO SPRAY HIS FIELDS WITH A TOXIC CHEMICAL THAT WAS NOT CERTIFIED. IT WAS THE ONLY METHOD THAT OFFERED HIM ANY HOPE OF SUCCESS. UNFORTUNATELY, WHEN THE FARMER BEGAN TO SPRAY HIS FIELDS, THE FEDERAL AGENT FROM THE FDA WAS IN THE AREA. THE FEDERAL AGENT'S OPINION OF THE FUNGUS WAS THAT IT WAS NOT AT A STAGE OF SIGNIFICANT CONCERN. HE OFFERED THE FARMER A CHOICE: STOP THE CONTAMINATION OF THE FLORA OF THE REGION OR FACE A FINE OF A SUBSTANTIAL AMOUNT. THE FARMER HALTED THE SPRAYING OF HIS ALFALFA FIELDS.

Answer _____

There are 47 "F"'s in the paragraph. If you were not able to locate all the "F"'s the first time around, you are not alone. Few people are able to identify all of the "F"'s on the first pass. Try this exercise once again to see if you can locate all of the "F"'s contained in the paragraph.

THE FARMER FOUND THAT HIS FIELD OF ALFALFA HAD A CERTAIN TYPE OF FUNGUS ON IT. THE FUNGUS WAS PART OF A FAMILY OF PARASITICAL MICROBES. THE ONLY ANSWER THAT THE FARMER HAD FOUND TO FIGHT THE FEISTY FUNGUS WAS TO SPRAY HIS FIELDS WITH A TOXIC CHEMICAL THAT WAS NOT CERTIFIED. IT WAS THE ONLY METHOD THAT OFFERED HIM ANY HOPE OF SUCCESS. UNFORTUNATELY, WHEN THE FARMER BEGAN TO SPRAY HIS FIELDS, THE FEDERAL AGENT FROM THE FDA WAS IN THE AREA. THE FEDERAL AGENT'S OPINION OF THE FUNGUS WAS THAT IT WAS NOT AT A STAGE OF SIGNIFICANT CONCERN. HE OFFERED THE FARMER A CHOICE: STOP THE CONTAMINATION OF THE FLORA OF THE REGION OR FACE A FINE OF A

SUBSTANTIAL AMOUNT. THE FARMER HALTED THE SPRAYING OF
HIS ALFALFA FIELDS.

                                                          Answer____

If you found all 47 "F"'s this time, you've done a terrific job. If you found
a few more "F"'s this time, but were unable to locate all 47 "F"'s ...once again,
you are not alone. Most people overlook the "F" contained in the word "of."
The following paragraph illustrates all 47 "F"'s.

THE FARMER FOUND THAT HIS FIELD OF ALFALFA HAD A	6
CERTAIN TYPE OF FUNGUS ON IT. THE FUNGUS WAS PART OF	4
A FAMILY OF PARASITICAL MICROBES. THE ONLY ANSWER	2
THAT THE FARMER HAD FOUND TO FIGHT THE FEISTY	4
FUNGUS WAS TO SPRAY HIS FIELDS WITH A TOXIC	2
CHEMICAL THAT WAS NOT CERTIFIED. IT WAS THE ONLY	1
METHOD THAT OFFERED HIM ANY HOPE OF SUCCESS.	3
UNFORTUNATELY, WHEN THE FARMER BEGAN TO SPRAY HIS	2
FIELDS, THE FEDERAL AGENT FROM THE FDA WAS IN THE	4
AREA. THE FEDERAL AGENT'S OPINION OF THE FUNGUS WAS	3
THAT IT WAS NOT AT A STAGE OF SIGNIFICANT CONCERN.	2
HE OFFERED THE FARMER A CHOICE: STOP THE	3
CONTAMINATION OF THE FLORA OF THE REGION OR FACE A	4
FINE OF A SUBSTANTIAL AMOUNT. THE FARMER HALTED	3
THE SPRAYING OF HIS ALFALFA FIELDS.	4
	47

This exercise illustrates that even when one is giving his or her full, undi-
vided attention to inspection, the human eye has a natural tendency to overlook
some things. These events are natural. As such, mass inspection is not 100% effective.

Drawback 2: Mass Inspection Only Identifies Problems—It Does Not Fix Them.

Once produced, the quality of the product or service, good or bad, is already built in. Mass inspection cannot undo what has already been done. It can
only determine if the product or service meets the quality standards. In effect,
mass inspection is only a safeguard to reduce the defects delivered to consumers.
To illustrate this point, answer the following questions.

You have a sore throat, your nose is running, and your voice is very hoarse.

- Do you need someone to tell you that you have a cold?   __ Yes   __ No
- If someone were to tell you that you have a cold, would your symptoms
  be removed once the problem was identified?   __ Yes   __ No

The answers to these questions are relatively obvious. Once you have all of the symptoms of a cold, you do not need to be told that you have one. And once the symptoms are firmly in place, the cold cannot be eliminated simply because it was detected. Only two options are available: (1) prevent colds from occurring in the first place, or (2) allow the cold to run its normal course.

The same theory holds true in any process. The only way to ensure quality is to build quality into the product and service up front: that is, to prevent defects from occurring in the first place, not by identifying if a problem exists after it has been produced. Thus: *Mass inspection does not fix quality problems; it can only identify whether or not quality problems exist.*

In short, mass inspection is not an effective way to ensure quality. Yet until competitive pressures emerged, little attention was given to these issues. Business's primary goal was to produce products and services—at any cost. The pressures to produce and maximize profits overrode all other concerns. In the process, suggestions for improvements were left unheard, people were powerless, costs increased, and inferior products and services were delivered to the customer. As profits rose, companies grew more careless and less interested in quality and customer satisfaction.

1B: THE EXPENSE OF NOT DOING THINGS RIGHT

During the "Golden Years," America enjoyed tremendous prosperity. Businesses grew wealthy, plants operated at, or near, full capacity, there was a growing demand for more service, and consumer buying seemed endless. But sweeping changes began to take place during the 1970s. Competition emerged, sales began to slump, companies lost billions of dollars, many giant corporations were on the brink of bankruptcy, small companies were folding, thousands of workers were laid off, and one by one, plants began to close. The "Golden Years" were rapidly coming to an end.

Many industries experienced tremendous economic hardship, due to increasing costs, declining productivity, and the emergence of foreign competition. The factors contributing to each aspect are described below.

Higher Costs

The methods used to produce products and services in many firms generate tremendous waste. Historically, performance was measured on the quantity, not the quality, of the products and services produced. This led to the production of many defects. Defects are a waste of the organization's productive resources and waste increases cost. Waste within the organization occurs in the following areas:

Labor.   It costs as much to produce a defect as it does to produce quality. Each defect produced represents a waste of labor.

Materials.   Depending on the severity of the problem, defects are either scrapped or reworked. Scrapped or additional materials required to remedy a problem represent a waste of materials and increase cost.

Machines. Defects represent a waste of the machinery used to produce products and services. Additional costs are also incurred if machinery is required to fix or remedy the defects produced.

Methods. Defects also generate waste in the methods and procedures used to produce a product or provide a service.

The waste of each productive resource increases costs directly. For every labor hour paid to produce a defect, another must be paid to correct the problem. Each additional resource required to find and fix defects increases the costs required to produce high-quality products and services. These additional costs have traditionally been passed on to the customer in the form of higher prices.

Basic economics have proven the relationship between price and demand: As price increases, demand decreases. Additionally, as price increases, consumers tend to look for alternatives that cost less. Basic economics govern nearly all buying decisions.

The expense of not doing things right has a domino effect that directly affects each person in our society.

When costs increase, prices increase automatically. When price increases, fewer consumers are able to buy. Businesses, in turn, make less money. When business makes less money, less production is required, and fewer people are needed. Each time someone is laid off, less money is available and this reduces one's standard of living. This domino effect is illustrated in Figure 1-2.

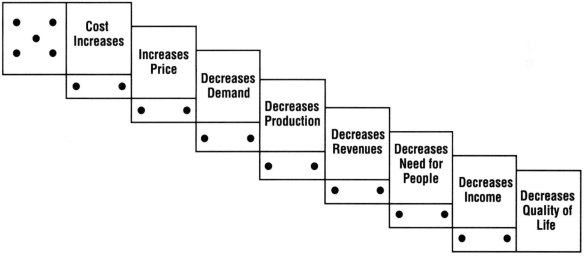

Figure 1-2

Productivity Levels

Compounding the problems created by rising costs during the 1970s, U.S. productivity was seriously declining. Much has been said about the issue of productivity throughout the years, yet few really understand the direct relationship between productivity and the economy. Declining productivity seriously affects our economic well-being. Statistics have proven that declining productivity:

• Creates excessive inflation
• Reduces standards of living
• Increases levels of unemployment and underemployment
• Severely inhibits the ability to compete

Productivity is the measure of resources (*inputs*) required to produce products and services (*outputs*). Inputs are the people, environment, materials, measurements, methods, equipment, and so on, that are utilized to produce products and services. Outputs are the final products and services produced for the consumer market. Figure 1-3 illustrates the basic productivity model.

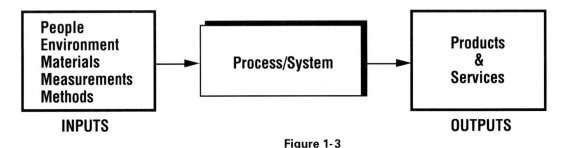

Figure 1-3

As the amount of resources (inputs) required to produce finished products and services (outputs) increases, productivity declines. That is, more resources and costs are required to produce the same level of products and services. As productivity declines, more is put into the system and less is put out by the system.

Declining productivity creates two primary problems:

1. The additional resources required to produce products and services for the market increases costs. Increased costs force prices up. This, in turn, hinders one's ability to compete effectively in the areas of cost and quality.
2. Declining levels of productivity represent lost opportunities in the market.

Overall, productivity directly affects a nation's competitive ability and market share. Three of the primary factors affecting productivity are: waste, technology, and human resources. To improve productivity, waste must be eliminated and sound investments need to be made in technology and human resource development. Improvements made in these areas reduce the amount of productive resources (inputs) required to produce finished products and services (outputs). When fewer inputs are required to produce outputs, the cost to produce goods and services declines. Reduced costs enhance the organization's ability to be more competitive in price. When price decreases, demand increases. As demand increases, prosperity also increases. Productivity improvement is critical in today's fiercely competitive global market.

Increased Competition

In 1950, the United States led the world in productivity; U.S. productivity was two and one-half times that of Germany's and almost seven times that of Japan's, as indicated in Figure 1-4. In 1966, U.S. productivity began to decline, while the productivity in other countries began to show dramatic growth. By 1979, U.S. productivity had been reduced to a little more than double that of Germany's and about one and one-half times that of Japan's. The United States remains the leader in overall productivity. Yet the rate of productivity growth in other countries exceeds the rate of growth within the United States.

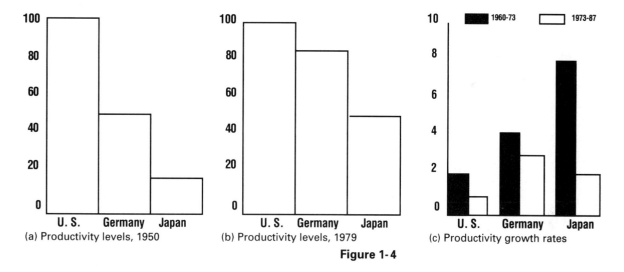

(a) Productivity levels, 1950   (b) Productivity levels, 1979   (c) Productivity growth rates

Figure 1-4

The improvements made by foreign competitors in the area of productivity have seriously threatened the U.S. position of economic leadership. Countries with higher productivity levels have two advantages. They can either obtain a greater share of the market or enjoy greater profitability. For example, if Japan's productivity level is higher than it is in the United States, Japan can obtain a greater share of the market by selling its products and services at lower prices. Or they can sell their products and services at the same price as in the United States and enjoy greater profit margins. In either event, the most productive country enjoys greater prosperity and higher standards of living.

The declining level of productivity in the United States and the continued growth of productivity in other countries have reduced U.S. competitive strength and market share, both at home and abroad. Figure 1-5 illustrates the overall decline of U.S. market share. Figure 1-5(a) illustrates the decline of U.S. manufactured goods in the United States. The percentage of goods supplied by U.S. manufacturers has dropped from 99% in 1960 to approximately 87% in 1989. Translated in everyday terms, 13 cents of every dollar spent within the United

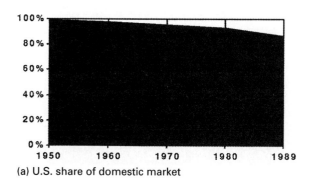

(a) U.S. share of domestic market

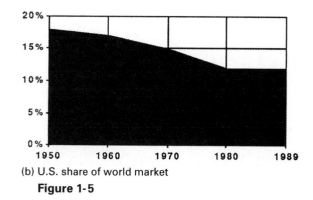

(b) U.S. share of world market

Figure 1-5

States goes to foreign competitors. Figure 1-5(b) illustrates the decline of U.S. manufactured goods supplied to other countries. The percentage of manufactured goods provided abroad has dropped from 18% in 1950 to just above 12% in 1989.

The loss of market share both at home and abroad may not seem significant. Yet measured in terms of dollars and cents, these declines represent an approximate cost of $125,000,000,000 in lost production and 2,000,000 jobs. These losses affect everyone directly or indirectly.

The graphs in Figure 1-5 represent *all* goods manufactured in the United States. Some markets have been harder hit than others. For example, take a quick look at the products listed below and see if you can determine the one thing they all have in common.

Automobiles	Cameras
Stereo	Medical equipment
Color TV sets	Hand tools
Electronic motors	Food processors
Microwave ovens	Computer chips
Machine tools	Industrial robots
Electron microscopes	Optical equipment

The one thing that all of these products have in common is that U.S. world market share dropped 50% during the 1970s. Today, American manufacturers' share of the U.S. color television market has dropped to 10%. Telephones made in the United States once captured 88% of the market. Today, it is 25%. U.S. world market share in machine tools has dropped from 79% to 35% (see Figure 1-6).

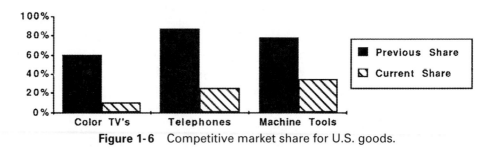

Figure 1-6   Competitive market share for U.S. goods.

Significant losses have also occurred in the automotive market. In 1960, U.S. products held 95.9% of the U.S. auto market. In 1970, the U.S. market share dropped to 84.8%. In 1988, that figure dropped to 68.9%, as indicated in Figure 1-7.

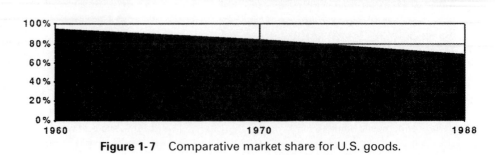

Figure 1-7   Comparative market share for U.S. goods.

In just 28 years, U.S. automotive manufacturers lost approximately 27% of the domestic automotive market. To make matters even worse, while the United States has experienced a decline in overall market share, foreign competitors have been gaining a larger share of the world's automotive market.

In the U.S. automotive market alone, foreign auto sales have risen from approximately 5% in 1960 to 31.1% in 1988 (Figure 1-8). During this period of time, foreign market share has risen over 26%.

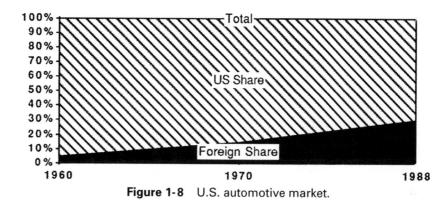

Figure 1-8   U.S. automotive market.

Japan's performance alone has been a key factor for the significant increase in foreign competition within the U.S. automotive market. During the 1970s, Japan held 3.7% of the U.S. automotive market. Ten years later, that figure rose sharply to 21.2%. While foreign imports have been restricted, the level of growth in Japanese market share within the United States has leveled off. Yet the number of Japanese manufacturing companies producing goods within the United States has grown significantly. In 1989, Japanese transplant production in the United States nearly doubled the amount produced in 1987. By 1992, that figure is expected to more than double.

The competitive pressures felt throughout these industries are just an example of the pressures facing *all* profitable industries—manufacturers and services alike, throughout the world. Manufacturing has made tremendous strides in reversing this declining trend in productivity, since its collapse in the early 1970s. Recent figures indicate that the average rate of productivity growth in manufacturing is above 3%. Yet the overall rate of productivity growth in the United States remains below 2%. Today, the primary drag on U.S. productivity comes from the service sector. These pressures will grow more intense as global competition continues to mount.

1C: BUILDING A STRONGER OFFENSE

An old adage that sums up today's economic challenge is: "The only thing certain is uncertainty." And change and uncertainty are definitely on the horizon. In the past, the United States enjoyed a very sizable world market share and many companies grew very wealthy. Then soaring prices, recession, and a flood of foreign competition reversed this. The rising trend of foreign competition has created immense uncertainty. Slumping sales, rising inflation, unemployment, plant closings, and many bankrupt companies are merely symptoms of the problems that have resulted from increased global competition. To solve the problem, the root causes need to be addressed. The primary causes of today's economic problems are waste, declining productivity, inferior quality, and customer dissatisfaction.

The rising trend of international competition will not disappear. The only way to survive and prosper in today's fiercely competitive market is to build a stronger offense. Building a stronger offense requires changes on everyone's behalf. Today, survival and prosperity require a relentless and continual drive to improve quality, reduce costs, and satisfy the customer.

Change Is Necessary

The problems that exist today did not occur overnight. And the solutions to these problems will not take place overnight either. But one thing is certain — change is necessary! The process of change is not easy. Change is very difficult and often resisted. Yet the alternatives to change are not very appealing. If we fail to accept the challenge of change, we will experience even greater levels of economic hardship, higher unemployment, and reduced standards of living.

The changes required for economic leadership and a strong competitive position in today's global economy are focused on the following items:

- Satisfying the customer
- Improving quality
- Eliminating waste
- Removing the barriers within the organization
- Building a sense of teamwork
- Developing human resources
- Investing in technology

Today, everyone shares a vested interest in the changes required — our futures depend on it. The road to economic success calls for a true spirit of cooperation and a firm commitment to *quality* and customer satisfaction.

Satisfying the Customer.   Today, customers have an endless variety of choices available to them from every nation around the world. Success in today's economy depends largely on one's ability to provide high-quality products and services that satisfy the customer's needs and wants, delivered on a timely basis, at competitive prices.

Improving Quality.   The historical methods of mass production emphasized *quantity*. Yet higher costs, decreasing sales, and declining market share have proven that increased production does not guarantee profits. Today, customers want high-quality products and services. Given this, economic excellence is now based on quality, not quantity. As a result, continuous quality improvement is required throughout *all* phases of the business: from design to customer delivery and service. Everyone in the organization must be firmly committed to improve quality and satisfy the customer.

Eliminating Waste. As mentioned previously, mass production generates tremendous waste. On average, 25 to 30% of sales is spent on finding and fixing defects and errors. This is often referred to as *defect detection*. To reduce and eliminate waste in a process effectively, the emphasis must be focused on *defect prevention*. Defect prevention is designed to prevent defects or errors in the process, rather than finding and fixing them after they have occurred.

Removing the Barriers within the Organization. Real quality improvement and customer satisfaction require the total cooperation of all resources within an organization. Every effort must be made to ensure that all of the organization's resources are working together to provide world-class quality products and services that satisfy customers at a competitive price. Tremendous efforts must be made to remove any barrier that prevents the organization from achieving this goal.

Building a Sense of Teamwork. Removing the barriers within the organization is only part of the total solution. Solid partnerships need to be formed with suppliers, departments, and all persons within the organization. Today, everyone shares a common goal to improve quality, productivity and customer satisfaction. This goal can be realized only by building a true spirit of cooperation and teamwork throughout the entire organization.

Developing Human Resources. People are the organization's greatest and most unique resource. The greatest opportunities for growth and advancement lie in the development of human resources. Organizations need to unleash the full potential of their human resources by soliciting ideas, drawing on experiences, seeking creative involvement, and developing their people in every aspect of the business.

Investing in Technology. Technological advancements play an extremely important role in increasing one's competitive advantage, yet technology alone will not accomplish the task. The blending of both technological advancements and human resource development is critical in becoming more competitive and productive.

Many changes are required to meet the competitive challenges in today's rapidly changing new world economy. Today, survival and prosperity call for a united effort and a relentless drive to improve quality, reduce costs, and satisfy the customer continuously. In today's fiercely competitive market, these requirements are not optional — they are the tickets to the game.

REVIEW QUESTIONS

1. From the following, identify three reasons for the emphasis on quantity.
   (a) Quantity ensures quality
   (b) Stockholders wanted greater returns on investments.
   (c) Everything produced was sold.
   (d) Customers were satisfied with products and services produced.
   (e) Production methods ensured high-quality products and services.
   (f) More production led to greater profits.

2. Which of the following are true statements?
   (a) Mass inspection identifies all the defects.
   (b) Mass inspection cannot identify all of the defects.
   (c) Mass inspection does not fix defects.
   (d) Mass inspection is an effective method of production.

3. List three examples of how mass inspection increases costs.

4. Describe the relationship between cost and market share.

5. The level of productivity growth rate in the United States
   (a) has remained relatively steady
   (b) is declining
   (c) is increasing

6. Productivity is the relationship between _____ and _____.

7. Foreign competition
   (a) is increasing
   (b) remains relatively stable
   (c) is decreasing

8. List four of the changes required to improve one's competitive edge in today's global market.

Chapter 2

The Evolution of Statistical Process Control

In Chapter 1 you learned how the emergence of global competition is challenging the way business is conducted. In this chapter you will learn the vital role that statistical process control (SPC) plays in quality improvement. Chapter 2 is divided into three units. Unit 2A discusses the struggle Japan faced to improve product quality after World War II. Unit 2B outlines the requirements of continuous process improvement. Unit 2C defines statistical process control and how it can be used to solve problems and improve the quality.

INSTRUCTIONAL OBJECTIVES

When you have completed this chapter, you will be able to:

- State the key developments in Japan's struggle to improve quality.
- Identify the key aspects of Deming's quality improvement philosophy.
- Define the commitments required to improve quality.
- Name the two primary sources of process improvement.
- Describe the voice of the process and the voice of the customer.
- Identify the three primary phases of process improvement.
- Cite the difference between statistics and data.
- Outline the major benefits of statistical process control.

LEARNING ACTIVITIES

_____2A: Meeting the Challenge
_____2B: Continuous Process Improvement
_____2C: Statistical Process Control: The Voice of the Process.

2A: MEETING THE CHALLENGE

Despite the competitive challenges facing U.S. industry today, this is not the first time in history that nations have been confronted with similar problems. Many people can recall the problems Japan faced during the 1960s. Overall, the quality of goods built in Japan was inferior. At that time, Japan was best known for building junk. In fact, it was embarrassing to be caught owning a product labeled "Made in Japan."

After World War II, the Japanese began to rebuild their country and improve its economic condition. In doing so, Japan's government made a public commitment to improve the quality. To assist them in their efforts, the United States sent Dr. Edwards Deming to Japan to teach the Japanese how to improve quality through the use of statistical quality control methods. Deming taught the Japanese how to improve quality and reduce costs by improving the process constantly. Continuous process improvement is driven by the customer. All of the work that is done to create a product or service for the customer is part of the process. Therefore, process improvement is a systematic method which ensures that processes continuously meet and exceed customer needs over time in the most efficient manner possible.

The *Deming wheel* (Figure 2-1) illustrates the continuous process improvement cycle. This model is also called the *Shewart cycle,* or the *plan/do/check/act* (PDCA) *cycle.*

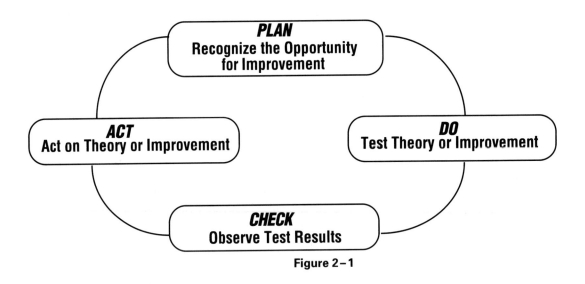

Figure 2–1

First, it is important to recognize the opportunity for improvement and identify the changes required to improve the process. Opportunities for improvement come from two primary sources, the customer and the process. Second, the theory or changes made to improve the process should be tested on a small scale. Third, the results should be observed and analyzed to determine if the results improved the process. Fourth, if the results are successful, act on the opportunity to improve the process by implementing the change on a full scale. Then, repeat the first step. This is a continuous cycle for process improvement—it has no end.

The process of change was slow. It took Japan nearly 30 years before their efforts to improve quality began to pay off. Yet the work of Deming and the commitment Japan made to improve quality have paid large dividends. Today, Japan is considered a leader in world-class quality. Figure 2-2 illustrates Japan's progress in developing their leadership position in quality. The United States is currently faced with the same challenges that Japan faced in the 1950s. Deming is frequently called upon by many U.S. business leaders to help them implement the solutions he delivered successfully to Japan.

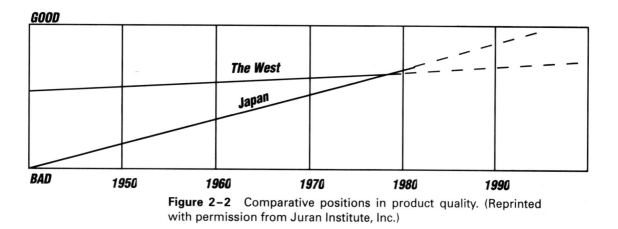

Figure 2–2 Comparative positions in product quality. (Reprinted with permission from Juran Institute, Inc.)

After visiting many U.S. firms, Deming issued a 14-point plan that defines the commitment required to provide high-quality products and services at competitive prices.

Dr. W. Edwards Deming's 14 Obligations of Management

1. Create a constancy of purpose toward improvement of product and service, with a plan to become competitive, stay in business, and provide jobs.
2. Adopt the new philosophy. We are in a new economic age, created by Japan. Western management must awaken to the challenge, must learn their responsibilities, and take on leadership for change.
3. Cease dependence on inspection to achieve quality. Eliminate the need for inspection on a mass basis by building quality into the product in the first place.
4. End the practice of awarding business on the basis of price tag. Instead, minimize total cost. Move toward a single supplier for any one item on a long-term relationship of loyalty and trust.
5. Improve constantly and forever the system of production and service, to improve quality and productivity, and thus constantly decrease costs.
6. Institute training on the job.
7. Institute leadership. The aim of leadership should be to help people, machines and gadgets to do a better job. Supervision of management is in need of overhaul, as well as supervision of production workers.
8. Drive out fear, so that everyone may work effectively for the company.

9.   Break down barriers between departments. People in research, design, sales, and production must work as a team to foresee problems of production and in use that may be encountered with the product or service.

10. Eliminate slogans, exhortations, and targets for the work force that ask for zero defects and new levels of productivity.

11. Eliminate work standards (quotas) on the factory floor. Substitute leadership. Eliminate management by objective. Eliminate management by numbers, numeric goals. Substitute leadership.

12. Remove barriers that rob the hourly worker of his right to pride in workmanship. The responsibility of supervisors must be changed from stressing sheer numbers to quality. Remove barriers that rob people in management and engineering of their right to pride in workmanship. This means, abolishment of the annual merit rating and management by objective.

13. Institute a vigorous program of education and self-improvement.

14. Put everybody in the organization to work to accomplish the transformation. The transformation is everybody's job.

Deming's approach is not complex. Simply stated, Deming believes that the first order of business is to improve quality. Quality improvement must be led by management, but the support and involvement of every person is needed. Quality improvement automatically leads the way to improvements in productivity, cost reduction, competitiveness and customer satisfaction.

Today's competitive challenge is great, as it calls for the reversal of a system that has been in existence for many years. The process of change will be very slow and difficult. Realistically, the changes required to restore quality and pride in workmanship may take years. Yet, as Deming has stressed, the alternatives to *not taking action* are even less appealing. Due to the nature of our world economy, *those who do not take action will not survive.*

The only way to remain in business is to provide world-class quality products and services that satisfy customer needs at competitive prices. To that end, quality is rapidly becoming the leading operating priority throughout *all* organizations. Although management must lead the effort, everyone in the organization must be totally committed to continuous process improvement. In short, our future depends on our ability to compete effectively in world markets.

2B: CONTINUOUS PROCESS IMPROVEMENT

Quality is a customer-driven process. Customers want high-quality products and services that meet their specific needs at a cost that represents value. In addition, they want products and services that are convenient, error-free, and delivered in a timely fashion. Customers may be internal or external. Internal customers may be a department within the organization, the next person in line, and so on. External customers are the people who use the final product or service.

A process is the blending of interdependent resources that provide products or services to meet customer needs. These interdependent resources are commonly grouped into five categories: people, equipment, materials, methods, and environment. All work that is done to produce a product or provide a service is part of the process (see Figure 2-3).

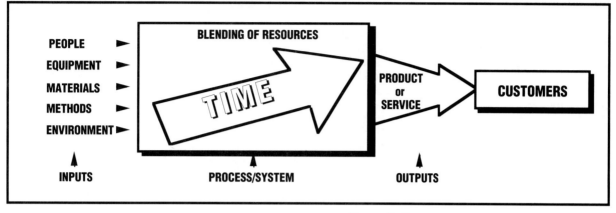

Figure 2–3

To improve any process, measurements are needed. Measurements are used to identify trends, problems, or improvement opportunities within the process. The two primary sources of data for process improvement are: The *voice of the customer* and the *voice of the process*.

Data from the *customer* can be received directly or indirectly. These data indicate how customer needs are being met.

Data from the *process* are direct and frequent feedback from output measurements in a statistical format (i.e., control charts, run charts, Pareto charts, etc.) These data enable one to determine how closely and consistently the process target goals are being met.

Through these two measurement systems, the opportunity for process improvement can be identified. The improvement opportunity from the "voice of the customer" is the difference between what the customer wants and what they get. The improvement opportunity from the "voice of the process" is the difference between the desired output and what is actually being produced. Data from these two sources represent opportunities for continuous process improvement. The model shown in Figure 2-4 incorporates the Deming cycle or the plan–do–check–act (PDCA) cycle over time to achieve continuous process improvement.

Plan.   Assess the process improvement opportunity. Identify the changes to inputs or the way inputs are used in the process and establish the criteria for improvement.

Do.   Implement the improvement on a small scale and collect data to analyze the new performance.

Check.   Compare the results of the new performance with the improvement criteria.

Act.   If results are successful, implement the change or improvement on a full scale. If not, modify the approach and repeat steps in the cycle until the criteria are met.

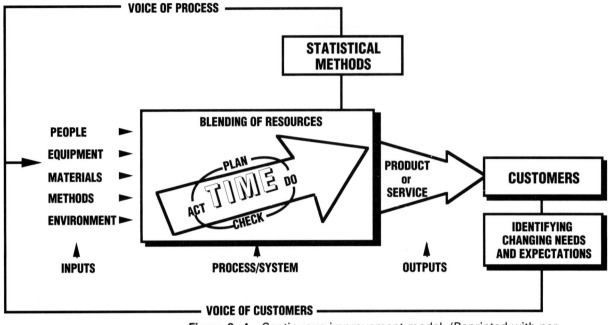

Figure 2–4 Continuous improvement model. (Reprinted with permission from Ford Motor Company © 1990.)

This method of continuous process improvement provides a framework for integrating a variety of statistical tools, such as quality function deployment, statistical process control, design of experiments, basic market research, problem-solving techniques, and team building skills. These tools have been widely applied in manufacturing and they hold tremendous value and potential in administrative processes as well. Continuous process improvement in all aspects of the organization is absolutely essential to providing world-class products and services that meet and exceed customer satisfaction at competitive prices.

2C: STATISTICAL PROCESS CONTROL: THE VOICE OF THE PROCESS

As indicated previously, the opportunities for continuous process improvement come from two primary sources: The voice of the customer and the voice of the process. The *voice of the customer* is information received directly or indirectly from customers regarding how well their needs and requirements are being met. The *voice of the process* is direct and frequent feedback from measurements taken on the output produced by the process. To obtain data from the process, statistical methods are used.

The Definition of Statistics

When most people hear the word "statistics," they usually shy away from it as though it were something foreign. Yet many people use statistical information every day. To illustrate this, consider the following examples:

- The average temperature for this time of year is ___.
- The number of cars produced last year was ____.

- Unemployment rose ___% last month.
- The consumer price index declined ___% this week.
- The automobile accidents reported during this holiday period are ____.
- Three out of four doctors recommended brand X over all other leading brands.
- Lou Whitaker's batting average is ____.
- The U of M had ____ yards rushing in their last game.

Each of these items is a statistic. With such widespread use of statistical information, statistics are not really foreign—they are just not thought of as statistics. The term *statistics* has two definitions. The most common definition of statistics generally refers to the collection of numerical data: that is, the "facts and figures" of a certain area of interest. The facts and figures may be the yards gained rushing by an NFL team, the level of income earned by an average American, the closing stock prices on the New York Stock Exchange, or the total number of cars produced for a given period of time.

A second definition for the word *statistics* refers to a specific field of study through which numerical data are systematically collected, described, organized, summarized, and analyzed. The value of studying statistics is that it provides the necessary tools to analyze and interpret numerical data in order to draw conclusions and make decisions regarding future events. The balance of this book deals with the second definition of statistics.

Many problems are solved on intuition alone. In these instances, information is given and we are asked to draw conclusions or make decisions. When this occurs, we quickly sort through the facts to identify the important information and make decisions. The value of one's intuition cannot be underestimated; however, when complex problems arise, decisions based on intuition alone are often inadequate. Complex problem solving, decision making, and process improvement require a more systematic approach.

Statistical tools can be used to:

- Define process problems, improvement opportunities, and set priorities
- Describe and summarize process characteristics
- Analyze process performance
- Determine the causes of variation in a process
- Identify improvements required to solve problems and reduce variation
- Evaluate changes made on the process
- Predict process performance over time
- Prevent defects versus detecting them

Continuous process improvement has three primary phases: *monitor the process, control the process,* and *improve the process* (Figure 2-5). To improve any process, it is important to know three things:

1. What are the customer and process requirements?
2. What is the process actually producing?
3. What can be done to improve the process?

Process Control and Improvement		
Phase 1 *Monitoring* **What is the process currently producing?**	**Phase 2** *Controlling* **Only stable, common-cause variation.**	**Phase 3** *Improving* **Continuously reduce variation in the process.**

Figure 2–5

Statistical process control is the primary vehicle used to measure and analyze the output of *any* process: whether you are processing customer orders or manufacturing products to be sold to customers. SPC is the use of statistical techniques to analyze a process or its output (Figure 2-6). From these data, actions can be taken to achieve and maintain a state of statistical control, prevent defects or errors in the process, and improve the capability of the process over time. In effect, statistical techniques provide the facts that indicate how a process has performed in the past, how it is performing currently, or make predictions on its future performance. Therefore, SPC provides the *basis for actions* required to improve process performance and satisfy customer needs.

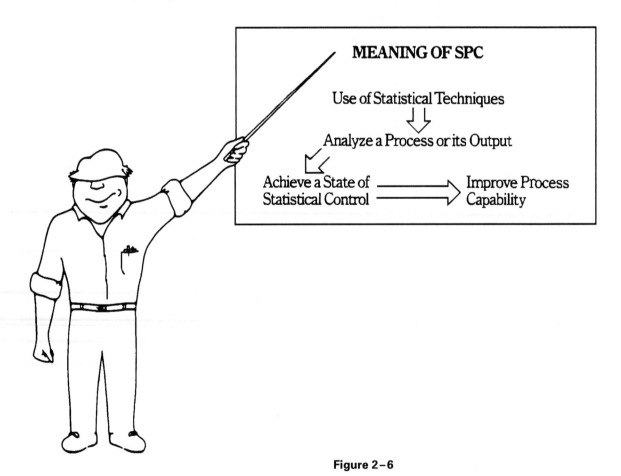

Figure 2–6

Statistical process control is used to:

- Reduce and eliminate errors, scrap, and rework in the process
- Improve communication throughout the entire organization
- Encourage active participation in quality improvement
- Increase involvement in the decision-making process
- Simplify and improve work procedures
- Manage the process by facts, not opinions

SPC is not only a better way of running a business—it is the *only* way.

A variety of statistical tools are available to monitor, analyze, control, and improve the performance of any process. Improvements made to the process improve quality and customer satisfaction. They also reduce costs. In the remainder of this book we concentrate on the statistical tools used to solve complex process problems and improve quality.

REVIEW QUESTIONS

1. Describe the steps taken by the Japanese to improve quality.
2. According to Deming, what must be done to improve quality?
3. Can management alone improve quality?
4. What are the two primary sources of data for process improvement?
5. How are data from the voice of the customer obtained?
6. What methods are used to obtain data from the voice of the process?
7. List the three primary phases of process improvement.
8. Which of the following are statistics?
   (a) The temperature is 87°.
   (b) The average temperature for the year is 60°.
   (c) Notre Dame gained 87 yards rushing.
   (d) Today's humidity is 65%.
   (e) The league's batting average is .345.
   (f) The average processing time is 30 minutes.
9. Is statistical process control a method for detecting or preventing defects? Explain why.
10. Name four primary benefits of statistical process control.

Chapter 3

Defining Problems and Setting Priorities

In Chapters 1 and 2 you have learned how the global economy is rapidly changing the way business is conducted and the changes required to improve quality. The remaining chapters of this book define the basic statistical tools that are used to analyze, monitor, and control the *process* quality. In this chapter we describe the methods that are commonly used to define and prioritize problems or opportunities for continuous process improvements.

The chapter contains four units. Unit 3A describes the preliminary decisions required to collect data. Unit 3B explains how check sheets are used to collect data. In Unit 3C we discuss how various graphs can be used to organize, summarize, and illustrate data. In Unit 3D, you will learn how Pareto charts can be used to define and prioritize problems or opportunities for improvement.

INSTRUCTIONAL OBJECTIVES

When you have completed this chapter, you will be able to:

- List the preliminary steps for data collection.
- Identify the difference between countable and measurable data.
- Define the application of four basic check sheets.
- State the use of check sheets and graphs in solving complex problems.
- Define and apply three basic graphs used to display data.
- Construct and analyze a Pareto chart.

LEARNING ACTIVITIES

_____3A: Collecting Data
_____3B: Check Sheets
_____3C: Graphs
_____3D: Pareto Charts

3A: COLLECTING DATA

The first step in defining any problem or to identify opportunities for improvement within a process is to collect data from the actual process. Since most processes produce large amounts of data, random samples are selected from the process. In randomly selected samples, every piece of data produced by the process has an equal chance of being selected. Random samples provide the data that are necessary to define problems or identify improvement opportunities within any process. Before random samples are taken, however, four preliminary steps are required.

Step 1: *Establish the Purpose for the Collection of Data*.   Let's say that you are interested in reducing the number of errors or defects occurring in a particular department. To define the problem properly, random samples of items produced in the department need to be collected. Sample data provide a good representation of the events actually occurring in the process. Therefore, the purpose of collecting data is to gain an understanding of the product defects/errors actually produced in the department over a given period of time.

Step 2: *Define the Type of Data That Are to Be Collected*.   Once the purpose of collecting data has been established, the type of data that needs to be collected can be determined. A number of variables affect the quality of any process. These variables may be:

- The quality of incoming parts and materials
- The machines and equipment used within the department
- The people who conduct or run the process
- The methods used to produce products or services
- The instruments, devices, and methods used to measure output
- The environmental factors affecting the process

Based on the number of variables affecting the quality of any product or service, a decision needs to be made on the type of data required to define the problem or opportunity. Decisions made on the type of data required may be based on one of the variables, a combination of the variables, or all of the variables operating in the process.

Using the example introduced in Step 1, the best way to gain an understanding of the defects/errors produced in the department is to collect data on the types of defects or errors actually produced at the end of the process. These data will then be used to summarize the various types and number of defects actually produced in the department.

Step 3: *Determine the Characteristics of the Data to Be Collected*. After the purpose of the data has been established and the type of data to be collected has been defined, the characteristics of the data to be collected need to be determined. Data can be collected in two basic forms.

- *Measurable data:* data that can be measured. A few examples of measurable data are length, size, weight, height, time, velocity, and so on. Measurable data are collected by measuring samples randomly selected from the process.

- *Countable data:* data that can be counted. A few examples of countable data are the number of defects, problems, percentage of defects, problems, and so on. Countable data are collected by counting the actual number of defects or problems produced in a given sample.

The characteristics of the data to be collected are based on the type of data required. For example, to determine the types of defects produced in a process, a count of the number of defects identified in each sample would be required. If data are needed on the measurements of parts produced by a given machine or length of incoming calls, sample measurements need to be randomly collected from the process.

Step 4: Identify Who Collects Data and When Data Are to Be Collected. As mentioned earlier, sample data from the process must be randomly selected. Randomly selected samples will ensure a good representation of the events actually occurring in the process. Samples may be selected during the hour, by each person, machine, department, and so on. Identification of who collects the data and when it is to be collected depends on the data required to define the problem or improvement opportunity. One of the most important points in any data collection activity is to ensure that everyone understands the purpose of collecting data and their roles and responsibilities in collecting the data. It is also important to maintain accurate records. The date, person, time, methods, and instruments used to collect the data should be accurately recorded. This information will establish a sound tracking system to identify and solve problems that are occurring in the process.

These steps provide a systematic method used to guide the data collection activities. By following these guidelines, you will be able to detect the problems occurring in the process and to define improvement opportunities.

3B: CHECK SHEETS

Once the preliminary data collection decisions have been made, the data can be collected. One of the most common tools used to collect data is the *check sheet.* Check sheets allow data to be collected in an easy, systematic, and organized manner. Accuracy is the most important aspect of any data collection activity. The quality of the actions and decisions taken on the data collected is only as good as the quality of data collected. An important term to keep in mind during any data collection activity is GIGO. GIGO means "garbage in – garbage out." If the quality of data is good, the decisions and actions taken from the data will also be good. Conversely, if the quality of data is poor, the decisions and actions taken on the data will also be poor.

A variety of check sheets are used to collect data from a process. The most commonly used check sheets are:

1. Defective item check sheets
2. Defective location check sheets
3. Defective cause check sheets
4. Checkup confirmation check sheets

The selection of the most appropriate check sheet is usually determined by the purpose, type, and characteristics of the data that need to be collected. Custom check sheets can also be designed to fit specific needs.

Defective Item Check Sheet

To reduce the number of defects or problems in any given product or service, it is important first to identify what types of problems are occurring. One way to do this is to use the *defective item check sheet.* These check sheets list the major categories of defects or problems identified in the samples collected. Data can easily be collected by placing a mark in the appropriate column whenever a defect or problem has been identified. The data collected for defective items represent countable data.

Defective item check sheets reveal an accurate picture of the types of defects occurring during the time samples are selected from the process. However, these check sheets do not indicate any changes made in the process. Changes may be a new person, machine, method, shift, and so on. Any change should be noted on the check sheet.

For example, let's say that you have been assigned the task of reducing the number of customer complaints in your department. The first thing you will need to do is to collect some data. Following the procedures required prior to collecting data, the following decisions were made.

1. The purpose of collecting data is to gain an understanding of the types of complaints occurring in the department for a period of two weeks.
2. The type of data that needs to be collected is a list of the complaints received from randomly selected samples and the number of times each complaint occurred during the study.
3. The characteristics of the data to be collected are countable data. That is, the data will be a count of the various complaints received in the department, as well as the total number of times they occurred from the samples selected during a two-week period of time.
4. Each operator in the department will select five sample complaints each hour and collect data on the number and type of complaints identified in the samples selected for a period of two weeks.

Based on these decisions, a defective item check sheet can be used to collect the data needed to define the problems occurring in the department. An example of the data collected on a defective item check sheet is shown in Figure 3-1.

CUSTOMER COMPLAINT REPORT

Department______________ Date_______

Operator	*Defect*	*Shift 1*	*Shift 2*	*Shift 3*
20	Bent Stem	17		
	Short Overall Length	15		
30	Undersized Stem	7		
	Oversized Stem	20		
50	Bad Grind on Head		32	
	Bad Grind on Grooves		10	
	Bad Grind on Valve Stem		25	
	Undersize Grooves		7	
90	Undersize Stem			52
	Oversized Stem			29
100	Pitted			18
	Cracks in Head			52
70	Undersized Groove	35		
	Bent Valve Stem	25		
	Undersized Stem	12		
TOTALS		131	74	151

Figure 3-1

Defective Location Check Sheet

Defective location check sheets are used to pinpoint or identify the location of certain problems or defects. These check sheets are particularly helpful when collecting data associated with the external appearance of any product, such as the presence of scars or bubbles.

Once a number of samples have been selected from the process, the data can be used to identify the most frequently occurring problem or defect. Once this has been determined, the causes can be identified and corrective measures can be taken to improve the process. For example, the defective location check sheet shown in Figure 3-2 was used to investigate the defects occurring in the in-

RIPPLE INVESTIGATION CHECK SHEET

Date ___________ **Product Type**______

Inspector _______ **Time** ___________

REMARKS:_______________________________

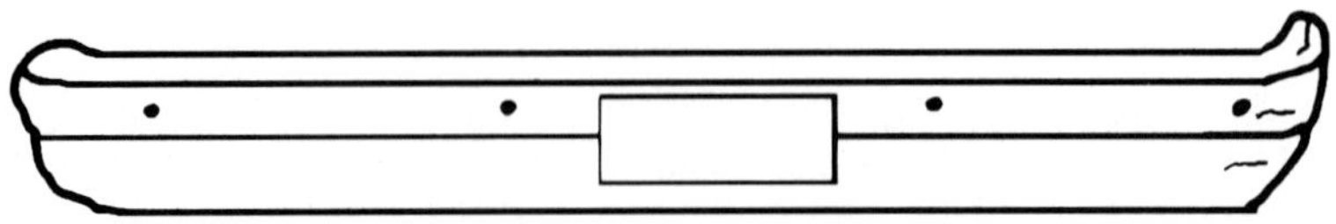

Figure 3-2

jection mold process for bumpers. After a number of samples had been selected, the data revealed that most of the defects identified were ripples in the upper right side of the bumper. The potential causes of the problem were then investigated. As a result, the team was able to determine that the temperature used in the injection process was not balanced properly, causing the right side of the bumper to set more quickly than the left side. Once the cause of the problem was identified, it was corrected and solved.

Defective Cause Check Sheet

The *defective cause check sheet* is used to identify potential causes of a problem or defect. This check sheet is more complex because more data need to be collected. The data may include the equipment, operator, time, day, type of defect, and so on. Defective cause check sheets are used to identify the possible causes of problems and to make more rapid adjustments to the process.

The defective cause check sheet shown in Figure 3-3 was used to determine the causes of errors in coding process sheets. Errors were recorded by category, operator, machine, time, and day. After reviewing the chart, most of the errors occurred on Wednesday and more errors were detected by operator B. With these data, the errors can be isolated and the cause(s) can be more readily determined.

		Monday		Tuesday		Wednesday		Thursday		Friday	
Equipment	Operator	AM	PM	AM	PM	AM	PM	AM	PM	AM	PM
Code Machine 1	A	O X	• •	X X	OO OXO	XXX X	O O	X O •	• • •	X	O O
	B	X X O	X O	• •	X •	• • • XXOO • • X	XXO XOX OOO	X • O	X X	•	X X
Code Machine 2	A	X	X X	• • X	X X	•OX X X	X X O O	• •	X X	• X •	• •
	B	OOO	X O •	O	X O	XXXX • • X X OOXO	OOX • • X X X O	OOO	X X	• • O	X O X
KEY:	x-Customer Code Error			o-Zip Code Missing			•-Ship To Missing				

Figure 3-3

Checkup Confirmation Check Sheet

Check sheets can also be used to ensure that proper routines and procedures are followed. In these cases, *checkup confirmation check sheets* are used (Figure 3-4). These check sheets list a complete set of items that need to be checked or inspected. The task is then to go through each item listed and indicate the results. Checkup confirmation check sheets are generally used in final inspections, machine maintenance checks, operation checks, service performance checks, and so on. One of the primary purposes of using this type of check sheet is to ensure that all areas covered in routine inspections are not overlooked.

Department Check Sheet

Date _____   Operator _____
Item _____   Department _____

	Accepted	*Rejected*
Item 10 Filled In	_____	_____
Column Total	_____	_____
Signature	_____	_____
Department Sign-off	_____	_____
Systems Coding	_____	_____

Figure 3–4

Many other check sheets, not described in this unit, are used to collect data. Selecting the most appropriate check sheet depends on the type of data required. One of the most important things to remember in selecting a check sheet is to ensure that it is easy to use, identifies the data that need to be collected, and is well understood by everyone involved in the data collection activity.

Check Sheet Summary

Defective item check sheet: lists the number of defects/errors by category

Defective location check sheet: drawing or pictorial view of defects/errors

Defective cause check sheet: defines errors, machines, time, day, operator, etc.

Checkup confirmation check sheet: checklist used in final and routine inspections

3C: GRAPHS

As indicated in the preceding unit, the initial task of defining complex problems is to collect clear and accurate data. Check sheets make data collection a relatively easy task. Once a sufficient amount of data has been collected, it needs to be organized in a format that can easily be understood. This is often done with graphs. *Graphs* are diagrams that summarize the data visually. In effect, a graph reveals a picture of the actual events and requires little explanation. A variety of graphs are used to summarize data. The most commonly used graphs are described below.

Line Graphs

Line graphs are used to plot events as they occur. The primary purpose of a line graph is to identify any trends or relationships occurring in a given process. The line graph shown in Figure 3-5 illustrates the number of units produced on a daily basis. The straight goal line then allows one to measure the actual production against the daily production goals.

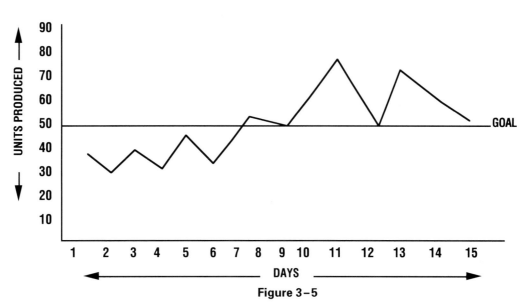

Figure 3-5

The vertical axis on this graph lists the number of units produced, and the horizontal axis lists the days of production. This line graph is used to determine whether production goals are being met and any trends occurring in the levels of production. As you can see, the first 7 days of production were below the goal. Production actually met or exceeded the goals from day 8 on. Line graphs can be used to summarize actual events and point out any problems in the process.

Bar Graphs

Bar graphs summarize and organize data into columns. These columns illustrate the overall relationship and appearance of the data. By comparing the relative lengths of the bars on the graph, the relationship between the various categories can easily be understood. The bar graph shown in Figure 3-6 was used to determine which defect or errors occurred most frequently in the process of copying documents. Data were collected on the types of defects found and the number of times the defect occurred. The data were then summarized and plotted on a bar

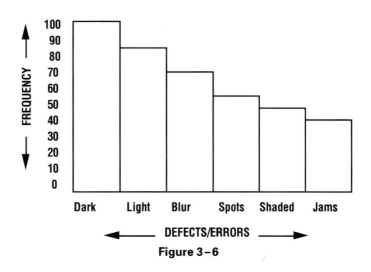

Figure 3-6

graph. Based on these data, the most significant defects were ranked and the problem-solving activities were focused on addressing the most significant defect: the copies were too dark.

Circle or Pie Graphs

Circle or *pie graphs* are used to indicate the relationship of a specific item to the whole. The relationship of each item is usually expressed as a percentage. Figure 3-7 illustrates the various categories of employees.

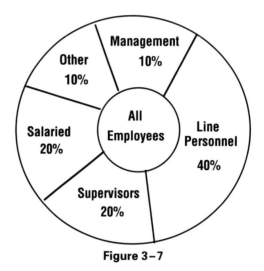

Figure 3–7

The intent of this unit was to familiarize you with the various graphs that are used to organize and summarize data. Throughout the remaining chapters, you will be shown how to construct and analyze the various graphs used to analyze, monitor, and control processes. Most of the graphs used to monitor and control processes are line and bar graphs.

3D: PARETO CHARTS

One of the statistical tools commonly used to define problems and set priorities is the *Pareto chart,* a bar graph that summarizes and organizes the data collected on the check sheet. Pareto charts illustrate the problems detected and how frequently the defect occurred in the process.

Once a sufficient amount of data has been collected, it can be summarized and plotted on a Pareto chart. The vertical axis on the Pareto chart lists the number of times the event or problem occurred. Each problem or defect is listed along the horizontal axis according to its frequency of occurrence. Data organized in this manner make it easy to define and prioritize problems occurring in the process. An example of a Pareto chart is shown in Figure 3-8.

In analyzing this Pareto chart, the most frequently occurring defect is the number of bent valves produced. The least frequently occurring defect is the number of cracked heads. Corrective actions are commonly focused on the most frequently occurring problem. However, further analysis should be made to determine which defect contains the highest costs. For example, if the cost of a bent

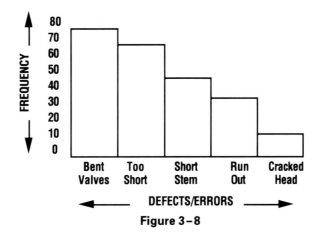

Figure 3–8

valve is $1 and the cost of a cracked head is $100, which area should be addressed first? The Pareto chart indicates that there were 75 bent valves at $1 each, the costs associated with it are $75. There were 10 cracked heads at $100 each, for a total cost of $1000. Addressing the cracked heads first would reduce the department's overall costs quicker.

In summary, Pareto charts provide the vital information needed to identify and prioritize problems in any process. Once the frequency of defects or errors has been prioritized, the cost associated with each category should be examined before corrective action is taken. That is, the defects or problems containing the highest cost should be addressed first. This procedure will enable you to improve the process and reduce costs in a more efficient manner.

Constructing a Pareto Chart

Step 1: Classify the Data. A decision must be made as to how the data should be classified. The major classifications are generally based on the following areas:

- Cost of scrap or waste
- Number of defects, errors, or problems
- Amount of scrap or waste
- Part numbers, products, department, or service
- Personnel, machines, or equipment

Step 2: Define the Period of Time. Identify an appropriate period of time to conduct the study. Any period of time can be used; however, it should be convenient and easily implemented within the normal work environment. Once the classification of data and period of time have been defined, a check sheet needs to be constructed to collect the data.

Step 3: Collect the Data by Classification. Summarize the data collected on the check sheet by counting the number of times that each event occurred. Then rearrange the data in decreasing order of occurrence.

Step 4: Draw a graph. Draw a vertical line to indicate the frequency of occurrence and a horizontal line indicating all of the events or problems detected.

Divide the vertical axis into a scale that reflects the totals of the data collected. Then divide the horizontal axis into equal segments, one for each category of events or problems recorded.

Step 5: List Each Event in Its Order of Frequency.   At the far left side of the horizontal axis, list the event or problem that occurred most frequently, then the next most frequent, the next, and so on, until all of the events have been listed.

Step 6: Draw the Bars on the Graph.   Draw a line for the total number of times each event or problem occurred for the categories listed on the horizontal axis with the corresponding values on the vertical axis.

Step 7: Add a Legend.   Indicate the title of the chart, the period of time covered, the person who prepared the chart, sources of the data, date prepared, and any other relevant information necessary to identify the data.

Application

Now that the procedure for constructing a Pareto chart has been defined, let's look at a typical application for the Pareto chart. John Deer was assigned the task of reducing the amount of scrap valves in his department. There were nine machine operators in the department and two shifts ran the entire production. John felt he needed to collect data on the process in order to define the problem. He constructed a check sheet to identify the major types of defects occurring in the process. He then instructed each operator to list the types of defects and to count the number of times each defect occurred during their shift. The check sheet shown in Figure 3-9 was used to collect the data.

Operator	Defect	First Shift	Second Shift	Total
10				
20				
30				
40				
50				
60				
70				
80				
90				

Figure 3-9

After a sufficient amount of data had been collected, John constructed a Pareto chart on the scrap valves produced. He followed the seven-step procedure to construct his Pareto chart.

Step 1: Classify the Data.   John decided to classify the data according to the amount and type of defects identified during the data collection activities.

Step 2: Define the Period of Time.   To obtain an adequate sampling of the on-going events, John collected data for two weeks.

Step 3: Collect the Data by Classification.   Check sheets were turned in daily at the end of the second shift. At the end of the 2-week period, John summarized the data as indicated in Figure 3-10.

Defect	Operator	No. of Defects	Defect	Operator	No. of Defects
Bent Valve Stems	10	48	Oversized Stem	10	0
	20	0		20	0
	30	0		30	30
	40	0		40	0
	50	0		50	0
	60	0		60	0
	70	0		70	0
	80	0		80	0
	90	0		90	0
	Total:	48		Total	30
Short Overall Length	10	0	Bad Grind	10	0
	20	76		20	0
	30	0		30	0
	40	0		40	21
	50	0		50	0
	60	0		60	25
	70	0		70	0
	80	0		80	0
	90	0		90	28
	Total:	76		Total:	74
Undersized Stems	10	0	Undersized Grooves	10	0
	20	0		20	0
	30	179		30	0
	40	27		40	100
	50	0		50	250
	60	4		60	75
	70	0		70	100
	80	0		80	200
	90	0		90	0
	Total:	210		Total:	725

FIGURE 3–10   Computation sheet for Pareto analysis subject: scrap valves, department 1872.

With this information, John rearranged the data and ranked each defect in its descending order of occurrence (Figure 3-11).

Rank	Category	Data
1	Undersized Grooves	725
2	Undersized Stems	210
3	Short Overall Length	76
4	Bad Grind on Grooves	74
5	Bent Valve Stems	48
6	Oversized Stems	30
	Total	1163

Figure 3-11 Computation sheet, Pareto analysis.

Step 4: Draw a Graph. John was now ready to construct a Pareto chart. To do so he drew a vertical axis to list the number of defects found. Then he drew a horizontal axis to list the categories of defects (Figure 3-12).

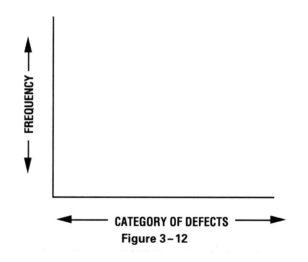

Figure 3-12

Step 5: List Each Event in Its Order of Frequency. After the graph was constructed, John listed the types of defects found on the horizontal axis. Starting at the far left, he noted each defect in decreasing order of frequency (Figure 3-13).

Step 6: Draw the Bars on the Graph. John then plotted the total number of defects under each category (Figure 3-14).

Step 7: Add a Legend. The final step needed was to indicate the *title, period of time covered, source of data, who prepared the chart,* and any additional material required to help describe the chart.

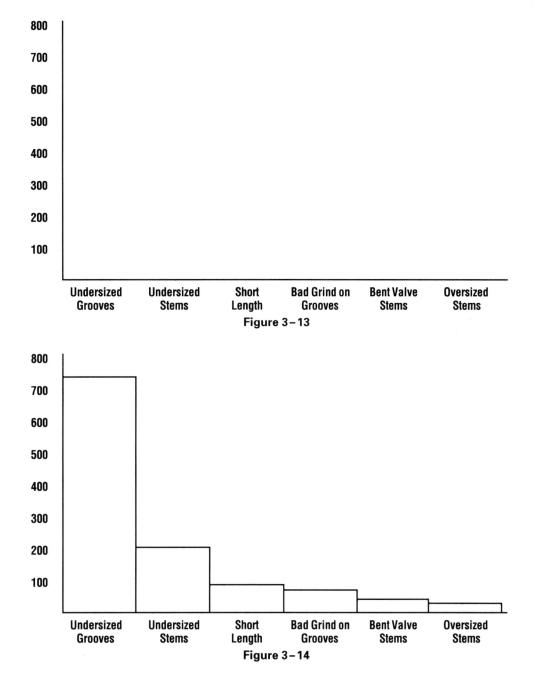

Figure 3-13

Figure 3-14

The Pareto chart defined the most critical problems occurring in the department: *undersized grooves* and *undersized stems*. After considering the costs associated with each defect, these two categories also proved to be the most costly to the department. Given these data, the department could begin to work on reducing the number of scrap valves produced. Through this analysis, everyone clearly understood the goals and worked together to correct the problems and reduce costs in the department. Defining problems and setting priorities are the first steps that need to be taken to solve complex problems. Preliminary data collection decisions, check sheets, graphs, and Pareto charts can be used to accomplish this task.

REVIEW QUESTIONS

1. List the four basic steps required prior to collecting data.

2. Which check sheet is used to provide a picture of the data?
   (a) Defective item check sheet
   (b) Defective location check sheet
   (c) Defective cause check sheet
   (d) Checkup confirmation check sheet

3. Which check sheet is used to define the defect, machine, time, day, and so on?
   (a) Defective item check sheet
   (b) Defective location check sheet
   (c) Defective cause check sheet
   (d) Checkup confirmation check sheet

4. A check sheet that lists the number of defects by category is called_____.

5. Match the following graphs and definitions.
   (a) Bar graphs   _____ Used to indicate the relationship of specific items to the whole
   (b) Circle/pie graphs   _____ Used to plot events as they occur
   (c) Line graphs   _____ Used to summarize and organize data into columns

6. Classify the following data in terms of measurable or countable data.
   (a) Time expended to respond to customer calls
   (b) The number of calls received during the course of one day
   (c) The diameter of a part
   (d) Number of defects produced
   (e) Order processing time
   (f) Coding errors

7. Match the following terms and definitions.
   (a) Check sheets   _____ Used to organize and summarize data
   (b) Pareto chart   _____ Used to collect data
   (c) Graphs   _____ Prioritizes problems according to frequency

8. Construct a Pareto chart on the following data.
   (a) Employee suggestions
       | Environmental Factors | 650 |
       | Salary/wages | 955 |
       | Management | 452 |
       | Teamwork | 892 |
       | Work methods | 756 |
   (b) Cost to rectify field service complaints
       | Delivery | $ 3,500 |
       | Clerical | 5,500 |
       | Shipping | 5,250 |
       | Installation | 17,500 |
       | Miscellaneous | 2,500 |

Chapter 4

Analyzing the Process

In Chapter 3 you learned the basic requirements and techniques used to collect, record, and summarize data. In addition, you learned how the Pareto chart can be used to define and prioritize quality problems or opportunities for continuous improvement. In this chapter you will learn how data can be used to analyze a process. This chapter is divided into two parts. Unit 4A describes the basic concepts of variation and the information that can be obtained from these data. Unit 4B illustrates how the histogram is used to illustrate the basic characteristics of data.

INSTRUCTIONAL OBJECTIVES

When you have completed this chapter, you will be able to:

- Describe the concept of variation.
- Classify common and assignable causes of variation.
- Apply two statistical tools used to describe data.
- Identify the normal, skewed, and bimodal distributions.
- Construct a histogram.
- Analyze and interpret the information in a histogram.

LEARNING ACTIVITIES

_____4A: Variation
_____4B: Describing Data Using Histograms

4A: VARIATION

The first concept required to analyze data is variation. Simply stated, the concept of *variation* indicates that no two items are alike. At first glance certain items may appear to be the same; however, differences always exist. For example, if you were to examine two bolts taken from the same production lot, the bolts would appear to be identical. Yet if the bolts were examined closely with precise measuring instruments, differences between the two bolts would be detected. The same thing holds true for processing invoices, the procedures followed for incoming calls, the route you take to work each day, and so on. In reality, no two items are ever identical. Everything varies to some degree in some way, shape, or form from one another. Variation occurs in all things, regardless of product, service, or process.

The causes of variation can be divided into two categories: common causes or assignable causes of variation.

Common Causes. Common causes of variation are based on events that occur naturally. These events are normal and *cannot* be entirely eliminated. A few examples of common-cause variation are: differences in people and methods used, varying temperatures, levels of humidity, lighting, machinery, materials, measurements, and so on. Common causes of variation are normal and natural events that occur in all processes. Common-cause variation in products, services, or processes can never be eliminated entirely. However, the variation resulting from common causes in any product, service, or process is stable and can be predicted.

Special or Assignable Causes. Special or assignable causes of variation are based on abnormal or unnatural events that occur in the process: that is, events that are not normally factored into the routine of processes, products, or services. Special or assignable causes of variation *can* be eliminated. Some examples of special or assignable causes of variation are: personnel not adequately trained, procedures not followed, computer and equipment malfunctions, broken tools or machine wear, air-conditioner failures, flat tires, doors left opened in the wintertime, and seized components. Special or assignable causes of variation create an unpredictable and unstable amount of variation in the process. These causes of variation can and should be eliminated.

The importance of analyzing variation in any process cannot be overstated. The outcomes of any process vary to some degree. By developing a sound understanding of the sources of variation operating within a process, you will be able to answer the following questions:

- How is the process currently behaving?
- What changes occur in the process over time?
- Is the process capable of producing what is expected?
- Is the process stable or "in control"?
- What are the causes of variation in the process?

In summary, variation is a natural phenomenon which illustrates that no two items are ever the same. Given this as a basis, statistical process control (SPC) provides the statistical tools used to measure how things differ in any given process. These tools provide sound measures for monitoring, controlling, and improving any process.

4B: DESCRIBING DATA USING HISTOGRAMS

To analyze variation in any process, a number of random samples need to be selected. Once the samples have been collected, summary measures are used to describe the data. Summary measures are statistical methods used to describe data in an organized and concise manner. Two statistical methods are commonly used to describe data. The first method is a bar graph, called the *histogram,* which presents a picture of the variation present in the data. The second method numerically describes the central location, dispersion, and shape of the data.

The Histogram

The histogram is a bar graph that is used to present a picture of what is actually being produced in a process over a given period of time. All products and services are designed to be produced or conducted within certain limits or standards. Yet, in reality, everything varies to some degree. The histogram identifies these differences and defines the variation that is occurring in the process.

Like the Pareto chart, the histogram is used to sort observations or measurements into categories and to describe the frequency of each observation. The basic difference between the Pareto chart and the histogram lies in what is being measured. The Pareto chart measures the *number* of problems or defects identified in the process and then ranks these items according to their frequency of occurrence. The histogram is used to measure the *amount of variation* within the process from various sample measurements selected from the process and the frequency of their occurrence.

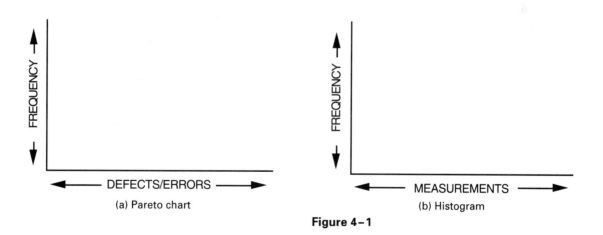

Figure 4-1

As indicated in Figure 4-1, the Pareto chart summarizes the frequency of defects or errors. The number of defects, errors, and so on, represent countable data. The histogram, on the other hand, summarizes the frequency of measurements selected from the process. This type of data represents measurable data. Measurable data allow you to determine the spread or distribution of variation within the process and provide a picture of what is actually being produced.

Histograms are constructed from a frequency table. The *frequency table* categorizes each sample measurement and tallies the total number of times the measurement occurs. Figure 4-2 provides an example of a frequency table.

Class	Boundaries	Tally	Total
1	55–59	I	1
2	60–64	II	2
3	65–69	IIII	4
4	70–74	IIII II	6
5	75–79	IIII	4
6	80–85	III	3

Figure 4-2   Frequency table.

The histogram is then constructed from the information contained in the frequency table (Figure 4-3). The vertical axis of the histogram lists the frequency of occurrence for each sample in a given category. The horizontal axis lists the various sample measurements selected from the process. Once the graph has been constructed, the summarized data can be plotted on the graph.

The specifications for this process call for a lower limit of 65 and an upper limit of 79. The random samples taken from process indicate that the variation exceeds the stated specifications. Based on this information, the histogram illustrates that too much variation exists in the process. Since the process is producing output that exceeds acceptable standards, the amount of variation within the process needs to be reduced to produce output within acceptable limits.

In addition to analyzing the variation in the process, the histogram is also used to study the shape of the distribution. The distribution of the variation in the data can take on several shapes. The most common shapes are: normal, bimodal, skewed to the left, or skewed to the right.

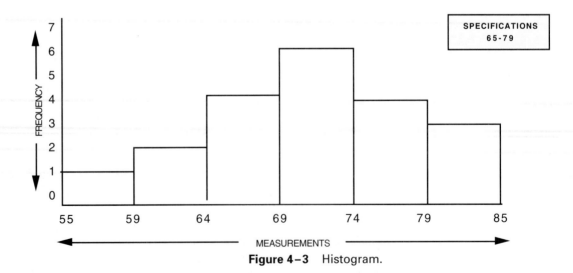

Figure 4-3   Histogram.

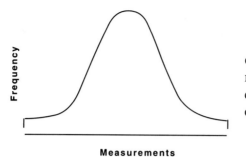

Normal Distribution

The shape of data in this type of distribution is bell-shaped. Most of the measurements are grouped around the center, with fewer measurements trailing off to the left and right.

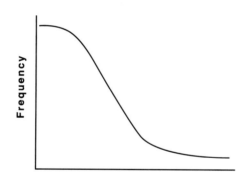

Skewed to the Left

The term *skewed* means that most of the data are pulled to one side. When data are *skewed to the left,* most of the data is grouped on the right side and the tail trails off to the left. When this occurs, more of the measurements are larger.

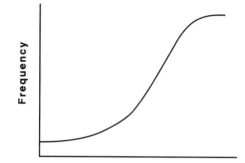

Skewed to the Right

When data are *skewed to the right,* most of the data are grouped on the left side of the graph and the tail trails off to the right. Measurements in this type of distribution tend to be smaller.

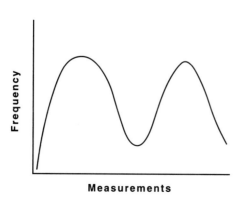

Bimodal Distribution

The data in this distribution have two peaks (high points). Whenever this occurs, two frequently occurring measurements processes or samples were selected from two populations.

Determining the shape of the data provides a better understanding of the data's overall characteristics and tendencies of variation in the process.

Constructing a Histogram

Step 1: Collect the Sample Data. Whenever sample data are used, it is important to remember that an adequate number of samples are needed to ensure a good representation of the events or variation occurring in the process. Therefore, as a general rule of thumb, a minimum of 50 samples should be collected.

Step 2: Determine the Range of the Sample Data. The *range* is the difference between the largest and smallest samples:

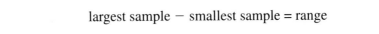

largest sample − smallest sample = range

Step 3: Determine the Number of Classes. This is a very important step in constructing a histogram because it determines how useful the information will ultimately be. To demonstrate this point, consider the three examples shown in Figure 4-4. Each histogram is based on the same data, yet each presents a different picture of the variation.

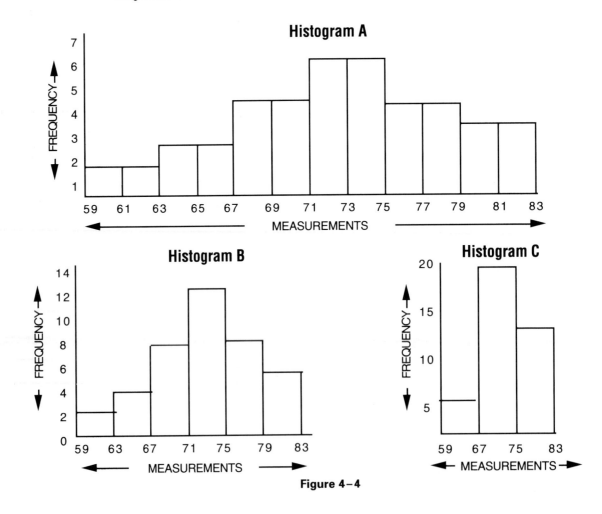

Figure 4–4

Histograms are used to gain an understanding of the variation in the process. As illustrated in Figure 4-4, the number of classes selected largely determines the usefulness of the histogram. The simplest rule of thumb is to use 5 to 7 classes for 50 or fewer samples. Use 8 to 10 classes for 50 to 100 samples. Use 10 to 15 classes for 100 to 250 samples. Use 15 to 20 classes for 250 or more samples.

Class Selection Summary	
Classes	*Sample Size*
5–7	0–50
8–10	51–99
10–15	100–250
15–20	Over 250

Step 4: Determine the Size of the Class Interval. The *class interval* is the width or size of each class. To determine the appropriate size of the class interval, the following formula is used:

$$\text{class interval} = \frac{\text{range}}{\text{number of classes}}$$

The range was calculated in Step 2, and the number of classes was determined in Step 3. To determine the size of the class interval, divide the range by the number of classes. The class interval for each class should always be *equal* and it is always better to round to whole numbers.

Step 5: Determine the Class Boundaries. The class boundaries establish the smallest and largest samples to be included in each class. It is important to ensure that no gaps occur in the data and that no sample overlaps into more than one boundary.

Step 6: Construct a Tally Sheet or Frequency Table. Construct a table to list the *classes, boundaries, tally,* and *total number of occurrences* for each class (Figure 4-5).

Class	*Boundaries*	*Tally*	*Total*
1	0.5–0.9		
2	1.0–1.4		
3	1.5–1.9		
4	2.0–2.4		
5	2.5–2.9		
6	3.0–3.4		

Figure 4–5

Step 7: Transfer Data from Check Sheet to Tally Sheet. To transfer the data from the check sheet to the tally sheet, mark a line in the tally column each time a sample falls within one of the classes (Figure 4-6). Once you have classified all of the samples on the check sheet, add the number of samples for each class and enter the total in the last column. The histogram can then be constructed from the data on the tally sheet.

Class	Boundaries	Tally	Total
1	0.5–0.9	||	2
2	1.0–1.4	||||	4
3	1.5–1.9	||||	4
4	2.0–2.4	||||	4
5	2.5–2.9	||	2
6	3.0–3.4	|	1

Figure 4–6

Step 8: Draw the Graph and Plot the Data. To construct the histogram, a graph is drawn with a vertical axis to list the number of times each sample occurred (frequency) and a horizontal axis to list the class boundaries for the samples. Once the graph has been constructed, the data in the table are plotted onto the graph to form the histogram (Figure 4-7).

Histogram

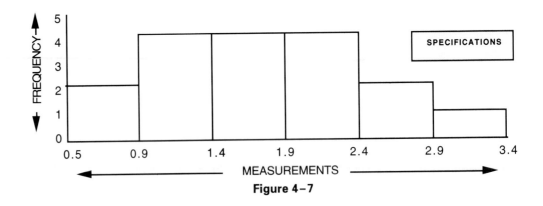

Figure 4–7

Step 9: Add a Legend. Legends make it easy for others to understand and interpret the information on the histogram. Therefore, it is important to list on the histogram the name, department, source of data, date, and any other pertinent information (Figure 4-8).

Histogram

Name _____   Date _____

Source_____   Department_____

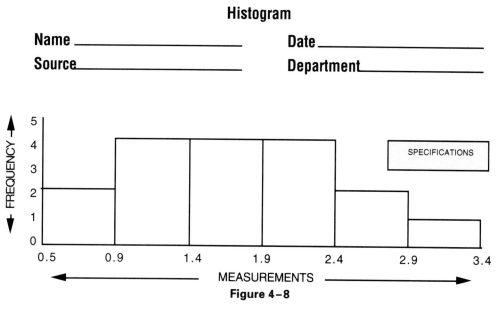

Figure 4-8

Application

Now that the steps used to construct a histogram have been explained, the following example will be used to illustrate how each step is applied.

Step 1: Collect the Sample Data. The samples shown in Figure 4-9 were collected to determine the variation in the number of orders processed.

Number of Orders Processed									
14	18	11	8	15	5	15	14	7	08
10	4	13	14	10	11	8	16	8	11
4	13	14	15	12	8	9	9	12	8
11	11	7	13	11	4	8	16	10	16
13	11	8	10	9	10	12	9	11	13
6	9	7	7	10	7	5	11	11	10
15	8	12	12	12	11	9	12	12	14
7	13	17	6	10	11	12	14	11	10
12	10	10	9	14	10	13	10	10	12
7	9	11	16	6	14	13	9	6	10
12	7	17	16	15	6	6	9	5	13
08	13	10	11	10	14	12	12	10	8
14	11	9	10	11	14	4	11	9	14
12	11	7	8	12	8	9	17	5	13
14	6	15	8	13	13	15	13	9	12
10	11	9	12	13	10	11	11	12	12
8	15	9	9	11	16	14	7	13	7
9	11	11	12	12	9	9	7	12	13
14	6	12	13	13	11	10	8	7	9
9	11	10	15	8	5	10	8	9	8
10	10	8	13	08	7	5	8	13	7
13	14	15	6	10	6	12	5	10	9

Figure 4-9

Step 2: Determine the Range of the Sample Data. The range of the data is obtained by subtracting the smallest from the largest sample. The smallest sample is 4 and the largest is 18. Therefore, the range is $18 - 4 = 14$.

Step 3: Determine the Number of Classes. In this example, 220 samples were collected. Using the basic rule of thumb, 10 to 15 classes should be used for 100 to 250 samples. Since 220 samples is at the higher end of the scale, 15 classes will be used.

Step 4: Determine the Size of the Class Interval. The class interval is computed by dividing the range by the number of classes. Dividing a range of 14 by 15 classes is .933. Rather than using odd numbers, .933 can be rounded to 1.

Step 5: Determine the Class Boundaries. To ensure that each sample is applied to only one class, there should be no gaps or overlaps in the class boundaries. Since the class interval is 1, each class will contain samples that are an equal distance apart. Figure 4-10 illustrates how the class boundaries are established.

Class	Boundaries
1	4 < 5
2	5 < 6
3	6 < 7
4	7 < 8
5	8 < 9
6	9 < 10
7	10 < 11
8	11 < 12
9	12 < 13
10	13 < 14
11	14 < 15
12	15 < 16
13	16 < 17
14	17 < 18
15	18 < 19

Figure 4-10 (The < sign indicates any number less than the number to the right of the < sign.)

Step 6: Construct a Tally Sheet or Frequency Table. The tally sheet makes it easy to summarize the data. To construct one, simply draw a table with four columns to indicate the classes, boundaries, tallies, and totals (Figure 4-11).

Step 7: Transfer Data from Check Sheet to Tally Sheet. Using the sample data collected, a line is made in the tally column to indicate the class boundary that each sample falls within. Then the total number of samples for each class is entered in the total column (Figure 4-12). The histogram will then be constructed from the data in the tally sheet.

Class	Boundaries	Tally	Total
1	4 < 5		
2	5 < 6		
3	6 < 7		
4	7 < 8		
5	8 < 9		
6	9 < 10		
7	10 < 11		
8	11 < 12		
9	12 < 13		
10	13 < 14		
11	14 < 15		
12	15 < 16		
13	16 < 17		
14	17 < 18		
15	18 < 19		

Figure 4–11

Step 8: Draw the Graph and Plot the Data. The data from this table can now be transferred to the histogram. The histogram is simply a bar graph with the vertical axis listing the frequency of occurrences for each class and a horizontal axis listing the boundaries for each class (Figure 4-13).

Step 9: Add a Legend. To add a legend to the histogram, the person constructing the histogram, department, date, time period, machines, operators, and any meaningful information is listed on the histogram.

Analysis of the Histogram

Once the histogram has been constructed, vital information on the process can be obtained. For example, the histogram can be used to determine the status of the following conditions in the process.

Class	Boundaries	Tally	Total
1	4 < 5	IIII	4
2	5 < 6	IIIIIII	7
3	6 < 7	IIIIIIIIII	10
4	7 < 8	IIIIIIIIIIIIIII	15
5	8 < 9	IIIIIIIIIIIIIIIIIIIII	21
6	9 < 10	IIIIIIIIIIIIIIIIIIIIIIIII	25
7	10 < 11	IIIIIIIIIIIIIIIIIIIIIIIIIII	27
8	11 < 12	IIIIIIIIIIIIIIIIIIIIIIIIIIII	28
9	12 < 13	IIIIIIIIIIIIIIIIIIIIIIIII	25
10	13 < 14	IIIIIIIIIIIIIIIIIIIIII	22
11	14 < 15	IIIIIIIIIIIIIIII	16
12	15 < 16	IIIIIIIIII	10
13	16 < 17	IIIIII	6
14	17 < 18	III	3
15	18 < 19	I	1

Figure 4–12

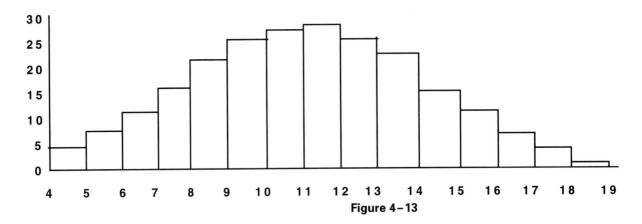

Figure 4-13

1. What most commonly occurs in the process?
2. How much dispersion is contained in the data?
3. What is the shape of the data?
4. Do the products or services meet the requirements?
5. Do any problems exist in the process? If so, what are the problems?

Referring to the histogram shown in Figure 4-14, we'll address each of these questions.

Histogram

Name _____   Date _____
Source _____   Department _____

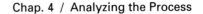

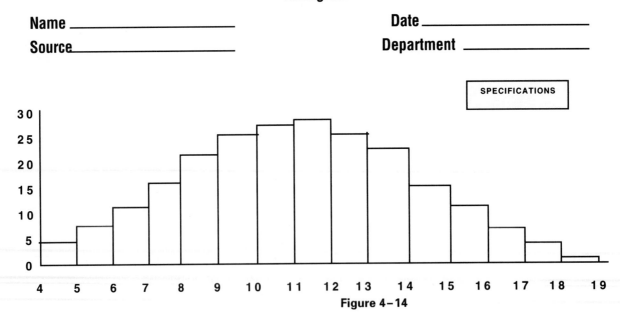

Figure 4-14

The histogram illustrates the overall appearance of the samples selected from the process. Additionally, the following process information can also be obtained.

1. *What most frequently occurs in the process?*   The most frequent sample is determined by the tallest bar on the histogram. The most fre-

quently occurring sample was 11 < 12. This indicates that 11 orders are processed most frequently on a daily basis.

2. *How much dispersion exists in the data?* The amount of dispersion is determined by the spread of the data. The dispersion in this example ranges from 4 to 19. If 1 to 25 orders are to be processed daily, the amount of dispersion in this histogram would be acceptable. If 9 to 15 orders are to be processed daily, the dispersion in this histogram would not be acceptable.

3. *What is the shape of the data?* The shape of the data provides valuable information in determining solutions to problems that exist in the process. The shape indicates what the process is producing. If the data are skewed, modifications can be made to improve the process. The shape of the data in this distribution is Normal. That is, the data forms a bell-shaped pattern. This type of variation is normal and the only way it can be reduced is to change the process.

4. *Does the product or service meet the requirements?* By comparing the samples to the product or service requirements, this determination can easily be made. If the process does not meet the requirements, improvements will be required.

5. *Do problems exist in the process? If so, what are they?* Once again, the purpose of the histogram is to gain an understanding of what is occurring in the process. If the product or service does not meet the requirements, a problem exists in the process. Problems can be identified by determining whether the samples are smaller or larger than the stated requirements.

In summary, all data have variation. That is, no two items are ever identical. Variation can be summarized and described by a histogram or statistical summary measures. A histogram is a bar graph that presents a picture of the data. Histograms can reveal the following data characteristics:

1. The most common or average value
2. The dispersion of the data
3. The shape of the data
4. The relationship of the data to the requirements
5. Any problems that exist in the process

Histograms are useful tools that are frequently used to chart the capability and characteristics of the process. Once an understanding of what is being produced and its relationship to the requirements have been identified, measures can be taken to reduce and eliminate any defects or problems in the process.

REVIEW QUESTIONS

1. What are the two categories of variation?

2. Identify the common cause of variation.
   (a) Department personnel
   (b) Temporary personnel
   (c) Different shifts
   (d) Computer failure
   (e) Procedures used to process paperwork
   (f) Paper jam in copy machine
   (g) Paper misfeed
   (h) Machine breakdown

3. Which cause of variation can be eliminated?

4. Which statistical tool provides a picture of process variation?

5. Which statistical tool is used to prioritize problems in a process?

6. Using the following data, what is the range?

11.1	32.4	21.0	11.2	4.4	27.4	18.5	15.1	10.7	25.0
12.2	4.7	14.8	16.0	7.4	10.0	3.5	14.5	8.12	19.1
12.5	7.8	16.4	22.3	6.1	32.8	16.4	6.0	15.8	18.2
12.6	23.5	22.6	19.1	9.2	26.2	16.2	3.2	12.9	13.7

7. Using the basic rule of thumb, how many classes would you select?
   (a)   5–7   (b)   8–10
   (c)   10–15   (d)   15–20

8. If six classes were used, what is the size of each class interval?

9. Construct a frequency table and histogram for the data in Question 6.

10. Using the histogram constructed in Question 9, answer the following questions:
    (a) How would you describe the shape of the data?
    (b) What is the most common measurement?
    (c) If the process requirements were to produce items within 8–23, would this process meet the requirements?
    (d) How many measurements fall below the requirements?
    (e) How many measurements exceed the requirements?
    (f) What is needed to improve the performance of the process?
    (g) Which area would you consider to be the highest priority to improve?

Chapter 5

Describing Data Using Statistics

In Chapter 4, you learned how histograms can be used to identify the basic properties of data at a glance. These basic properties can also be expressed numerically. Each numerical expression used to summarize and describe the properties of data is a statistic. In this chapter you will learn how statistics are used to summarize and describe the following properties of data:

1. Measures of location
2. Measures of dispersion
3. Measures of shape

This chapter is divided into three units. In Unit 5A we describe the statistics used to determine the central tendency or *location* of data. In Unit 5B we describe the statistics used to determine the spread of data or *dispersion*. In Unit 5C we discuss how the measures of location and dispersion can be used to determine the *shape* of the data.

INSTRUCTIONAL OBJECTIVES

When you have completed this chapter, you will be able to:

- Define three measures of location or central tendency of data.
- Compute the mean, median, and mode of data.
- Compute the range and standard deviation of data.
- Conduct a simple test to determine the shape of data.

LEARNING ACTIVITIES

_____5A: Measures of Location
_____5B: Measures of Dispersion
_____5C: Measures of Shape

5A: MEASURES OF LOCATION

Most data have central tendencies. *Central tendencies* identify the location where most of the data are located. *Measures of location* are the summary measures used to describe the central tendency or location of data. Measures of location are also referred to as the central tendency. There are three primary statistics used to summarize and describe data's measures of location: *mode, median,* and *mean.*

The Mode

One of the statistics commonly used to describe data's measures of location is the *mode,* which is the value that occurs *most frequently.* In the frequency table displayed in Figure 5-1, the mode is 8. That is, the value of 8 occurred more frequently in the data. In effect, the mode defines the positional value where most of the data are located.

Value	*Frequency*	
1		
2		
3		
4				
5					
6							
7									
8	|||||||||	Mode
9								
10							

Figure 5–1 Frequency table.

The Median

Another statistic frequently used to describe the measures of location of data is the median. The *median* is the *middlemost value.* The median divides the data into two parts: Half of the measurements fall above the median and the other half fall below it. To determine the *median,* the data must be arranged in sequential order. If the data contain an *odd* number of samples, the median will always be a unique number located in the middlemost position of an ordered group of data. If the data contain an *even* number of samples, the median is the number halfway between the two middlemost values.

The following group of ordered data contains 47 samples. Therefore, the formula for computing the median for an odd number of sample data is needed.

1	5	6	7	8	8	9	10	11	13
2	5	6	7	8	8	9	10	11	14
3	5	6	7	8	8	9	10	11	
4	6	7	7	8	9	9	10	12	
4	6	7	7	8	9	9	10	12	

To identify the middlemost value for an odd number of samples, add 1 to the total number of samples and divide the sum by 2. Using these data, there are 47 samples. To find the median, the following calculations are needed.

$$\frac{47+1}{2} = \frac{48}{2} = 24$$

The 24th sample represents the middlemost sample. The value of the 24th sample represents the median for this group of data; therefore, the median in this case is 8.

1	5	6	7	8	8	9	10	11	13
2	5	6	7	8	8	9	10	11	14
3	5	6	7	8	8	9	10	11	
4	6	7	7	⑧	9	9	10	12	
4	6	7	7	8	9	9	10	12	

If these data contained an even number of samples, the median would be calculated differently. To identify the median for an even number of samples, the two middlemost samples need to be identified. To identify these values, divide the total number of samples by 2. Then add 2 to the total number of samples and divide that sum by 2. These two values indicate the position of the two middlemost samples in data. The median is the value halfway between the values identified in the two middlemost samples. Therefore, the values of the two middlemost samples are added together and divided by 2 in order to determine the median value for data containing an even number of samples.

The following example illustrates how the median is computed for data containing an even number of samples.

1	5	6	7	8	8	9	10	11	13
2	5	6	7	8	8	9	10	11	14
3	5	6	7	8	8	9	10	11	15
4	6	7	7	8	9	9	10	12	
4	6	7	7	8	9	9	10	12	

These data contain 48 samples. To identify the two middlemost samples, the following calculations are needed:

$$\frac{48}{2} = 24 \quad \text{and} \quad \frac{48+2}{2} = 25$$

The median for these data is a value halfway between the values found in the 24th and 25th samples. To find the median, the values found in the 24th and 25th samples are added together and divided by 2.

1	5	6	7	8	8	9	10	11	13
2	5	6	7	8	8	9	10	11	14
3	5	6	7	8	8	9	10	11	15
4	6	7	7	⑧	9	9	10	12	
4	6	7	7	⑧	9	9	10	12	

$$\frac{8+8}{2} = \frac{16}{2} = 8$$

The median for this group of data is 8.

The Mean

The third statistic used to describe measures of location is the mean. The mean is calculated by adding each sample and dividing the sum by the total number of samples. The mean represents the *average value* of samples. The formula used to compute the mean is:

$$\overline{X} = \frac{X_1 + X_2 + X_3 + X_4 + \cdots + X_n}{n}$$

where $\overline{X}$ (pronounced "ex-bar") = the mean or average value
X_1, X_2, etc. = each individual sample
n = number of samples

This formula can be condensed to read as follows:

$$\overline{X} = \frac{\Sigma X}{n}$$

where $\overline{X}$ = mean or average value
X = value of each sample
n = number of samples
Σ is the Greek capital letter *sigma*, which means "the sum of"

The mean for the following data is computed as follows.

1	5	6	7	8	9	10	11
2	5	7	7	8	9	10	12
3	6	7	8	8	9	10	12
4	6	7	8	8	9	10	13
4	6	7	8	9	9	11	14
5	6	7	8	9	10	11	15

1. Add each value to compute the sum. The sum of these data is 384.
2. Divide the sum by the total number of samples. The total number of samples is 48. Therefore, the mean is 384 ÷ 48 = 8.

To illustrate how the formula is used to compute the mean, the formula can be translated to read as follows:

$$\bar{X} = \frac{\Sigma X}{n}$$

$$= \frac{384}{48}$$

$$= 8$$

In summary, three statistics can be used to summarize and describe the measures of location for sample data.

> *Mode:* represents the most *frequent* value.
> *Median:* represents the *middlemost* value.
> *Mean:* represents the *average* value.

Although each summary measure can be used to describe the *central location* of the data, each provides a slightly different picture. The summary measure used to determine the data's central tendency depends largely on the information required. It is also important to point out that summarizing data by a single summary measure can be very misleading. For example, if you were given the mean value for three groups of data and the mean was the same for each group, you might conclude that each group has the same characteristics. However, this may not be the case. To illustrate this point, consider the following data.

Group	*1*	*2*	*3*
	66	52	43
	69	82	97
	66	53	91
	68	78	44
	66	61	67
	67	72	90
	67	67	54
	67	71	50
Sum	536	536	536
Mean	67	67	67

The mean for each group is 67. Yet the data in each group are quite different, as illustrated in the corresponding frequency distributions shown in Figure 5-2.

To obtain a better understanding of the data's characteristics, measures of location need to be complemented by measures of dispersion.

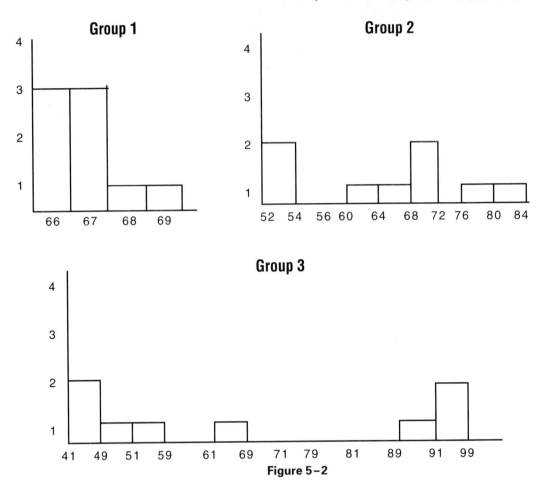

Figure 5–2

5B: MEASURES OF DISPERSION

Measures of dispersion describe the amount of variation or spread of the data around its central tendency. That is, the measure of dispersion describes how the data are *scattered* around a central location. As illustrated in the previous example, the data in group 1 contained little scatter or dispersion around its central location of 67. Yet the data in groups 2 and 3 had a lot of scatter or dispersion.

Two primary statistics are used to summarize and describe the amount of dispersion in the data: range and standard deviation.

The Range

The *range* is the easiest way to measure the amount of dispersion in data. The range is determined by subtracting the smallest value from the largest value in the data:

$$\text{largest value} - \text{smallest value} = \text{range}$$

Using the data 43, 97, 91, 44, 67, 90, 54, and 50, the range is calculated by subtracting 43 from 97. The range for these data is 54.

Although the range is an easy way to measure dispersion, it only takes extreme values into account. The range does not provide any information about the amount of dispersion between the highest and lowest values. Given this, the range can be misleading, as you will see in the next example.

The range for the groups of data shown in Figure 5-3 is 8. Even though the range for each group is the same, the amount of dispersion is quite different. Therefore, whenever using the range, keep its limitations in mind.

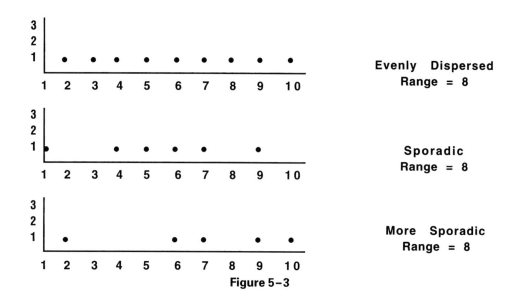

Figure 5-3

The Standard Deviation

The second statistic used to measure dispersion in data is the *standard deviation.* The standard deviation provides a more accurate picture of the dispersion or spread of the data. The standard deviation identifies the *average* amount of dispersion around the data's mean or central location. That is, the standard deviation indicates how close or how far the data are scattered away from the mean. The larger the standard deviation, the greater the distance the data is from the mean, and vice versa. The following formula is used to compute the standard deviation.

$$\sigma = \sqrt{\frac{\Sigma X - \overline{X}}{n - 1}}$$

Now, don't let this formula throw you. All formulas look Greek at first glance, but once they are broken down into step-by-step operations they are not as difficult as they first appear.

First, a translation of the formula will be given, followed by a step-by-step procedure for calculating the *standard deviation* for sample data. In this formula,

$\sqrt{}$ is the mathematical symbol for the square root, Σ is the Greek letter sigma, which means "the sum of," and

σ = standard deviation for sample data

X = each individual value or data in the sample

$\bar{X}$ = the mean, the average value for sample data

n = total number of values or data in the sample

The following steps are required to calculate the standard deviation for samples.

Step 1: Compute the Mean.   The mean is the sum of individual values divided by the number of values:

$$\bar{X} = \frac{X_1 + X_2 + X_3 + X_4 + \cdots + X_n}{n} \qquad \text{or} \qquad \bar{X} = \frac{\Sigma X}{n}$$

Step 2: Construct a Table.   A table is generally constructed to keep the calculations for the standard deviation in order.

X	$\bar{X}$	$(X - \bar{X})$	$(X - \bar{X})^2$
			Σ

Step 3: List Each Value (X) and the Mean ($\bar{X}$).   Once the table has been constructed, list each individual value in the first column and the mean value in the second column.

Step 4: Subtract the Mean from Each Value (X –$\bar{X}$).   Subtract the mean from each individual value and place the difference in the third column. Be sure to indicate negative values when the individual values are smaller than the mean.

Step 5: Square the Difference of Values and Means $(X - \bar{X})^2$. To complete this step, take each number in the third column of the table and multiply it by itself. Enter the squared difference for each individual value in the fourth column. Remember that any time a negative number is multiplied by another negative number, the answer is always a positive number.

Step 6: Compute the Sum of the Fourth Column $[\Sigma(X - \bar{X})^2]$. Add each value in the fourth column to determine the sum of all squared differences.

Steps 1 to 6 represent the computations required for the top half of the equation under the $\sqrt{}$.

Step 7: Divide the Sum by the Number of Values $- 1$ $(n-1)$. Count the number of values and subtract 1 from the total. Then divide the sum of squared differences computed in Step 6 by the number of values, less 1.

Step 7 represents the computations required for the bottom half of the equation.

Step 8: Find the Square Root. The square root of a number is the number that when multiplied by itself is that given number. For example,

$$\sqrt{25} = 5, \text{ because } 5 \times 5 = 25$$

$$\sqrt{16} = 4, \text{ because } 4 \times 4 = 16$$

and so on

To find the square root of any number, enter the number in the calculator and depress the square root key ($\sqrt{}$). To complete Step 8, enter the value computed in Step 7 in your calculator and depress the square root key. The answer is the value of the standard deviation for the sample data.

Application

Now that the steps required to compute the standard deviation have been completed, the following example will be used to illustrate how each step is applied. The sample data contain the following information:

Paperwork Processing Errors	
26	23
23	20
22	21
25	25
21	26

Step 1: Compute the Mean ($\overline{X}$).   Add each value and divide the sum by the number of values. The sum of values listed above is 232, and there are 10 samples. Therefore, the mean is $232 \div 10 = 23.2$. To make the calculations easier, 23.2 will be rounded to 23.

Step 2: Construct a Table.   The following format will be used to compute the data.

X	$\overline{X}$	$(X - \overline{X})$	$(X - \overline{X})^2$
			Σ

Step 3: List Each Value (X) and the Mean ($\overline{X}$) in the Table.

X	$\overline{X}$	$(X - \overline{X})$	$(X - \overline{X})^2$
26	23		
23	23		
22	23		
25	23		
21	23		
23	23		
20	23		
21	23		
25	23		
26	23		
			Σ

Step 4: Subtract the Mean from Each Value $(X - \bar{X})$.

X	$\bar{X}$	$(X - \bar{X})$	$(X - \bar{X})^2$
26	23	3	
23	23	0	
22	23	-1	
25	23	2	
21	23	-2	
23	23	0	
20	23	-3	
21	23	-2	
25	23	2	
26	23	3	
			Σ

Step 5: Square the Differences $(X - \bar{X})^2$. To square the differences, multiply each value in the third column by itself. *Remember that the squared value of either a positive or a negative value is always a positive value.*

X	$\bar{X}$	$(X - \bar{X})$	$(X - \bar{X})^2$
26	23	3	9
23	23	0	0
22	23	-1	1
25	23	2	4
21	23	-2	4
23	23	0	0
20	23	-3	9
21	23	-2	4
25	23	2	4
26	23	3	9
			Σ

Step 6: Sum the Differences $[\Sigma (X - \bar{X})]$. Add the numbers in the fourth column. The sum of all squared differences is 44.

X	$\bar{X}$	$(X - \bar{X})$	$(X - \bar{X})^2$
26	23	3	9
23	23	0	0
22	23	-1	1
25	23	2	4
21	23	-2	4
23	23	0	0
20	23	-3	9
21	23	-2	4
25	23	2	4
26	23	3	9
			Σ 44

The equation can now be read as follows:

$$\sigma = \sqrt{\frac{44}{n - 1}}$$

Step 7: Divide the Sum by the Number of Samples, Less One. There are 10 samples in this example, less 1 = 9. To compute this step, divide 44 by 9. The answer is 4.88. This number can be rounded to 5 to make the computations easier.

$$\sigma = \sqrt{\frac{44}{9}}$$
$$= \sqrt{4.88} \text{ or } \sqrt{5}$$

Step 8: Find the Square Root. The square root of 5 is 2.236. Rounded to one decimal, it is 2.2.

$$\sigma = \sqrt{5}$$

The standard deviation is 2.2. Therefore, the *average amount of dispersion* is 2.2 units around the mean. That is, most of the data are located 2.2 units on each side of the data's central value of 23 (Figure 5-4).

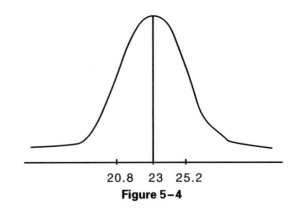

20.8   23   25.2

Figure 5-4

The standard deviation in this example indicates a small amount of dispersion in the data.

Whenever summary measures are used to describe data, there is always an element of risk. The risk lies in the summary measures' ability to present an accurate picture of the data's characteristics. As we mentioned earlier, describing data with a single summary measure, such as its mean, can be very misleading. Therefore, measures of location (mean, median, or mode) should always be complemented by a measure of dispersion (range or standard deviation). These measures provide information on the data's central location and dispersion. It is important to point out that these summary measures can be misleading if the data are skewed, that is, pulled to one side. Therefore, to ensure that you have an accurate picture of the data, the shape of the data should be examined.

5C: MEASURES OF SHAPE

Measures of shape identify the shape or distribution of the data. A simple test can be conducted to determine the shape of the data. Data have two basic shapes: symmetrical or skewed. *Symmetrical data* form a bell-shaped curve when plotted on a frequency distribution. In Figure 5-5, the right side of the curve mirrors the left side of the curve.

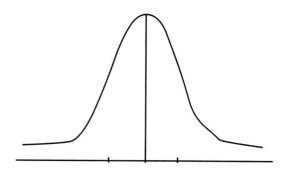

Figure 5-5

Rather than plotting the data on a graph to determine the distribution's shape, the following test is used.

If the mean, median, and mode are close in value, you can conclude with reasonable confidence that the data are symmetrical or normally distributed.

If the data are symmetrical, the summary measures of location and dispersion accurately reflect the true characteristics of the data (Figure 5-6).

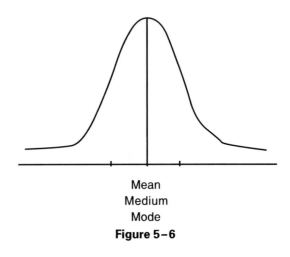

Mean
Medium
Mode
Figure 5–6

Data that are not symmetrical are skewed or nonsymmetrical. *Skewed data* are the data located in an extreme direction away from the mean or pulled to one side of the mean. In these instances, the values of the mean, median, and mode are not close or equal. If the data are skewed, the summary measures used to describe data will not reveal an accurate description of the data's characteristics. Data can be either skewed to the left or skewed to the right (Figure 5-7). Skewness is determined by the direction of the tail. Data that trail off to the left are *skewed to the left*. Data that trail off to the right are *skewed to the right*.

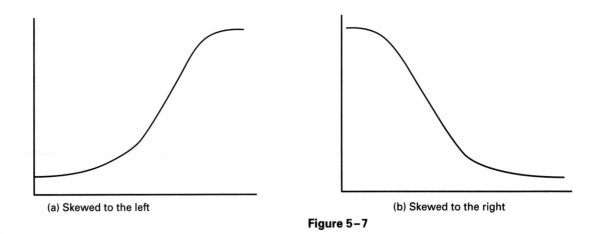

(a) Skewed to the left   (b) Skewed to the right

Figure 5–7

The values of the mean, median, and mode can be used to determine if data are skewed to the right or to the left.

1. If the mode is greater than the median, and the median is greater than the mean, the data are skewed to the left (Figure 5-8).

2. If the mode is less than the median, and the median is less than the mean, the data are skewed to the right (Figure 5-9).

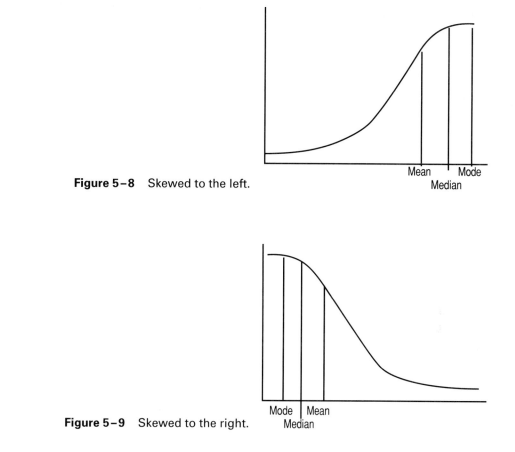

Figure 5–8 Skewed to the left.

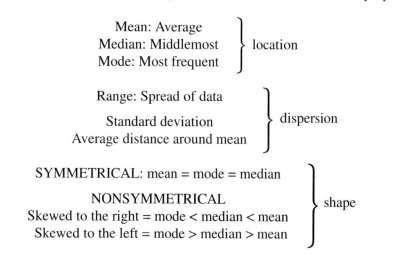

Figure 5–9 Skewed to the right.

Under skewed conditions, the mean is *not* an accurate reflection of the data's true characteristics. This usually occurs in data that have extreme values. These extreme values pull the mean out of balance. Whenever this occurs, the median portrays a more accurate measure of location. The median is the measure that is least affected by extreme values in the data.

In summary, variation in data can be summarized and described by a histogram or statistical summary measures. Statistical summary measures can be used to describe accurately three basic properties of data: *location, dispersion,* and *shape.* The statistical summary measures used to describe each property are:

Mean: Average
Median: Middlemost   } location
Mode: Most frequent

Range: Spread of data
Standard deviation   } dispersion
Average distance around mean

SYMMETRICAL: mean = mode = median

NONSYMMETRICAL   } shape
Skewed to the right = mode < median < mean
Skewed to the left = mode > median > mean

REVIEW QUESTIONS

1. Which of the following tools are used to describe the basic properties of data?
   (a) A histogram   (b) A statistic
   (c) A Pareto chart   (d) A measure of location

2. Which of the following items is a basic property of data?
   (a) Location   (b) Specification
   (c) Shape   (d) Dispersion

3. Which of the following is used to describe the *average* value?
   (a) Mode   (b) Mean   (c) Median

4. Find the mode for the following groups of data.
   (a) 2, 3, 3, 1, 2, 3, 1
   (b) 4, 6, 3, 2, 2, 5, 4, 1, 3, 2, 3, 2, 2, 3
   (c) 1.0, 7.0, 5.0 1.0, 4.0, 10.0, 5.0, 1.0
   (d) 102 mm, 104 mm, 99 mm, 100 mm, 99 mm
   (e) 3 in., 2 in., 9 in., 6 in., 2 in., 9 in., 2 in., 6 in.

5. Find the mean for the following data.
   (a) 10, 3, 5, 8, 14
   (b) 20, 5, 10, 15, 25
   (c) 3 in., 4 in., 1 in., 2 in., 2 in., 3 in., 5 in., 3 in., 4 in.
   (d) 99.75 mm, 100.04 mm, 102.21 mm, 99.99 mm, 100.01 mm
   (e) 102 nm, 104 nm, 99 nm, 115 nm, 100 nm

6. Find the median for the following data.
   (a) 20, 5, 10, 15, 25
   (b) 20, 5, 10, 25
   (c) 102 mm, 104 mm, 99 mm, 115 mm, 100 mm
   (d) 102 mm, 99 mm, 104 mm, 100 mm, 115 mm, 104 mm
   (e) 3 in., 21 in., 9 in., 15 in., 6 in., 18 in., 12 in.

7. True or false? The characteristics of data can be summarized by a single summary measure.

8. The best summary measure used to determine the dispersion in data is:
   (a) Range   (b) Standard deviation

9. True or false? If the mean for three different groups of data were the same, you can conclude that the data for all three groups are the same.

10. Measures of _____ provide a summary measure of variation.

11. Determine the range for the following data.
    (a) 13, 23, 11, 25, 18, 11, 14, 24
    (b) 67, 57, 93, 87, 91, 88, 65, 90, 79, 97
    (c) 91, 90, 54, 67, 50, 98, 44, 29

12. Determine the standard deviation for the following data.
    100, 98, 102, 97, 84, 56, 73, 68, 111, 121

13. Five random samples were selected to determine the lifespan of seals. The data contained values of 16, 12, 23, 25, and 18.
    (a) What is the mean for these data?
    (b) What is the range?
    (c) What is the median?
    (d) Is there a mode?
    (e) Compute the standard deviation for these data.

14. True or false? Any summary measures can be used to accurately reflect the characteristics of data.

15. True or false? Data are either symmetrical or skewed.

16. True or false? Data that are symmetrical are pulled to one side of the mean.

17. If the mean, median, and mode are close in value, the data are_____.

18. If data are skewed, the _____ is a more accurate measure of location.

19. What are the three basic measures of location?

20. What are the two basic measures of dispersion?

21. What are the two basic measures of shape?

Chapter 6

Predicting Outcomes and Estimating Populations

Up to this point, we have discussed the statistical techniques used to organize, summarize, and describe the basic properties of data. These statistical tools provide valuable insight on what has occurred in the process. The area of statistics covered in this chapter will allow you to make predictions on the likelihood of future events and estimate the characteristics of populations based on sample data. This area of statistics is based on the theory of probability. Probability indicates the likelihood of future or unknown events.

INSTRUCTIONAL OBJECTIVES

When you have completed this chapter, you will be able to:

- Define probability.
- Compute probabilities for simple events.
- Compute probabilities for combined events.
- Describe the characteristics of normal distribution.
- Determine the probability of events using the area under the curve.
- Construct a normal curve given the mean and standard deviation.
- Estimate the characteristics of a population using sample data.
- Identify and define various statistical symbols used in SPC.
- Describe random sampling techniques and state their importance.
- Define the central limit theorem and its use.
- State the relationship between the mean and standard deviations of populations and samples.

LEARNING ACTIVITIES

____6A: The Theory of Probability
____6B: Normal Distribution
____6C: Random Sampling
____6D: The Central Limit Theorem

6A: THE THEORY OF PROBABILITY

Probability is the cornerstone of nearly all decision making. Many decisions are formulated on the likelihood of an event's occurrence based on *theories* or *experience*. Probabilities based on experience are more common than those based on theory. For example, if you were to hear that a major accident has occurred on the route you normally take to work, you will probably take an alternate route to avoid the delay. Your decision to take an alternate route is based on the probability that a traffic jam is *likely* to occur. Probabilities based on experience provide the basis of most decisions.

Another aspect of probability concerns itself with precise statements regarding events that are likely to occur. For example, given 100 samples, 20 are likely to be defective. Precise statements of probability are based on theory. This aspect of probability utilizes mathematical computations that indicate the *likelihood* of certain events. Although it is impossible to state what *will* happen, the theory of probability allows us to state what is likely to happen.

Probability allows us to make predictions about the outcome of future events and to estimate the characteristics of populations, based on sample data. The outcome of any event is influenced by chance. Chance can be defined as the interaction of various factors that collectively influence the outcome of an experiment. For example, when you flip a coin, the following chance factors influence the outcome:

- The number of times the coin is shaken
- The air currents present when the coin is released
- The force involved when the coin is thrown
- The angle at which the coin hits the surface
- The texture of the surface, which affects the bounce of the coin

Chance factors affecting the outcome of any event cannot be controlled or eliminated. Given this, it is impossible to know the outcome of any event. The theory of probability allows us to predict the outcomes that are likely to occur over time, based upon repeated observations and experiments. The probability of an event is a number indicating the likelihood of some future or unknown event. This number is derived by comparing the number of successful outcomes to the number of all possible outcomes.

Before the mechanics of probability can be discussed, some basic terms need to be defined.

Probability: number that expresses the likelihood of some future or unknown event.

Experiment: series of tests conducted to determine the outcomes or results of some unknown or future event.

Trials or observations: individual tests conducted in an experiment. For example, if a coin is tossed ten times to determine the probability of likely outcomes, the ten coin tosses represent the experiment and each toss of the coin represents one trial or observation in the experiment.

Event: outcome of each trial or observation in the experiment.

In summary, probability is a number that summarizes the likelihood of future or unknown events. These numbers are based on the outcome of each trial or observation conducted in an experiment. Probability is usually stated in reference to an event. An event might be described as the number of times heads appeared in a series of coin tosses, the number of parts conforming to requirements, the hours of television watched, the number of errors in processing an order, the number of service calls made, and so on. The probability of an event is stated as *P*(event). The *P* is used to denote probability and the event in question is contained within the parentheses.

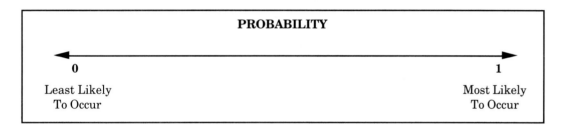

P(tossing heads)   *P*(service calls)   *P*(defects or problems)

The probability of an event is expressed as a number between 0 and 1. On a scale, 0 represents events that are *not likely* to occur, and 1 represents events that are *likely* to occur.

PROBABILITY

0   1

Least Likely   Most Likely
To Occur   To Occur

The closer the number is to 0, the more unlikely it is that the event will occur. Conversely, the closer the number is to 1, the greater the likelihood that the event will occur.

Probabilities are always expressed as a number between 0 and 1. The probability of any event can be stated as a decimal, a percentage, a fraction, or a ratio. For example, the probability of flipping heads on the toss of one coin can be expressed as:

- 1 out of 2 chances of occurring   The probability of a coin toss has two possible outcomes: heads or tails. Therefore, heads represents 1 of the 2 possible outcomes.

- $\frac{1}{2}$ Probability can be expressed as a *fraction* where the numerator represents the number of times the event (heads) can occur, and the denominator represents the number of all possible outcomes.

- 0.50   Probability can be expressed as a *decimal* by dividing the number of times the event (heads) can occur by the number of all possible outcomes. ($1 \div 2 = .50$.)

- 50%   Probability can be expressed as a *percentage*. To express the probability of an event as a percentage, multiply the decimal expression by 100. ($.50 \times 100 = 50\%$.)

All of these expressions represent a number between 0 and 1.

- $\frac{1}{2}$ is greater than 0 and less than 1.
- .50 is greater than 0 and less than 1.0.
- 50% is greater than 0 and less than 100%.

The probability of an event *cannot* be greater than 1.

The Probability of Simple Events

Simple events have only one outcome. In simple events, each possible outcome has an equal chance of occurring. For example, a toss of a coin is a simple event because only one outcome can occur (either heads or tails) and each possible outcome has an equal chance of occurring (heads = 50% and tails = 50%).

To determine the probability of a simple event, two things must be determined:

1. The number of times the event in question can occur successfully
2. The number of all possible events that can occur

The formula used to compute the probability of a simple event is

$$P(\text{event}) = \frac{\text{number of times the event can occur successfully}}{\text{number of all possible events that can occur}}$$

The following example illustrates how the probability of a simple event is calculated using this formula.

Probability of Rolling a 6 on One Die.   (A die is one unit of a pair of dice.)

P(rolling a 6)

The probability of rolling a 6 is classified as a simple event:

1. Only one outcome can occur in the roll of one die. Either a 1, 2, 3, 4, 5, or 6 will appear on the toss of one die.
2. Each outcome possible has an equal chance of occurring. No face on the die has a greater chance of occurring than the others.

Once the conditions for determining the probability of a simple event have been satisfied, the probability is computed in the following manner.

$$P(\text{event}) = \frac{\text{number of times the event can successfully occur}}{\text{number of all possible events that can occur}}$$

First, the formula is translated

$$P(\text{rolling a 6}) = \tfrac{1}{6}$$

The probability of rolling a 6 on one toss of the die is 1 out of 6. This probability is based on two factors. First, there is one face on the die equal to 6, so a 6 can occur only once in the toss of one die. Second, there are six faces on the die, so a total of six outcomes are possible in the toss of one die. Therefore, the probability of rolling a 6 on the toss of one die is $\tfrac{1}{6}$.

To express the probability of rolling a 6 on the toss of one die as a decimal or a percentage, the following calculations are needed:

$$P(\text{rolling a 6}) = \tfrac{1}{6}$$

$$\text{Decimal:} \quad = 1 \div 6$$

$$= .166 \quad \text{or } .017 \quad \text{(rounded)}$$

$$\text{Percentage:} \quad .17 \times 100 = 17\%$$

Any one of the following formats can be used to express the probability of rolling a 6 on the toss of one die:

	P(**Rolling a 6**)	
Fraction	**Decimal**	**Percent**
$\tfrac{1}{6}$	.17	17%

Another example of computing the probability of a simple event follows.

Probability of Flipping Tails on One Toss of a Coin [P(Tossing a Tail)]. A tail can occur only once when a coin is tossed and there are only two possible outcomes: a head or a tail. Since each possible outcome has an equal chance of occurring, it is classified as a simple event.

$$P(\text{tails}) = \tfrac{1}{2} \quad \text{or} \quad 50\%.$$

In the simple events covered thus far, the event in question had only one chance of occurring. Next, we address simple events when the event in question has more than one chance of occurring.

Clubs	Diamonds	Hearts	Spades
♣ K	♦ K	♥ K	♠ K
♣ Q	♦ Q	♥ Q	♠ Q
♣ J	♦ J	♥ J	♠ J
♣ 10	♦ 10	♥ 10	♠ 10
♣ 9	♦ 9	♥ 9	♠ 9
♣ 8	♦ 8	♥ 8	♠ 8
♣ 7	♦ 7	♥ 7	♠ 7
♣ 6	♦ 6	♥ 6	♠ 6
♣ 5	♦ 5	♥ 5	♠ 5
♣ 4	♦ 4	♥ 4	♠ 4
♣ 3	♦ 3	♥ 3	♠ 3
♣ 2	♦ 2	♥ 2	♠ 2
♣ 1	♦ 1	♥ 1	♠ 1

Figure 6–1   Suits.

Determine the Probability of Selecting a Queen from a Deck of 52 Cards [P(Selecting a Queen)].   (See Figure 6-1.) Given the following, the probability of selecting a queen from a deck of cards can also be classified as a simple event.

1. Whenever one card is selected from the deck, only one outcome is possible.
2. Each of the possible outcomes has an equal chance of occurring.

$$P(\text{event}) = \frac{\text{number of times the event can occur successfully}}{\text{number of all possible events that can occur}}$$

Since these two conditions have been satisfied, the same formula can be used to compute the probability of selecting a queen from a deck of cards.

There are four queens in a standard deck of 52 cards. Given this, there are four chances that the event (selecting a queen) can successfully occur. Since there are 52 cards in a standard deck of cards, 52 possible outcomes can occur. Therefore, the probability of selecting a queen from a deck of cards can be expressed as

$$P(\text{selecting a queen}) = \tfrac{4}{52} \quad \text{or} \quad 8\%$$

Probability of Events When All Possible Outcomes are Unknown

In many cases the number of all possible outcomes are not known. Under these circumstances, probability is determined by conducting an experiment to observe the events or outcomes that occur. The formula used to determine the probability of events under these conditions is

$$P(\text{event}) = \frac{\text{number of times the event occurred}}{\text{number of trials or observations}}$$

For example, if you were attempting to determine the probability of customer complaints, an experiment would be needed to determine the number of complaints received over a period of time. Let's assume that 5 customers filed complaints during a 100-day period of time. The probability of customer complaints could be expressed as follows.

$$P(\text{customer complaints}) = \tfrac{5}{100} \quad \text{or} \quad 5\%$$

Whenever experiments are conducted to determine the probability of an event when all possible outcomes are not known, it is important to keep the following in mind.

1. Experimentation provides only an *estimate,* not an exact measure of probability.
2. The number of observations conducted directly influences the accuracy and confidence of the estimated probability. Each additional trial reduces the margin of error contained in the estimate. More trials or observations provide better estimates on the probability of the event's occurrence.
3. Estimated probabilities are not universal. The results of an experiment can only be applied to data that have the exact set of conditions.

Probability of Combined Events

Up to this point, the probability of simple events has been addressed: that is, events that have only one outcome. In many cases, combined events occur. Two of the most common types of combined events are addressed next.

1. The probability of *two independent events occurring.*
2. The probability that *one of two mutually exclusive events will occur.*

Probability of Two Independent Events [P(Event 1 AND Event 2)]. The probability of two events occurring at the same time is a combined event. Events are independent when the occurrence of one event has no bearing on the occurrence of the other event. That is, if two dice are thrown, the outcome of one die has no bearing or affect on the outcome of the other die. Each event is independent and stands alone.

To compute the probability of two independent events, the probability of one event is multiplied by the probability of the second event:

$$P(\text{event 1 AND event 2}) = P(\text{event 1}) \times P(\text{event 2})$$

For example, what is the probability of tossing a head on two coins, P(heads and heads)? The outcome of tossing a head on one coin does not affect the outcome of tossing a head on the other coin, making the events independent. To compute the probability of two independent events, the probability of each event needs to be determined. The probability of tossing heads on one coin is $\tfrac{1}{2}$ and the probability of tossing heads on the other coin is $\frac{1}{2}$. To determine the probability that both independent events will occur, the probability of each independent event is multiplied.

$$P(\text{heads AND heads}) = P(\text{heads}) \times P(\text{heads})$$
$$= \frac{1}{2} \times \frac{1}{2}^{*}$$
$$= \frac{1}{4} \quad \text{or} \quad 25\%$$

To prove the accuracy of this probability, all possible outcomes that can occur when two coins are tossed are outlined below.

	Coin 1	Coin 2
1 Toss	H	H
2 Tosses	H	T
3 Tosses	T	H
4 Tosses	T	T

A total of four combinations can occur when two coins are tossed. *Heads* will occur only once on both coins. The probability of tossing *heads* on two coins is $\frac{1}{4}$. Next, consider the probability of rolling a 2 and a 6 on a pair of dice.

$$P(\text{2 on one die AND 6 on second die})$$

First the probability of each independent event must be determined. The probability of rolling a 2 on one die is $\frac{1}{6}$, and the probability of rolling a 6 on one die is also $\frac{1}{6}$. To compute the probability that both events will occur, multiply the probability of each independent event:

$$P(\text{2 on one die AND 6 on one die}) = P(\text{2 on one die}) \times P(\text{6 on one die})$$
$$= \frac{1}{6} \times \frac{1}{6}$$
$$= \frac{1}{36} \quad \text{or} \quad 3\%$$

Whenever the probability of two independents is required, each independent event is multiplied, regardless of the number of events. To determine the probability for a number of independent events, follow these two steps:

1.   Determine the probability of each independent event.

$$P(\text{event}) = \frac{\text{number of times the event can occur successfully}}{\text{number of all possible events that can occur}}$$

---

* Whenever you multiply fractions, multiple the numerator of each fraction, then multiply the denominators of each fraction. $\frac{1}{2} \times \frac{1}{2}$ —$1 \times 1 = 1$ and $2 \times 2 = 4$; the answer is $\frac{1}{4}$.

2. Multiply each independent probability:

$$P(\text{event 1}) \times P(\text{event 2}) \times P(\text{event 3}) \times P(\text{event 4}), \text{etc.}$$

For example, to determine the probability of flipping heads on five consecutive coin tosses, the following calculations are required.

1. The probability for each independent event is $\frac{1}{2}$.
2. The probability of flipping 5 heads is $\frac{1}{2} \times \frac{1}{2} \times \frac{1}{2} \times \frac{1}{2} \times \frac{1}{2}$.

The probability of flipping heads on 5 consecutive tosses is $\frac{1}{32}$ or 3%.

Probability That One Mutually Exclusive Event Will Occur [P(Event 1 OR Event 2)]. The probability that *at least one of two events will occur* is also known as a combined event. Events are *mutually exclusive* when only one of the two events can actually occur. That is, if one event occurs, the other event cannot possibly occur. To compute the probability of two mutually exclusive events, the probability of each event is added.

$$P(\text{event 1 OR event 2}) = P(\text{event 1}) + P(\text{event 2})$$

For instance, consider the probability of drawing an ace or a jack from a standard deck of 52 cards. These events are mutually exclusive because only one of these events can actually occur (ace *or* jack). To compute the probability of these mutually exclusive events, the probability of each event is required. The probability of drawing an ace is $\frac{4}{52}$ and the probability of drawing a jack is $\frac{4}{52}$. To determine the probability that either one or the other event will occur, the probability of each event is added.

$$
\begin{aligned}
P(\text{ace OR jack}) &= P(\text{ace}) + P(\text{jack}) \\
&= \frac{4}{52} + \frac{4}{52} \\
&= \frac{8}{52} \quad \text{or} \quad 15\%
\end{aligned}
$$

Here is another example of computing the probability of two mutually exclusive events. Determine the probability of rolling a 5 or a 6 in a single roll of one die: $P(\text{rolling a 5 OR a 6})$. First, the probability of each mutually exclusive event must be determined. The probability of rolling a 5 on one die is $\frac{1}{6}$, and the probability of rolling a 6 on one die is also $\frac{1}{6}$. To compute the probability that either a 5 or a 6 will occur, the probability of each event is added.

$$
\begin{aligned}
P(\text{rolling a 5 OR a 6}) &= P(\text{rolling a 5}) + P(\text{rolling a 6}) \\
&= \frac{1}{6} + \frac{1}{6} \\
&= \frac{2}{6} \quad \text{or} \quad 33\%
\end{aligned}
$$

Whenever the probability of two mutually exclusive events is required, the probability of each event is added, regardless of the number of events.

$$P(\text{event 1 OR event 2}) = P(\text{event 1}) + P(\text{event 2})$$

To determine the probability for a number of mutually exclusive events, the following steps are required.

1. Determine the probability of each event:

$$P(\text{event}) = \frac{\text{number of times the event can occur successfully}}{\text{number of all possible events that can occur}}$$

2. Add the probability of each event:

$$P(\text{event 1}) + P(\text{event 2}) + P(\text{event 3}) + P(\text{event 4}), \text{etc.}$$

For example, to determine the probability of rolling a 1 or 2 or 3 or 4 on a single roll of one die, the following calculations are needed.

1. The probability for each event is $\frac{1}{6}$.
2. The probability of rolling a 1, 2, 3, or 4 is $\frac{1}{6} + \frac{1}{6} + \frac{1}{6} + \frac{1}{6}$.

The probability of this mutually exclusive event is $\frac{4}{6}$ or 67%.

6B: NORMAL DISTRIBUTION

As described in the preceding unit, probability is a powerful tool used to estimate or predict the likelihood of future events. Probability can best be thought of as a yardstick that gages the likelihood of certain outcomes. These measures reduce uncertainty and enable you to make sound decisions. The concepts described thus far provide the framework governing the theories of probability. These concepts, in and of themselves, are of little value in predicting the outcomes of most processes. However, as the theory of probability is expanded to include the concepts of normal distribution, you will be able to see how probability can be used to determine the likelihood of events in any process.

As indicated earlier, variation occurs in all things. That is, everything varies to some degree. Therefore, it can be concluded that no process, product, or service is always the same. Anything that can be measured or counted contains variation. If you were to plot this variation on a graph, you would find that most variation tends to form a basic pattern or shape. This is commonly referred to as the *normal distribution curve* or the *normal curve* (Figure 6-2). The normal curve illustrates the natural or normal variation that occurs in most processes.

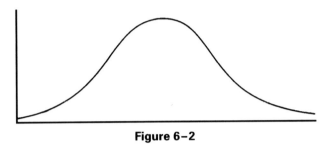

Figure 6–2

The concept of *normal distribution* is a natural phenomenon that was discovered in the eighteenth century by a group of astronomers and scientists. To their amazement, they found that repeated measurements always varied. When the measurements were plotted on a graph, one shape continued to occur. The measurements always formed a bell-shaped pattern. The importance of this discovery is that the distribution of nearly all measurable or countable data tends to form a bell-shaped pattern. This pattern is commonly referred to as the normal curve. The normal curve provides a simplified model that can be used to determine the probability of certain events in nearly all stable processes. Given this, the normal curve allows us to make predictions on the likelihood of certain outcomes.

To illustrate how the normal curve is used to determine the probability of certain events, the characteristics of normal distribution need to be examined.

1. The *area under the curve* represents 99.7% of the possible outcomes (Figure 6-3). Therefore, all but .3% of the outcomes produced in a *normally distributed* process will be distributed in the *area under the curve.*

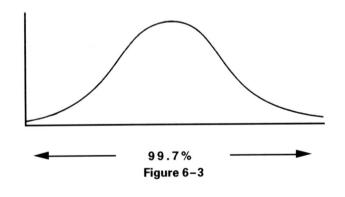

99.7%
Figure 6–3

2. The mean (average) is located at the center of the curve (Figure 6-4). The mean represents the average value of the outcomes *under the curve.*

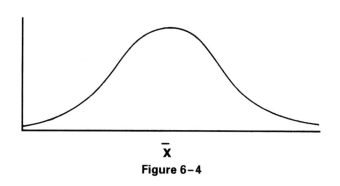

$$\overline{x}$$

Figure 6-4

3. The *area under the curve* is divided into six sections (Figure 6-5). Each section represents 1 standard deviation. Each standard deviation indicates the percentage of measurements in the area under the curve. The standard deviations to the left of the mean are negative and those to the right of the mean are positive. Of the variation in any *normally distributed* process, 99.73% falls within 6 standard deviations (+3 and −3 from the mean).

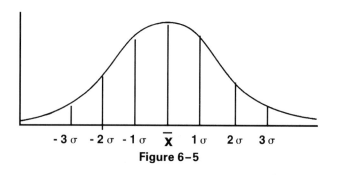

$$-3\sigma \quad -2\sigma \quad -1\sigma \quad \overline{x} \quad 1\sigma \quad 2\sigma \quad 3\sigma$$

Figure 6-5

4. Of the data in a *normally distributed* process, 68% will fall between +1 and −1 standard deviations from the mean (Figure 6-6).

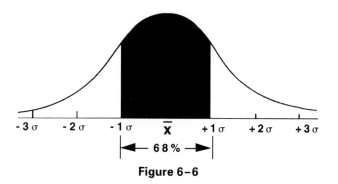

$$-3\sigma \quad -2\sigma \quad -1\sigma \quad \overline{x} \quad +1\sigma \quad +2\sigma \quad +3\sigma$$

$$\longleftarrow 68\% \longrightarrow$$

Figure 6-6

5. Of the data in a *normally distributed* process, 95.5% will fall between +2 and −2 standard deviations from the mean (Figure 6-7).

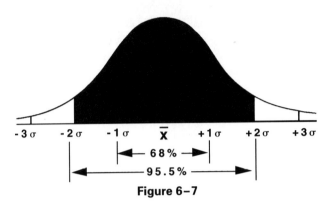

Figure 6–7

6. Of the data in a normally distributed process, 99.7% will fall between +3 and −3 standard deviations from the mean (Figure 6-8).

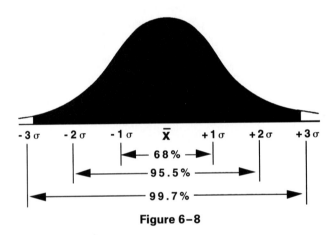

Figure 6–8

In terms of probability, the probability of selecting one sample from a *normally distributed* population that will fall within +1 and −1 standard deviations is 68%. Similarly, the probability of selecting a sample that is located within +2 and −2 standard deviations from a *normally distributed* population is 95.5%, and there is a 99.7% probability that a sample selected from the population will fall within +3 and −3 standard deviations (Figure 6-9).

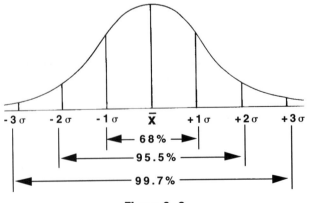

Figure 6–9

The normal curve for any process can be completely specified by two numbers: the mean and the standard deviation. The mean represents the average value of the data. The standard deviation is a measure of the average deviation or spread of data from the mean. Although each mean and standard deviation forms a unique curve or bell-shaped pattern, the characteristics of the normal curve are always the same.

The characteristics of the normal curve enable you to determine the probability of values that are likely to occur in any normally distributed process. To demonstrate this, consider the following example. A manufacturing process produced 500 switches. Each switch produced was measured and recorded. The mean was calculated to be 20.0 and the standard deviation was .3. Given these two numbers, the values for the normal curve can be computed. The mean of the 500 switches is 20.0; therefore, 20.0 is the value located at the center of the normal curve (Figure 6-10).

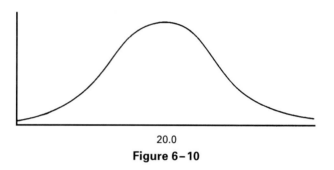

20.0

Figure 6-10

The standard deviation for the 500 switches is .3. To compute the values for each standard deviation, the calculations shown in Figure 6-11 are required.

Unit of Standard Deviation	=	Number of Standard Deviations	×	Value of 1 Standard Deviation	+	Mean	=	Standard Deviation Value
+1 σ	=	1	×	.3	+	20.0	=	20.3
+2 σ	=	2	×	.3	+	20.0	=	20.6
+3 σ	=	3	×	.3	+	20.0	=	20.9
−1 σ	=	−1	×	.3	+	20.0	=	19.7
−2 σ	=	−2	×	.3	+	20.0	=	19.4
−3 σ	=	−3	×	.3	+	20.0	=	19.1

Figure 6-11

These computed values can be inserted under the curve and the probability of likely outcomes likely are determined by the characteristics of the normal curve (Figure 6-12).

- 68% of the switches will be between 19.7 and 20.3.
- 95.5% of the switches will be between 19.4 and 20.6.
- 99.7% of the switches will be between 19.1 and 20.9.

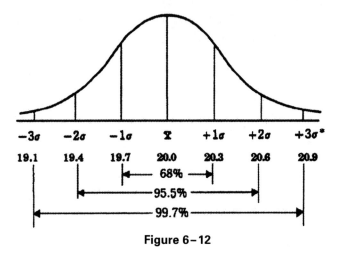

Figure 6–12

The normal curve is a model that can be used to estimate the probability of values that are likely to occur in *any* normally distributed process. The basic rules of probability can also be applied to the normal curve.

Probability of a Simple Event

$$P(\text{event}) = \frac{\text{number of times the event can successfully occur}}{\text{number of all possible events that can occur}}$$

A simple event may be to determine the probability of selecting a sample that is between 19.7 and 20.3. To compute the probability of this event, the following calculations would be needed:

$$P(\text{selecting a sample between the values of 19.7 and 20.3}) = \frac{68}{100}$$

The probability of selecting a sample between the values of 19.7 and 20.3 is 68%.

Probability That One of Two Mutually Exclusive Events Will Occur [P(Event 1 OR Event 2)]

$$P(\text{event 1 OR event 2}) = P(\text{event 1}) + P(\text{event 2})$$

This combined event could be stated as the probability of selecting a sample between the MEAN and the values of 19.7 or 20.3. To compute the probability of this event, the following calculations are required.

$P(\text{sample between mean and 19.7 or 20.3})$

$$= P(\text{mean and 19.7}) + P(\text{mean and 20.3})$$

$$= \qquad 0.34 \qquad + \qquad 0.34$$

$$= 68 \quad \text{or} \quad 68\%$$

Probability That Two Independent Events Will Occur [P(Event 1 AND Event 2)]

$$P(\text{event 1 AND event 2}) = P(\text{event 1}) \times P(\text{event 2})$$

This combined event could be stated as the probability of selecting two samples between the values of 19.7 and 20.3. To compute the probability of this event, the following calculations are needed.

$$P(\text{samples 1 and 2 are between 19.7 or 20.3}) = P(\text{sample 1}) \times P(\text{sample 2})$$
$$= 0.68 \times 0.68$$
$$= 0.46 \quad \text{or} \quad 46\%$$

In effect, probability can be used to describe or estimate the characteristics of any process. Given the relationship between probability and normal distribution, the values within any normally distributed process can be estimated and the events or outcomes that are likely to occur can be predicted.

6C: RANDOM SAMPLING

The normal curve is a model that defines the basic characteristics of variation in any normally distributed process. The curve represents an easy method for determining the probability of outcomes or events that are likely to occur. Yet even though the normal curve makes it easy to determine the probability of certain events, the mean and standard deviation need to be computed before the curve can be of any value. Since it is virtually impossible to count or measure every item produced by a given process, *random sampling* methods are used. Random samples are selected in a manner whereby every item in the process has an equal chance of being selected. Random sampling methods help to ensure that the samples provide an accurate picture of the entire process. The information obtained from random samples can be used to estimate and describe the characteristics of the entire population or process.

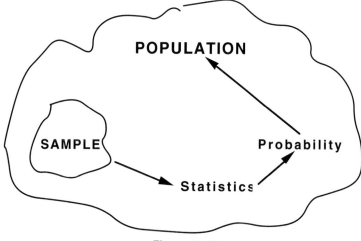

Figure 6–13

Therefore, by taking a series of random samples and calculating the mean and standard deviation of the samples, the mean and standard deviation of the entire population can be estimated.

> Samples ≈ populations
> Sample means ≈ population means
> Sample standard deviations ≈ population standard deviations
> (≈ means used to estimate or approximately equal to)

To demonstrate how samples can be used to estimate the characteristics of a population or process, it may be helpful to recall the example that was used earlier to describe the characteristics of a normal distribution. In that example the distribution of 500 switches was plotted onto a graph to illustrate the bell-shaped pattern (normal curve) that was formed (Figure 6-14). Given the characteristics of this population, you can observe the behavior of samples randomly selected from the population.

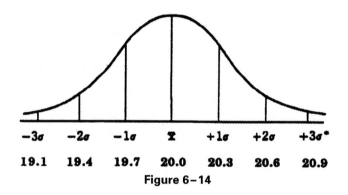

-3σ	-2σ	-1σ	$\overline{X}$	$+1\sigma$	$+2\sigma$	$+3\sigma$
19.1	19.4	19.7	20.0	20.3	20.6	20.9

Figure 6–14

The mean of this population was 20.0, with a standard deviation of .3. Now let's assume that a number of samples were randomly selected from the process in order to estimate the characteristics of the entire population. Each sample group contained five individual measurements, and five sample groups were selected from the population. Based on the samples selected from the population, the following data were recorded:

Sample 1	Sample 2	Sample 3	Sample 4	Sample 5
20.16	20.25	20.02	19.73	20.33
20.27	19.63	19.88	20.46	20.03
19.94	20.15	19.99	19.41	20.37
19.54	20.59	19.96	20.01	19.68
19.85	19.90	19.78	20.09	20.13

The mean $\overline{X}$ and the standard deviation (σ) were calculated for each sample selected from the population.

	Sample 1	Sample 2	Sample 3	Sample 4	Sample 5
	20.16	20.25	20.02	19.73	20.33
	20.27	19.63	19.88	20.46	20.03
	19.94	20.15	19.99	19.41	20.37
	19.54	20.59	19.96	20.01	19.68
	19.85	19.90	19.78	20.09	20.13
Sum	99.76	100.52	99.63	99.70	100.54
Mean	19.95	20.10	19.93	19.94	20.11
σ	.285	.363	.097	.395	.277

Each sample mean varies slightly from the population mean; however, the grand average for all sample means is 20.0.

$$\text{Grand average } \overline{\overline{X}} = (19.95 + 20.10 + 19.93 + 19.94 + 20.11) \div 5 = 20.0$$

The same holds true for the standard deviation. Each sample standard deviation tends to vary from the population's standard deviation, but the average standard deviation is .3.

$$\text{Average standard deviation} = (.285 + .363 + .097 + .395 + .277) \div 5 = .3$$

Figure 6-15 summarizes the relationship of random samples selected from a population. This exercise demonstrates how random samples can be used to estimate and describe the characteristics of the entire population.

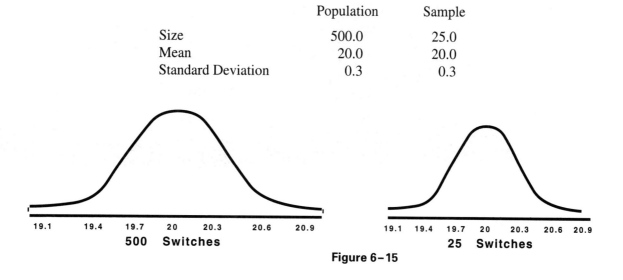

	Population	Sample
Size	500.0	25.0
Mean	20.0	20.0
Standard Deviation	0.3	0.3

Figure 6–15

6D: THE CENTRAL LIMIT THEOREM

The theory that explains how random samples can be used to estimate the characteristics of an entire population is known as the *central limit theorem,* which states two very important rules regarding the statistical behavior of data.

Rule 1: If the population *is* normally distributed, the means of samples selected from the population will also be normally distributed, regardless of the sample size.

Rule 2: If the population is *not* normally distributed, the means of 30 or more samples randomly selected from the population will be normally distributed.

The example used to demonstrate how random samples selected from a population of 500 switches could be used to estimate the characteristics for the entire population supports the validity of Rule 1 (Figure 6-16).

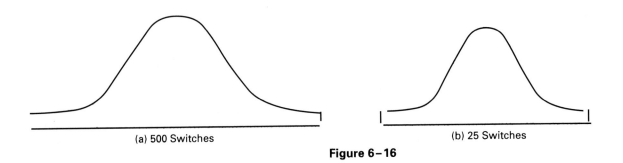

(a) 500 Switches   (b) 25 Switches

Figure 6–16

Rule 2 states that *regardless* of the population's distribution, the means of 30 or more samples selected from the process will be normally distributed (Figure 6-17).

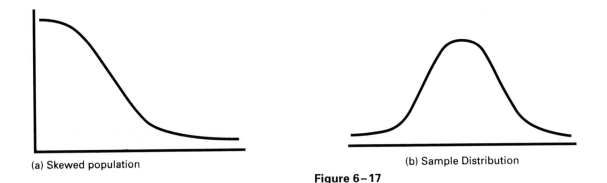

(a) Skewed population   (b) Sample Distribution

Figure 6–17

If you have some time and are interested in conducting an experiment to prove the validity of the central limit theorem, try the following exercise.

Experiment

A standard deck of 52 cards (Figure 6-1) is classified as an entire population. The distribution of this population is rectangular (Figure 6-18). To test the validity of Rule 2, randomly select 30 samples (2 cards per sample) from the deck. For each sample, record the values of each card, total the values and compute the average

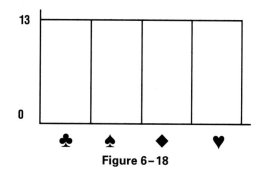

Figure 6–18

for each sample, using a tally sheet like the one shown in Figure 6-19. After you have selected 30 samples, plot the sample means on a graph. Through this experiment, you will find the sample means will form a normal curve (Figure 6-20). Regardless of the population's distribution, the means of 30 or more samples randomly selected from the population will be *normally distributed.*

Sample	Value Card 1	Value Card 2	Total	Average (Mean)
1				
2				
3				
4				
5				
6				
...				
...				
...				
30				

Figure 6–19 Ace = 1, 2, 3, 4, 5, 6, 7, 8, 9, 10, jack = 11, queen = 12, and king = 13.

The importance of the central limit theorem is that you can obtain the critical information needed to analyze and predict the outcomes of any process, based on the means of 30 or more samples selected randomly from the process.

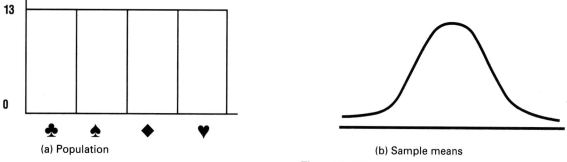

(a) Population

(b) Sample means

Figure 6–20

SUMMARY

In summary, probability is a number used to express the likelihood of future or unknown events. The theory of probability provides the basic foundations used to predict outcomes or estimate the characteristics of a population. The probability of any event is expressed as a number between 0 and 1.

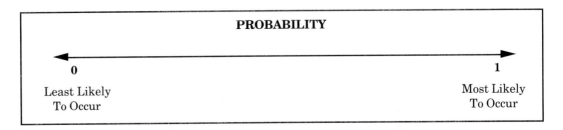

The rules of probability are designed to aid the computations necessary to determine the probability of an event.

Probability of Simple Events When All Outcomes Are Known

$$P(\text{event}) = \frac{\text{number of times the event can occur successfully}}{\text{number of all possible events that can occur}}$$

Probability of Simple Events When All Outcomes Are Not Known

$$P(\text{event}) = \frac{\text{number of times the event occurred}}{\text{total number of trials or observations}}$$

Probability That Two Independent Events Will Both Occur [P(Event 1 AND Event 2)]

$$P(\text{event 1 AND event 2}) = P(\text{event 1}) \times P(\text{event 2})$$

Probability That One of Two Mutually Exclusive Events Will Occur [P(Event 1 OR Event 2)]

$$P(\text{event 1 OR event 2}) = P(\text{event 1}) + P(\text{event 2})$$

The basic rules of probability can also be used to predict the characteristics or outputs of most processes. Every process contains a certain amount of variation. The natural or predictable variation in most stable processes is referred to as the normal distribution curve. The normal curve is the model used to predict or estimate the variation in nearly all processes. Figure 6-21 illustrates the probability of outcomes or events that are likely to occur in a normally distributed process.

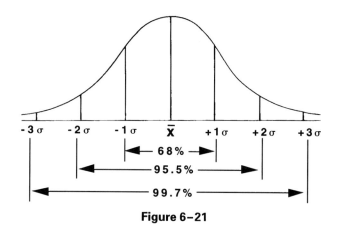

Figure 6–21

In a normally distributed process, 68% of the data will fall within -1 and $+1$ standard deviations of the mean, 95.5% of the data will be fall within -2 and $+2$ standard deviations of the mean, and 99.73% of the data will fall within -3 and $+3$ standard deviations of the mean. In effect, 99.73% of the data in a normally distributed population will fall within 6 standard deviations of the mean. Six standard deviations is equivalent to $+3$ and -3 standard deviations from the mean.

Random sampling methods eliminate the need to measure or count the entire population. Statistical theories have proven that the distribution of 30 or more sample means selected from a population will be normally distributed, regardless of the population's distribution. Based on this, the means of 30 or more random samples selected from a process can be used to estimate the probability of future or unknown events.

Estimating Populations

- The characteristics of random samples can be used to estimate the characteristics of the entire population.
- Sample means are used to estimate population means.
- Sample standard deviations are used to estimate the population standard deviations.

Given the statistical theories presented in this chapter, the characteristics of almost any process can be determined by a series of random samples. To determine the characteristics or estimate the probability of events in any process, the mean and the standard deviation need to be computed.

Once the values for the mean and standard deviation have been computed, the normal curve can be used to determine the probability of events. The mean is located at the center of the curve and the values of ±3 standard deviations are entered along the horizontal axis. The following calculations are required to compute the values of each standard deviation.

$$-1\sigma = -1(\sigma) + \overline{X} \qquad 1\sigma = 1(\sigma) + \overline{X}$$
$$-2\sigma = -2(\sigma) + \overline{X} \qquad 2\sigma = 2(\sigma) + \overline{X}$$
$$-3\sigma = -3(\sigma) + \overline{X} \qquad 3\sigma = 3(\sigma) + \overline{X}$$

Given this information, the probability of events can be estimated, using the normal curve (Figure 6-22). The normal curve represents the probability of values likely to occur in the process: 68% of the values will fall within −1 and +1 standard deviations of the mean, 95.5% of the values will fall within −2 and +2 standard deviations of the mean, and 99.7% of the values will fall within −3 and +3 standard deviations of the mean.

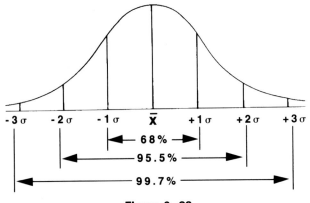

Figure 6−22

REVIEW QUESTIONS

1. The theory of probability states the _____ of future events.

2. If the probability of an event is 0, the outcome is _____ to occur.

3. Insert the formula for the following probabilities.
   (a) The probability of simple events when all outcomes are known
   (b) The probability of simple events when all outcomes are not known
   (c) The probability that two independent events will both occur
   (d) The probability that one of two mutually exclusive events will occur

4. A box contains 20 colored balls: 3 white, 7 red, and 10 green balls. What is the probability of picking a white ball?

5. A process has produced 1000 items and 15% are defective. What is the probability of drawing a defective on the first draw?

6. The probability of producing an item that is too small is .15 and the probability of producing an item that is too large is .10. What is the probability of selecting an item that is too large or too small?

7. The probability of finding a defective is .20. What is the probability of selecting two defectives?

8. A pair of dice are tossed. What is the probability of throwing a 6 on both?

9. A firm has a three-step inspection process. The probability of a defective in each step is .20. What's the probability that a defective will get by all 3?

10. What is the probability of selecting a jack or a queen from a deck of cards?

11. Using the normal curve, enter the location of the mean and $\pm 3\sigma$.

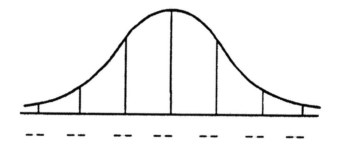

   (a) What percentage of probabilities is displayed under the normal curve?
   (b) What percentage of probabilities is located between $\pm 1\sigma$?
   (c) What percentage of probabilities is located between $\pm 2\sigma$?
   (d) What percentage of probabilities is located between $\pm 3\sigma$?

12. Using the normal curve, answer the following questions.

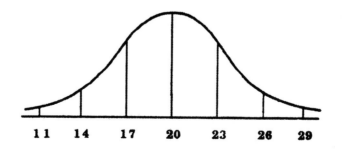

   11   14   17   20   23   26   29

   (a) What is the probability of selecting one item between 17 and 23?
   (b) What is the probability of selecting one item between 11 and 29?
   (c) What is the mean value?

      (d)   What is the value of -1σ?

      (e)   What is the value of 2σ?

      (f)   What is the probability of selecting two items between 17 and 23?

13. If a process has a mean of 15 and a standard deviation of 2, compute the values of $\pm 3\sigma$.

14. Fifty samples were randomly selected from a process. Compute the mean and standard deviation for the following data and draw the normal curve.

Sample 1	Sample 2	Sample 3	Sample 4	Sample 5
4	10	6	9	11
8	5	1	2	6
0	2	1	10	12
3	2	4	3	5
13	9	7	9	0

15. Using the data from Question 14,

      (a)   68% of the items will fall between ___ and ___.

      (b)   95.5% of the items will fall between ___ and ___.

      (c)   99.73% of the items will fall between ___ and ___.

16. State the two rules for the central limit theorem.

17. If the mean of 50 subgroups is plotted on graph, do you need to measure the entire population to determine the probability of values?

Chapter 7

Process Capability and Precontrol Charts

In Chapter 6 you learned how the theories of probability and normal distribution can be used to predict outcomes and estimate the characteristics of processes. In this chapter you will learn how to assess the variation in processes. The chapter contains two units. Unit 7A explains the importance of assessing the capability of the process. In Unit 7B you will learn a simple technique to monitor process variation and capability, using precontrol charts.

INSTRUCTIONAL OBJECTIVES

When you have completed this chapter, you will be able to:

- Define the term *process*.
- Describe the conditions of processes operating in control.
- State the characteristics of process capability.
- Identify four basic operating conditions.
- Compute the capability ratio of a given process.
- Compute the capability of process of a given process.
- Compute the capability in relation to mean of a given process.
- Identify the two significant process changes affecting quality.
- Construct a precontrol chart.
- Apply precontrol techniques to a given process.
- Monitor and analyze process characteristics, using precontrol.

LEARNING ACTIVITIES

_____7A: Process Capability
_____7B: Precontrol Techniques

7A: PROCESS CAPABILITY

As you have learned, a certain amount of variation is present in all processes. Variation affects the *quality* of products or services produced by the process. Therefore, process *variation* needs to be carefully monitored, analyzed, and controlled. Statistical process control (SPC) provides the basic statistical methods used to analyze the process and control the quality of parts and services produced.

A process can be defined as a set of conditions that are combined to produce a product, service, or result. These conditions are commonly classified as:

- Machines and equipment
- Methods and procedures
- Personnel
- Materials
- Measurements
- Environment

Each condition is a source of variation in the process. When these conditions are combined to produce a product or service, a natural and predictable amount of random variation occurs. Variation that occurs from these conditions *cannot* be entirely eliminated and are referred to as *common-cause variation.*

In most cases, common-cause variation can be described by the normal curve (Figure 7-1). That is, 99.7% of the common-cause variation will fall within ±3 standard deviations of the mean. Whenever processes exhibit stable and predictable variation, the process is operating *in control.* The parts or services produced by processes operating in control are the best that the process can produce, unless the process itself is changed or improved.

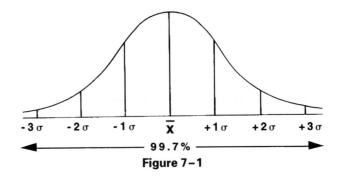

Figure 7–1

The term *process capability* refers to the inherent or natural ability of the process to produce parts or services over a period of time. Before the capability of any process can be determined, however, the process variation needs to be stable. That is, the process must be in control. Once you have established the common-cause variation operating within the process, you can determine if the process is *capable* of repeatedly meeting the stated requirements.

Process requirements are often stated in terms of upper and lower specification limits or boundaries. The difference between these two limits is called the specification spread (Figure 7-2). If the common-cause variation (normal distribution) of a process falls within the stated specifications, 99.73% of the

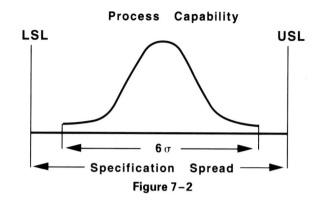

Figure 7–2

parts or services produced will meet the requirements. Thus you can conclude that the process is capable of repeatedly meeting the process requirements. If this is not the case, actions should be taken to improve the performance of the process.

Given this, statistical process control provides methods that measure the process's common-cause variation *(in control)* and the process's ability of repeatedly meeting the stated requirements *(capability)*.

Processes operating "in control" are not always "capable" of repeatedly meeting the process requirements. The following conditions can exist in any given process.

1. Processes can be in control and capable of repeatedly meeting requirements.
2. Processes can be in control and *not* capable of repeatedly meeting requirements.
3. Processes can be out of control but are capable of repeatedly meeting the requirements.
4. Processes can be out of control and *not* be capable of repeatedly meeting the requirements.

Figure 7-3 illustrates each of these conditions. Distribution (a) is in control and capable of repeatedly meeting the process requirements. Therefore, distribution (a) is operating within statistical process control.

Distribution (b) is also in control; however, the variation exceeds the process requirements. Therefore, the process is not capable of repeatedly meeting the stated requirements. Given this, distribution (b) is *not* operating within statistical process control.

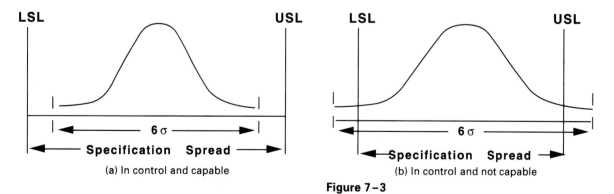

Figure 7–3

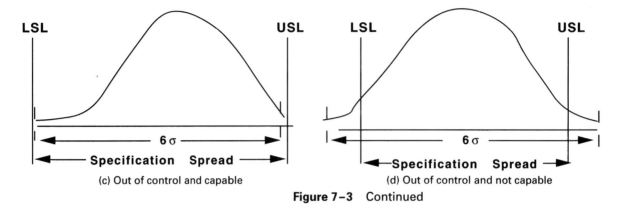

(c) Out of control and capable   (d) Out of control and not capable

Figure 7–3   Continued

Distribution (c) is out of control, yet the process variation falls within the requirements. Whenever a process is out of control but capable, the process is *not* operating within statistical process control.

Distribution (d) is also operating out of control and some of the variation exceeds the requirements. As a result, this process is out of control and not capable of repeatedly meeting the requirements. Distribution (d) is *not* operating within statistical process control.

To maintain statistical process control in any given process, two conditions must be satisfied:

1. The process must be in control. That is, the variation within the process does not exceed six standard deviations.
2. The process should be capable. That is, common-cause variation must fall within the process requirements.

The normal curve is used to identify common-cause variation within a process. Capability indexes are frequently used to determine if a process meets the requirements. Capability indexes are helpful because they express the capability of a process as a single number, making it easier to evaluate the process's capability.

Three indexes are used to evaluate the capability of any given process.

• Capability ratio (CR)
• Capability of process (CP)
• Capability in relation to mean (Cpk)

K is the comparison of the process's mean and the specification midpoint. The value of *K* tells you how the data are centered within specification limits.

Capability Ratio

The *capability ratio* (CR) is the ratio of the process's common variation (6σ) to the requirements (specification spread) (see Figure 7-2):

$$\text{capability ratio} = \frac{\text{capability } (6\sigma)}{\text{specification spread}}$$

Ideally, the capability ratio should be .75 or less to ensure and maintain good statistical process control over any given process. For example, if a process is operating in control and has an upper limit of $+1.2$ and a lower limit of -1.2, with a standard deviation of .30, would the process be capable of repeatedly meeting the requirements?

To answer this question using the capability ratio, the following calculations are required:

$$
\begin{aligned}
\text{process capability} &= 6 \text{ standard deviations} \\
&= 6 \times .30 \\
&= 1.80
\end{aligned}
$$

$$
\begin{aligned}
\text{specification spread} &= +1.2 \text{ and } -1.2 \\
&= 1.2 + 1.2 \\
&= 2.4
\end{aligned}
$$

$$
\begin{aligned}
\text{capability ratio} &= \frac{1.80}{2.4} \\
&= .75
\end{aligned}
$$

The capability ratio is .75 or 75%. Therefore, the process is capable of repeatedly meeting the requirements or stated specifications, as Figure 7-4 illustrates. Given this, the process is in control and capable of repeatedly meeting the requirements. Therefore, it is operating within statistical process control.

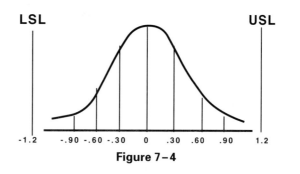

LSL   **USL**

-1.2   -.90 -.60 -.30   0   .30   .60   .90   1.2

Figure 7-4

Capability of Process

Another method of computing the capability of a process is capability of process (CP). The formula used to compute CP is the inverse of the capability ratio (CR) formula. CP is the ratio of the process's requirements (specification) to its common-cause variation (6σ):

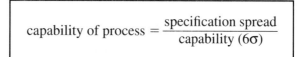

$$
\text{capability of process} = \frac{\text{specification spread}}{\text{capability } (6\sigma)}
$$

When capability of process is used to determine process capability, the value of CP should be 1.33 or greater.

- If the value of CP is between 1.0 and 1.33, the process is capable, but it should be monitored carefully as it approaches 1.0.
- If the value of CP is less than 1.0, the process is *not* capable.

Using the previous example, the capability of process would be computed as follows:

> Process specification ±1.2   Standard deviation: .30

$$\text{process capability} = 6 \text{ standard deviations}$$
$$= 6 \times .30$$
$$= 1.80$$

$$\text{specification spread} = +1.2 \text{ and } -1.2$$
$$= 1.2 + 1.2$$
$$= 2.4$$

$$\text{capability of process} = \frac{2.4}{1.80}$$
$$= 1.33$$

The CP for this process is 1.33, indicating that the process is capable of repeatedly meeting the requirements.

The capability of any process can be determined by either the capability ratio (CR) or capability of process (CP). The only difference between the two is the way the process capability is computed and interpreted.

- When CR is used, the process is capable when it is .75 or less.
- When CP is used, the process is capable when the value is 1.33 or greater.

> CR ≤ .75   CP ≥ 1.33

It is important to keep in mind that whenever the process's mean is not the same as the midpoint of the specification, CR or CP are less precise measures of process capability. Under these circumstances, the process mean should be centered before the CR or CP is computed.

One easy way to compare the process mean to the specification's midpoint is to compute the value of *K*. *K* indicates how the process variation is centered within the specification limits. The value of *K* is computed as follows:

$$K = \frac{\text{mean} - \text{midpoint}}{\text{tolerance} \div 2}$$

- If the value of K is a *positive number*, the process's mean is above the midpoint of the stated specifications.

- If the value of K is a *negative number*, the process mean is below the midpoint of the stated specifications.

- If the value of K is 0, the process mean is equal to the midpoint of the stated specifications.

The value of K does not relate to the capability of the process. It is simply a measure that tells you how the data is centered.

If the value of CR or CP indicates that the process is capable but the process is not centered, a portion of the variation will fall outside the requirements or specification limits. Figure 7-7 illustrates when K is a negative number or a positive number.

Capability in Relation to the Specification Mean

Cpk is considered the most useful index because the formula compensates for any shifts in the process's mean away from the specification's midpoint. This provides you with a more accurate measurement of the process's overall capability.

The following formula is used to compute the value of Cpk:

$$
\text{Cpk} = \text{the lesser of:}
$$
$$
\frac{\text{USL} - \text{mean}}{3\sigma} \quad \text{or} \quad \frac{\text{mean} - \text{LSL}}{3\sigma}
$$

Using the following example, the value of Cpk is computed as follows:

$$\text{USL} = 1.2 \qquad \text{mean} = 0$$

$$\text{LSL} = -1.2 \qquad \sigma = .30$$

First, the formula is translated by inserting the values into the formula.

$$\text{Cpk} = \text{the lesser of:}$$

$$\frac{\text{USL} - \text{mean}}{3\sigma} \quad \text{or} \quad \frac{\text{Mean} - \text{LSL}}{3\sigma}$$

$$\frac{1.2 - 0}{3(.30)} \quad \text{or} \quad \frac{0 - (-1.2)*}{3(.30)}$$

$$\frac{1.2}{.90} \quad \text{or} \quad \frac{1.2}{.90}$$

$$1.33 \quad \text{or} \quad 1.33$$

To interpret the meaning of the Cpk value, use the following index.

---

* Whenever you subtract a negative value, the subtraction sign is changed to an addition sign and the number to the right of the subtraction sign is changed to its inverse.

- A negative Cpk value indicates the process mean is outside the specification limits (Figure 7-5).

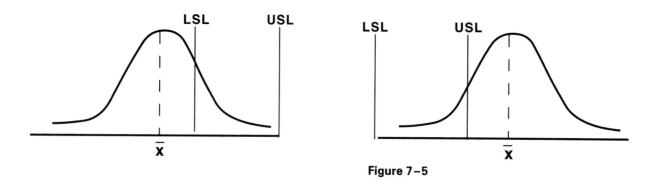

Figure 7–5

- A Cpk value of 0 indicates that the process mean is equal to one of the specification limits (Figure 7-6).

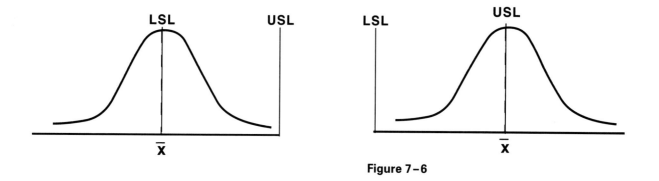

Figure 7–6

- If the value of Cpk is between 0 and 1.0, the process mean is within the specification limits, however, a portion of the process's variation falls outside of the specification limits (Figure 7-7).

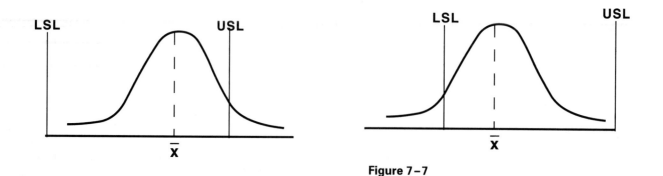

Figure 7–7

• If the value of Cpk is 1.0, one end of the process's variation falls on a specification limit (Figure 7-8).

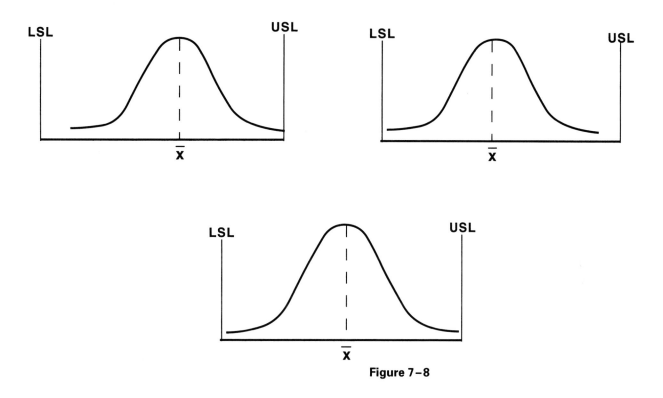

Figure 7-8

• If the value of Cpk is greater than 1.0, the process's variation falls completely within the specification limits (Figure 7-9).

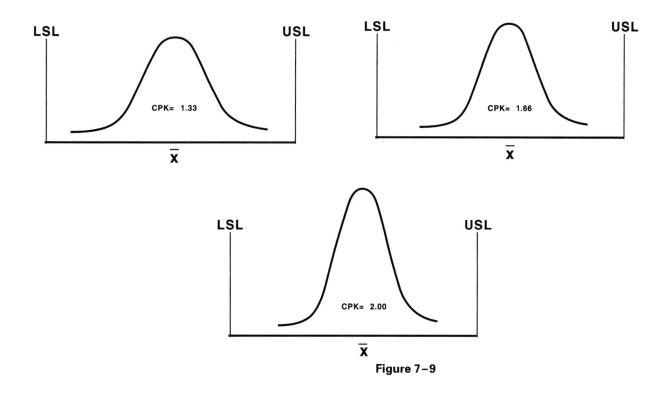

Figure 7-9

Therefore, whenever the value of Cpk is used to determine the capability of a process, the Cpk value must be larger than 1.0 before the process can be considered capable of repeatedly meeting requirements. Given this and the Cpk value of 1.33 for the process used in our example, we can conclude with confidence that the process is in control and capable (Figure 7-10).

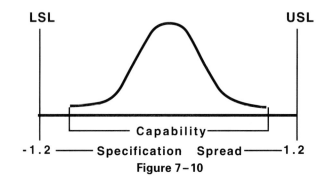

Figure 7–10

7B: PRECONTROL TECHNIQUES

Up to this point, you have learned that the quality of products and services is affected by variation. To improve quality, the variation in the process must be monitored and controlled continuously. Common causes of variation are always operating in the process. Common-cause variation cannot be entirely eliminated, but it can be predicted. When only common causes of variation are operating in a process, the variation in the process is normally distributed. Under these conditions, the normal curve can be used to describe the common-cause variation in the process.

Common-cause variation in almost any process is equivalent to 6 standard deviations. That is, 68% of the variation will fall within +1 and −1 standard deviations of the mean, 95.5% of the variation will fall within +2 and −2 standard deviations of the mean, and 99.73% of the variation will fall within +3 and −3 standard deviations of the mean (Figure 7-11). Whenever processes exhibit stable and predictable common cause variation, the process is in control.

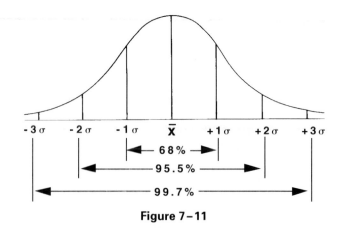

Figure 7–11

You have also learned that when processes are in control, it does not automatically mean that the process is capable of repeatedly meeting the require-

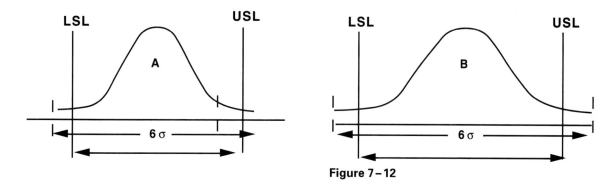

Figure 7–12

ments or specifications, as Figure 7-12 illustrates. The variation in the distributions is normal; however, the variation exceeds the process specifications in both cases. When this occurs, the process is not capable of repeatedly meeting the requirements. To improve the quality of products or services produced in any process, two conditions must be satisfied:

1. Processes must be in control.
2. Processes must be capable of repeatedly meeting the stated specifications or process requirements.

One way to ensure that these two conditions are satisfied is to utilize the tools that detect any significant changes in the process. Two of the areas that need to be continuously monitored in any process are:

• Shifts in the process *mean*
• Changes in process *variation*

Shifts in the process mean can cause a process once operating in control and capable of operating in control to be no longer capable of repeatedly meeting the stated specifications. The graphs in Figure 7-13 illustrate what occurs when a process mean has shifted.

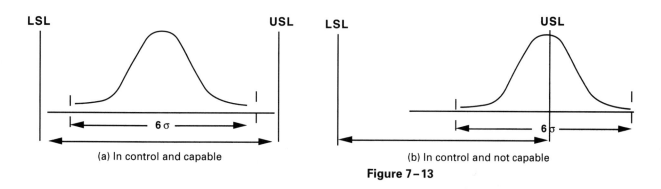

(a) In control and capable   (b) In control and not capable

Figure 7–13

Changes in process variation can also cause a process once operating in control and capable of operating in control to be no longer capable of repeatedly meeting the stated specifications. Figure 7-14 illustrates what occurs when a change in variation occurs.

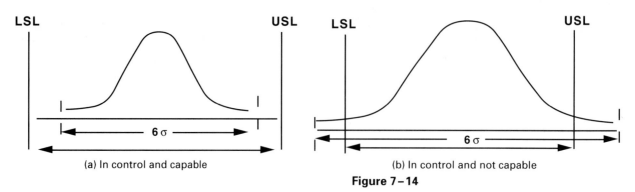

Figure 7–14

One of the tools that can be used to detect significant changes in a process on an ongoing basis is precontrol. Precontrol is based on the theory of normal distribution; however, fewer computations are required. Before this technique can be used, the following conditions need to be established:

1. The process is in control.
2. The process mean is centered.
3. The process performance is less than or equal to 100% of the stated specifications or requirements.

Process performance is a measure of common-cause variation in the process over an *extended* period of time (Figure 7-15).

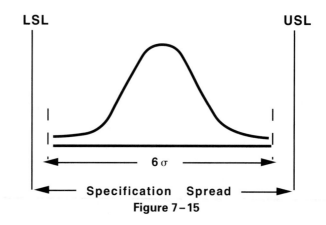

Figure 7–15

Precontrol divides process capability into three zones: low, middle, and high (Figure 7-16). The *low zone* represents 7% of the process's capability, the *middle zone* represents 86% of the process's capability, and the *high zone* represents 7% of the process's capability. Based on this, precontrol charts can be used to monitor and control process variation to ensure that the requirements are met continuously.

Precontrol can best be described as a *traffic light* that monitors and controls process variation. The areas beyond the high and low zones are the *red* areas. Whenever the variation exceeds the high or low zones, the process is not producing parts or services that meet the requirements. Under these conditions, the process should be stopped to identify and remove the cause.

The areas within the high and low zones are *yellow* areas. When the variation is within the high or low zone, the process variation is beginning to approach the process limits. Under these conditions, a change may be occurring in the process. The process can continue to operate, however, the variation needs to be monitored with caution.

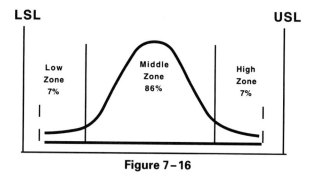

Figure 7-16

The area in the middle zone is a *green* area. Whenever the variation falls within the middle zone, the process is well centered and within specifications. Under these conditions, the process can run without interruption or caution.

Precontrol is a simplified method of detecting significant changes that can occur in any process. That is, precontrol charts can be used to detect shifts in the *mean* and the changes in variation.

Precontrol techniques provide guidelines to address:

- When the process should be adjusted
- When special causes of variation are operating in the process
- When the process should be left alone

Shifts in the Process Mean

If two consecutive items are selected from a process and both fall within the same yellow area on the precontrol chart, it is reasonable to believe that the process mean has shifted.

YELLOW	GREEN	YELLOW
x x		

YELLOW	GREEN	YELLOW
		x x

Whenever these conditions exist, some adjustments in the process are needed to recenter the *mean*.

Changes in Variation

If two consecutive items are selected from a process and one item falls within a yellow area and the second item falls within the other yellow area, it is reasonable to believe that the process variation has changed. Under these conditions, the special causes of excess variation need to be identified and eliminated.

YELLOW	GREEN	YELLOW
x		x

Before precontrol charts can be used to monitor and control process variation, the following conditions must be met:

1. The process is operating in control.
2. The process mean is centered.
3. Process performance ≤ 100% (*process capability over an extended period*).
4. Accurate measurement devices are available to measure process output.
5. The personnel involved in the process understand the requirements.
6. When necessary, process adjustments can be readily made by personnel.
7. Actions are *only* taken to reduce process variation and eliminate variation that exceeds the requirements.

Once these conditions have been met, the precontrol chart is constructed in the following manner.

1. To center the process, compute the mean of the process specification. The mean is calculated by adding the high specification limit to the low specification limit and dividing the sum by 2. For example, if the specifications call for an upper limit of 21.5 and a lower limit of 18.5, the following calculations are required:

$$21.5 + 18.5 = 40 \quad \text{and} \quad 40 \div 2 = 20$$

2. Divide the tolerance or specification spread by 4, to establish the values for each zone. The tolerance or specification spread is the difference between the upper and lower specification limits.

$$21.5 - 18.5 = 3.0 \quad \text{and} \quad 3.0 \div 4 = .75$$

3. Add one fourth ($\frac{1}{4}$) of the tolerance or specification spread to the mean to establish the value of the high zone.

$$20.0 + .75 = 20.75$$

4. Subtract one fourth ($\frac{1}{4}$) of the tolerance or specification spread from the mean to establish the value for the low zone.

$$20.0 - .75 = 19.25$$

Once the chart has been constructed, the setup procedure can be conducted.

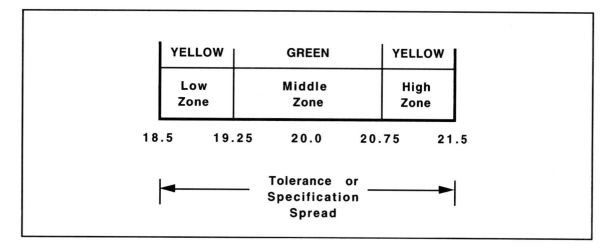

Setup Procedure

Run five consecutive items and measure each one.

- If all five items fall within the middle zone (green), the process is in control and capable. When this occurs, the process is ready to run.
- If five consecutive items do not fall within the middle zone (green), continue to adjust the process until it is centered. The process is properly centered when five consecutive items fall within the middle zone or (green) area.

Setup: The process is ready to run when five consecutive items fall within the middle zone or green area.

YELLOW	GREEN	YELLOW
	x x x x x	

Running Procedures

To ensure that the process remains in control, it must be monitored on a continuous basis. When precontrol charts are used, two consecutive items are selected from the process approximately every 15 to 30 minutes. This is only a guideline and the frequency of checks will vary from process to process.

Step 1: Measure the First Item.

- If the first item falls within the middle zone (green), continue to run the process.

- If the first item falls within the high or low zone (yellow), measure the second item. If the second item falls within the middle zone (green), continue to run the process.

> *Running:* When only one item falls within the high or low zone (yellow), continue to run the process.

YELLOW	GREEN	YELLOW
X	X	

OR

YELLOW	GREEN	YELLOW
	X	X

Step 2: If the First Item Falls in the Yellow, Measure the Second One.

- If the first item falls within the high or low zone (yellow), and the second item falls in the *same* zone, the process mean has probably shifted. When this occurs, the process needs to be recentered.

> *Running:* When two consecutive items fall within the same high or low zone (yellow), the process mean has shifted and needs to be recentered.

YELLOW	GREEN	YELLOW
X X		

OR

YELLOW	GREEN	YELLOW
		X X

The first chart indicates that two consecutive items fell within the low zone (yellow). This indicates that the process mean has shifted downward. To recenter the mean, the process needs to be adjusted upward. The second chart indicates that two consecutive items fell within the area high zone. This indicates that the process mean has shifted upward. To recenter the mean, the process needs to be adjusted downward. Whenever the process is adjusted, the setup procedure needs to be repeated to ensure that the process mean has been centered properly. After each adjustment, continue to run and measure the items until five consecutive items fall within the middle zone (green). Once the process mean is centered, run the process and check two items every 15 to 30 minutes or so.

Step 3: If Both Items Fall in Opposite Yellow Areas, Investigate.

- If the first item falls within a high or low zone (yellow) and the second item falls within the opposite high or low zone (yellow), it is reasonable to suspect that a change has occurred in the process's common-cause variation. Whenever this occurs, actions should be taken to identify and remove any special causes of variation.

> *Running:* When two consecutive items fall within opposite high and low zones (yellow), the variation has increased. Identify and remove any special causes of variation.

YELLOW	GREEN	YELLOW
x		x

- Whenever adjustments are made in the process, the setup procedure is repeated.

Step 4: If Any Item Falls in a Red Area, Stop the Process.

- If any item exceeds the high or low zone (red), the process should be stopped to identify the cause of the excess variation.

> *Running:* Whenever any item falls outside the high or low zones (red), the process output does not meet the requirements. Stop the process to remove the special causes of variation.

RED	YELLOW	GREEN	YELLOW	RED
x				x

- Whenever adjustments are made in the process, the setup procedure is repeated.

If no adjustments are needed after 25 consecutive checks, the frequency of the checks can be reduced. If any adjustments are made during 25 consecutive checks, continue to check two items approximately every 15 to 30 minutes.

In summary, precontrol charts can be used to monitor and control process variation on an ongoing basis.

> *Setup:* When five consecutive items fall within the middle zone (green), run the process.

YELLOW	GREEN	YELLOW
	x x x x x	

Running: When only one item falls within a high or low zone (yellow), run the process.

YELLOW	GREEN	YELLOW
x	x	

OR

YELLOW	GREEN	YELLOW
	x	x

Running: When two consecutive items fall within the low zone (yellow), the process mean has shifted downward and needs to be adjusted.

YELLOW	GREEN	YELLOW
x x		

Running: When two consecutive items fall within the high zone (yellow), the process mean has shifted upward and needs to be adjusted.

YELLOW	GREEN	YELLOW
		x x

Running: When two consecutive items fall within the opposite high and low zones (yellow), the process variation has increased and all special causes of variation need to be identified and removed.

YELLOW	GREEN	YELLOW
x		x

Running: Whenever any item exceeds the high and low zones (red), the process should be stopped to remove the special cause of variation.

RED	YELLOW	GREEN	YELLOW	RED
x				x

- Whenever any adjustments are made to the process, the setup procedure needs to be repeated.
- If no adjustments are required after 25 consecutive checks, the frequency of checks can be decreased.

REVIEW QUESTIONS

1. True or false? To improve quality, process variation needs to be controlled.
2. Process variation that falls within __ standard deviations is in control.
3. True or false? Process capability refers to processes that are in control.
4. True or false? A process is capable when it is in control and capable of repeatedly producing items according to the stated requirements.
5. The requirements for a process are 18.50 – 21.50. The standard deviation is .37. What is the capability ratio? Is it capable?
6. The ideal capability ratio is _____.
7. If the requirements for a process are 8–20 and the standard deviation is 2, what is the capability of process value?
8. Ideally, the capability of process should be _____ or greater.
9. True or false? The capability ratio more accurately reflects capability than the capability of process.
10. Are the process mean and specification midpoint always the same in a process?
11. If the mean is 12 and the requirements are 8 –20, what is the value of K? Describe the relationship between the mean and midpoint.
12. If K is a negative number, the process mean is _____ the midpoint.
13. If K is a positive number, the mean is _____ to the midpoint.
14. Given the following data, compute the Cpk value.
    (a) USL = 20, LSL = 8, mean = 14, standard deviation = 2.0
    (b) USL = 20, LSL = 8, mean = 14, standard deviation = 1.0
    (c) US> = 20, LSL = 8, mean = 16, standard deviation = 1.33
15. Describe the relationship between the mean and the specification limits when:
    (a) Cpk is 0.   (c) Cpk is between 0 and 1.
    (b) Cpk is a negative number.   (d) Cpk is 1.0.
16. If the requirements for a process are 12–14 and the mean is 13, construct a precontrol chart for the process.
17. Using the precontrol chart constructed in Question 16, answer the following questions.
    (a) What is the value indicating the lower zone boundary?
    (b) What is the value indicating the higher zone boundary?
    (c) Describe the zones that the following values would fall within:

13.2	12.0	12.6	13.8	15.0	12.8	11.0

18. Indicate the actions required under the following conditions.

YELLOW	GREEN	YELLOW
	x x x x	

YELLOW	GREEN	YELLOW
xx		

YELLOW	GREEN	YELLOW
		xx

YELLOW	GREEN	YELLOW
x		x

YELLOW	GREEN	YELLOW
x	x	

OR

YELLOW	GREEN	YELLOW
	x	x

RED	YELLOW	GREEN	YELLOW	RED
x				x

19. How often should pieces be selected from the process?

20. Can precontrol be used when the capability ratio exceeds 1.0?

21. What is required whenever an adjustment is made to the process?

Chapter 8

Control Charts

In Chapter 7 you learned the importance of analyzing process capability and how precontrol charts can be used to control process variation. In this chapter, another statistical method that is commonly used to control process variation is introduced. This method is called the control chart. A variety of control charts can be used to monitor process variation. Throughout this chapter you will learn the primary purpose and application of various control charts.

The chapter contains two units. In Unit 8A we describe the control charts commonly used to monitor process variation. Since signed numbers are often used in variable control charts, Unit 8B provides a brief review of signed number concepts.

INSTRUCTIONAL OBJECTIVES

When you have completed this chapter, you will be able to:

- Define the term *control chart* and state their use in process control.
- Select the appropriate control chart for variable and attribute data.
- List the steps required to construct a control chart.
- Classify common control charts and their application.
- Identify the conditions of common patterns on a control chart.
- State the conditions for processes operating in control via control charts.
- Identify the absolute value of numbers.
- Add and subtract signed numbers.

LEARNING ACTIVITIES

____8A: An Introduction to Control Charts
____8B: Signed Number Review

8A: AN INTRODUCTION TO CONTROL CHARTS

Another tool that is commonly used to monitor and control process variation on an on-going basis is the control chart. Like precontrol, control charts are used to ensure that the process is in control and capable of repeatedly meeting the requirements. The major difference between these two charts is that the control chart provides more detailed information on the process. The control chart can be used to detect machine wear, fluctuations in the process, differences in gages and measurement devices, operators, and so on. Each of these areas is discussed in greater detail throughout this unit.

The statistical theories covered up to this point provide the basis for all control charts. By way of a quick review, process variation affects the quality of all products and services. To improve the quality of any product or service, variation in the process must be continuously monitored, analyzed, controlled, and improved. A stable and predictable level of variation can be expected to occur in all processes. This is referred to as *common-cause variation.* For the most part, common-cause variation can be described by the characteristics of the normal curve. The normal curve allows you to predict 99.73% of the outcomes that are likely to occur in the process (Figure 8-1). Given this, the variation in the process can be monitored and controlled continuously to ensure that it meets the requirements.

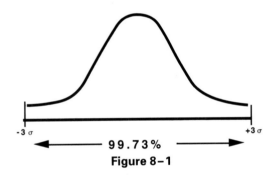

Figure 8-1

Any time the process variation exceeds the boundaries of the normal curve, it is generally the result of a *special* or *assignable* cause. Special or assignable causes of variation can be identified, controlled, and eliminated. A special or assignable cause of variation may be:

- Broken tools
- Temporary staff
- Machine wear
- Processing errors
- Inaccurate data
- Doors left open in the winter
- Air-conditioning failures

- Poor communications
- Computational errors
- Inaccurate measurements
- Improper adjustments
- Illness
- Procedures not followed
- Improper lighting

In effect, special or assignable causes of variation are *not* designed into the process. These causes of variation tend to force the process variation beyond the limits of the normal curve. In most cases, special or assignable causes of variation can be identified, corrected, and eliminated.

Common-cause variation in any process can be estimated by random samples selected from the process. Figure 8-2 illustrates the relationship between the population and sample means selected from the process. Based on statistical theories, the characteristics of an entire process can be estimated from samples randomly selected from the process. Given this statistical basis, control charts can be used to determine the stability of common-cause variation in the process (in control). Control charts also enable you to determine if the process output meets the

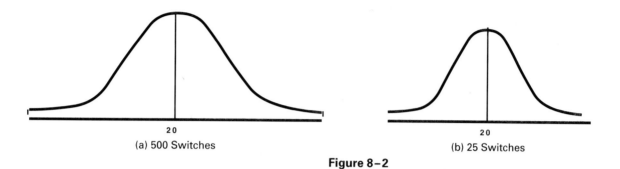

(a) 500 Switches   (b) 25 Switches

Figure 8-2

requirements (capability). The control chart does not actually control the process, it only provides critical information about the process. This information allows you to make sound decisions and take actions, when necessary, to improve the process.

Control charts can provide you with the following information:

- The operating characteristics of the process over time
- Common-cause variation that can be expected in the process
- Whether common cause variation meets the requirements
- The presence of special or assignable causes of variation

In summary, the control chart is merely a tool that provides critical information on the process. This information enables you to make sound decisions, take appropriate actions, and maintain statistical process control.

Control charts contain three lines: the upper control limit (UCL), the average or central line (CL), and the lower control limit (LCL) (Figure 8-3).

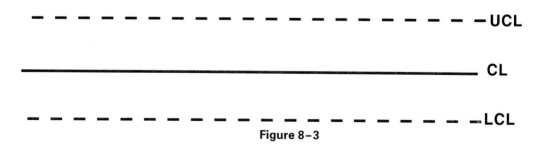

Figure 8-3

Control charts are based on the statistical theories of the normal curve and random sampling. By turning the normal curve 90°, the relationship between the normal curve and control charts becomes more evident (Figure 8-4). The upper control limit represents +3 standard deviations from the mean. The central line represents the mean and the lower control limit represents −3 standard devia-

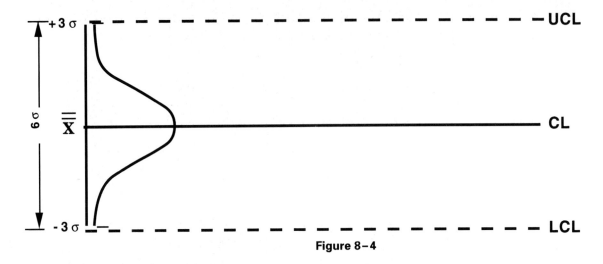

Figure 8-4

tions from the mean. These lines indicate the limits of the common-cause variation (normal curve) in the process.

The control limits and central line are computed from samples selected from the process. These samples provide an estimate of the common-cause variation in the process. A process is in control when the following conditions are met:

1. All points on the control chart are *within* the control limits.
2. No *patterns* are formed by the points on the control chart. Patterns may be runs, cycles, trends, and so on. Patterns can be detected by analyzing the points on the chart.

When a process is in control, common-cause variation is randomly distributed within the control limits. Figure 8-5 illustrates the characteristics of a process that is in control.

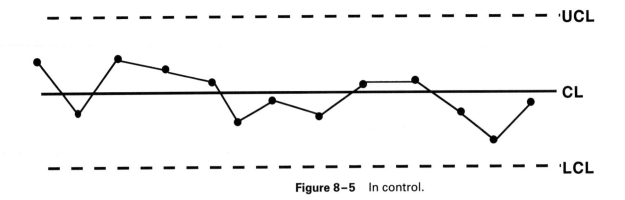

Figure 8-5   In control.

A process is out of control when any one of the following conditions exists:

1. Points exceed the upper or lower control limits.
2. Points within the control limits form a pattern.

Some of the more common out-of-control conditions are described below. Figure 8-6 shows a point exceeding the upper control limit (UCL).

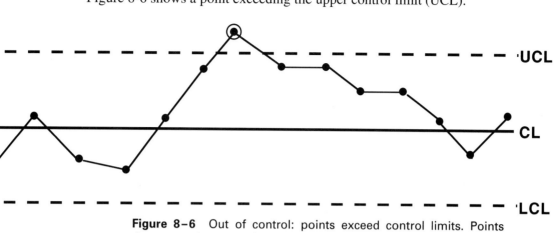

Figure 8–6 Out of control: points exceed control limits. Points that exceed control limits indicate that a special or assignable cause of variation is present. When this occurs, the process should be investigated to identify and remove any special causes or variation.

A process may also be out of control if the points within the control limits form a pattern. One common pattern is a run (Figure 8-7). A *run* is a series of consecutive points that fall on one side of the central line. Runs can be defined by any one of the following conditions:

- 7 consecutive points fall on one side of the central line.
- 10 of 11 consecutive points fall on one side of the central line.
- 12 of 14 consecutive points fall on one side of the central line.

A run indicates that the process mean has shifted or a change has occurred in the process. When this occurs, the process should be investigated to identify and remove the cause of the changes.

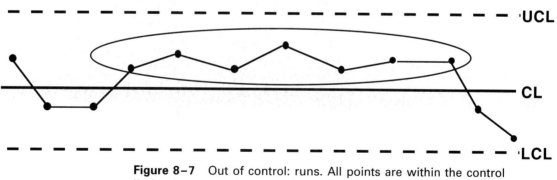

Figure 8–7 Out of control: runs. All points are within the control limits; however, 7 consecutive points fall above the central line. This is called a run.

Another common pattern is a trend (Figure 8-8). A *trend* is a steady progression of points in one direction. If the trend continues, the points will eventually exceed the control limits. Trends are usually due to machine, tool, or equipment wear.

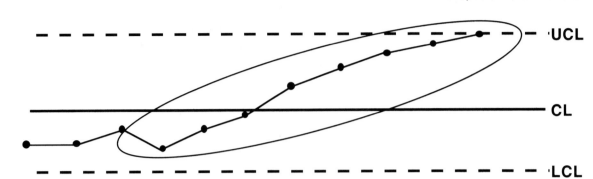

Figure 8–8 Out of control: trends. All points fall within the control limits, yet the points indicate a steady upward progression. This pattern is called a trend.

Another common pattern is called a cycle (Figure 8-9). A *cycle* is a series of points that form similar patterns over time. Whenever a cycle exists, the process should be investigated to identify and correct the cause.

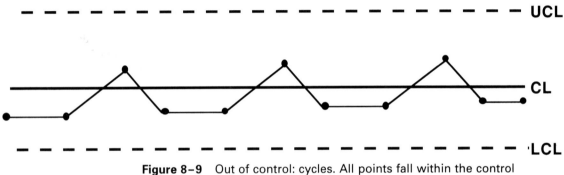

Figure 8–9 Out of control: cycles. All points fall within the control limits, yet a similar pattern repeats itself over time. This pattern is called a cycle.

Whenever points exceed the control limits or form a pattern, the process is out of control. When this occurs, a special or assignable cause of variation is usually present. Under these conditions, the process should be investigated to identify and remove any special causes of variation. If special or assignable causes of variation are not removed, the process variation is unpredictable and it will eventually exceed the requirements.

Control charts enable you to control process variation. When only common-cause variation exists, the variation in the process is randomly distributed within the control limits (in control). Once a process is in control you can determine if it is capable of repeatedly meeting the process requirements.

There are two basic types of control charts: variable and attribute control charts. *Variable control charts* are used for *measurable* data. Measurable data can be expressed as size, time, dimension, weight, temperature, sensitivity, hardness, resistance, diameter, and so on. The most widely used variable control chart is the *average and range control chart,* also called the $\bar{X}$–R *chart* ($\bar{X}$ is pronounced "ex-bar").

Attribute control charts are used for *countable* data. Countable data can be expressed as the number of errors, items, defects, defectives, and so on, or the percentage of defectives, defects, items, errors, and so on. It is important to note that defects and defectives are not the same. A *defect* occurs when one aspect of the whole unit is not acceptable or satisfactory. *Defective* means that the entire unit is not acceptable or satisfactory. Four of the most commonly used attribute control charts are *p*, *np*, *c*, and *u* charts.

Control Chart	Use
p	Percent defective
np	Number defective
c	Number of defects
u	Defects per unit

Figure 8-10 summarizes the various control charts commonly used to monitor and control process variation.

Variable *(Measurable Data)*	*Attribute* *(Countable Data)*
• Time • Size • Gages • Dimensions • Length • Weight	• Go/no-go gages • Clickers or counters • Number of defects • Number of errors • Percentages • Acceptable/not acceptable

Figure 8-10   Control charts.

Preliminary Decisions in Constructing a Control Chart

Before a control chart can be constructed, certain aspects about the process need to be defined:

1. What characteristic in the process should be investigated?
2. Is the characteristic countable or measurable data?
3. Which control chart should be used?
4. How many samples are needed?
5. How often should samples be selected from the process?
6. How should the samples be selected from the process?

Characteristics.   The characteristic to be analyzed needs to be determined. In general, the most critical characteristic or area should be analyzed first. In most cases, the greatest quality improvements are made by analyzing the most critical characteristic or area in the process.

Type of Data (Countable or Measurable).   Once the process characteristics have been determined, you can identify if the data are countable or measurable. The type of data collected in the process will have a direct bearing on the type of control chart that can be used. Regardless of the type of data collected, accurate and reliable measurement instruments are required. Remember: GIGO (garbage in – garbage out).

Control Chart. Once the characteristics and type of data have been identified, the appropriate control chart can be selected. Variable control charts (measurable data) can only be used to analyze one characteristic in the process. Attribute control charts (countable data) can be used to analyze more than one aspect or characteristic in the process. Figure 8-11 provides a brief summary of the control charts commonly used.

Variable Control Charts	*Attribute Control Charts*

• Used for measurable data:
  • Inches
  • Diameter
  • Weight
  • Height
  • Size
  • Hardness
	• Used for countable data:
	  • Accepted/rejected
	  • Number of defects
	  • Number of defectives
	  • Percentage of defectives
	  • Average defects per unit
	  • Go/no-go

Type	*Type*
• $X–R$ control chart	• p Chart—percent defective • np Chart—number defective • c Chart—number of defects • u Chart—average number of defects/unit
Guidelines	*Guidelines*
• Measurement is critical. • Precision is needed to evaluate the process. • Gaging or testing devices are accurate, dependable, and available. • One characteristic needs to be evaluated.	• Measurement is not possible. • Measurement is time consuming. • More then one characteristic needs to be evaluated. • 100% inspection is required.

Figure 8–11

Sample Size. The most important aspect of determining the appropriate number of samples is to ensure that a good representation of the entire process is obtained. As a general rule of thumb, the following guidelines can be used:

- *Variable control charts.* Approximately 20 to 25 sample means are required. To acquire this, 5 consecutive samples for 20–25 subgroups should be selected from the process.
- *Attribute control chart.* Approximately 20–25 sample means are also required. Less information on the process is obtained from attribute data. To compensate for this each subgroup should contain approximately 50 individual samples.

Timing of Sample Selection. The frequency of selecting samples from a process varies. Initially, the intent is to gain an understanding of the process characteristics. Once a level of statistical control has been established, samples can be selected less frequently. The most important thing to keep in mind is to vary the time that the samples are selected. That is, if a decision is made to select samples each hour, the samples should be selected at various times during the hour. The first samples can be selected on the hour, the second sample at quarter past the hour, the third sample at half past the hour, and so on.

Sample Selection.   Samples are only useful when they provide a good representation of the entire process. Therefore, samples must be randomly selected. Random selection means that every item in the process has an equal chance of being selected. For example, if you wanted to randomly select 10 samples from a bin of 1000 items, it would be necessary to select items from each area of the bin (top, middle, bottom) and not just from one area of the bin.

It is also important to note that samples should be selected from only one source or process. That is, all samples are produced under exactly the same conditions. Samples may be selected by department, machine, lot, task, operator, and so on. Random sampling from one source makes the task of identifying the possible causes of problems much easier.

Once the characteristics, type of data, control chart, number of samples, timing of sample selection, and process of selecting random samples have been established, the control chart can be constructed. Control charts enable you to analyze and control process variation on an ongoing basis. The primary purpose of these charts is twofold:

1. To ensure that the process variation is in control
2. To ensure that the process is capable of meeting the requirements

Once these two conditions have been met, the process can be monitored continuously to maintain or improve the quality of products or services produced by the process. Figure 8-12 briefly summarizes the concepts of variation and statistical process control.

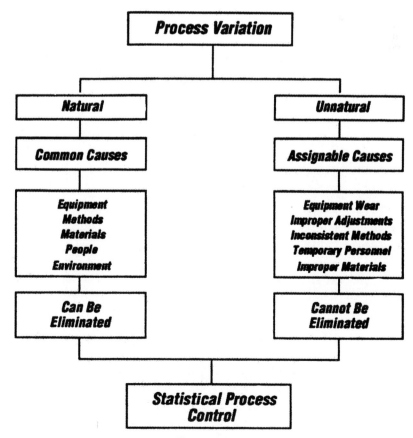

Figure 8-12

Three standard control chart forms are used to monitor and control process variation. One of these control charts is for variable data. The other control charts are for attribute data. Each chart is divided into three sections:

1. A legend
2. Record of data collected
3. Graphs

The *legend* lists all of the vital information about the process. This section describes who, what, why, and how the information for the chart was collected and constructed. The *record section* lists the actual measurements or numbers from samples selected from the process. The *graph section* is an area where the control limits and samples are plotted onto the graph. This section provides a visual analysis of the process characteristics. Samples of the three basic control charts commonly used are shown in Figures 8-13 to 8-15.

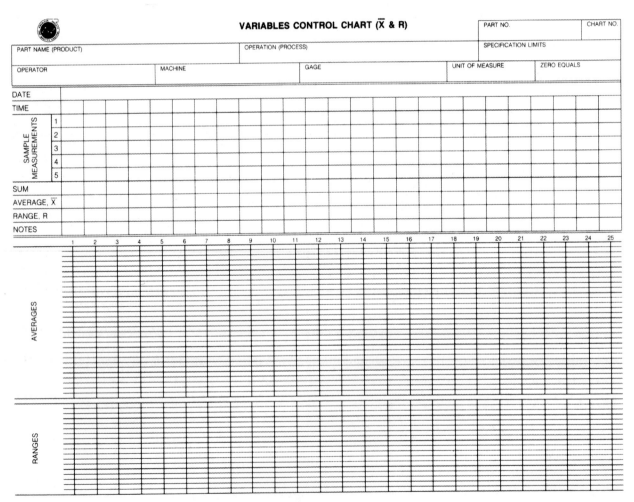

Figure 8-13

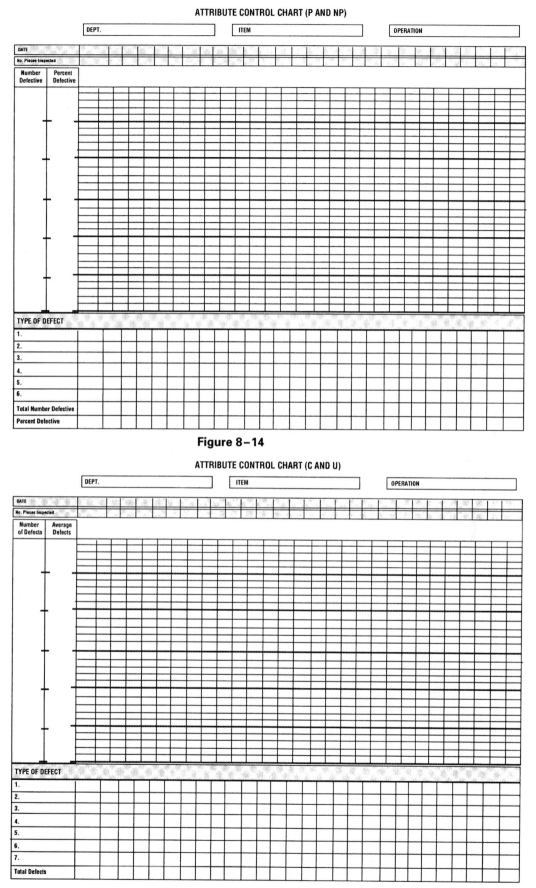

ATTRIBUTE CONTROL CHART (P AND NP)

DEPT. ITEM OPERATION

Figure 8–14

ATTRIBUTE CONTROL CHART (C AND U)

DEPT. ITEM OPERATION

Figure 8–15

8B: SIGNED NUMBER REVIEW

Variable control charts frequently contain signed numbers: that is, numbers that have both positive (+) or negative (−) values. Before variable control charts are discussed, a brief review of the basic operations of signed numbers will be presented.

Any number may have a positive (+) or negative (−) sign attached to it. The sign of any particular number is used to indicate its direction from a point of reference. The point of reference for signed numbers is 0. Positive numbers (+) are located to the right of the reference point 0 on the number line. Positive numbers are always greater than 0.

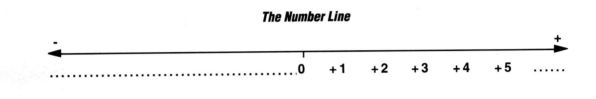

Negative numbers are located to the left of the reference point 0, on the number line. Negative numbers always less than 0.

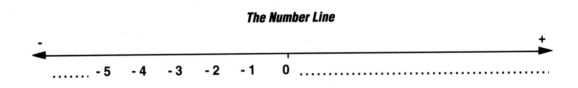

Normally, the + sign is omitted from a positive number. Therefore, any number without a sign generally indicates a positive number.

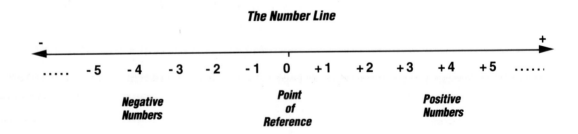

Another very important term frequently used to describe signed numbers is the absolute value. The *absolute value* of any number indicates the distance between the number and the point of reference of 0. For example, since −4 is 4

units away from 0, its absolute value is 4. Similarly, +4 is 4 units away from 0, and the absolute value of +4 is also 4.

The Number Line

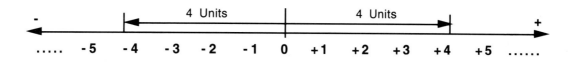

The absolute value of any number is simply the number without its sign.

The absolute value of	$-1 = 1$
The absolute value of	$+1 = 1$
The absolute value of	$+9 = 9$
The absolute value of	$-9 = 9$
And so on	

The number line is a very important concept in performing the basic mathematical operations of signed numbers. The number line defines the number of units that are to be added (+) or subtracted (−). For example, if you were adding two positive numbers, the number line could be used to illustrate the number of units that are to be added together.

Adding Signed Numbers

We will use the number line to determine the sum of 2 + 2. Starting at the reference point of 0, move 2 units to the right. Next, move 2 more units to the right. The sum is 4.

The Number Line

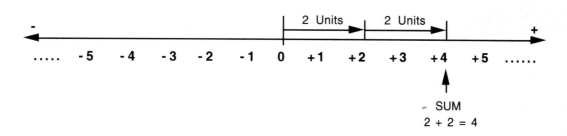

The same concept is used to add negative numbers. We use the number line to determine the sum of −3 plus (+) −1. First, move 3 units to the left of 0. Then, move 1 more unit to the left. The sum is −4.

The Number Line

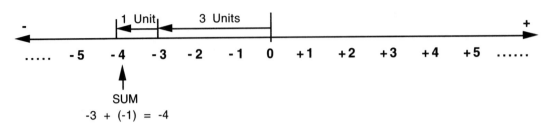

SUM

-3 + (-1) = -4

Of course, you would not need to draw a number line each time you wanted to add the values of like numbers (all positive or all negative numbers); however, the real beauty of the number line is seen when unlike numbers (positive and negative values) are added together. For example, use the number line to find the sum of −5 plus (+) 2. First, move 5 units to the left of 0. Then move 2 units to the right. The sum is −3.

The Number Line

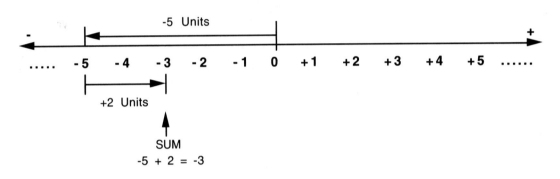

SUM

-5 + 2 = -3

Now, the number line will be used to find the sum of 5 plus −3. Since 5 is a positive number, you move 5 units to the right of 0. Then 3 is a negative number, so you move 3 units to the left. The sum is 2.

The Number Line

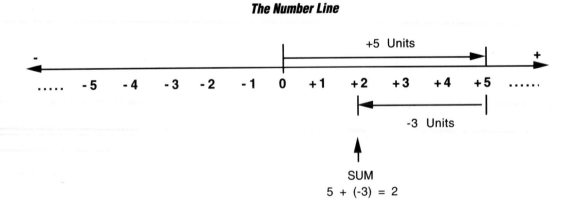

SUM

5 + (-3) = 2

Whenever positive numbers are used, the movement along the number line is from left to right. When negative numbers are used, the movement is from right to left.

The number line was used to illustrate the addition of signed numbers; however, it is not the most efficient method available. One of the more efficient methods is to follow these two basic rules.

1. If the signs of the numbers are all the same (either all positive or all negative values), add the absolute values of each number and use the same sign.

$$(+3) + (+4) + (+7) + (+11) = +25$$

or

$$(-3) + (-4) + (-7) + (-11) = -25$$

Notice that in each of these examples, the signs of the numbers are all the same (either positive or negative). Whenever the sign of all numbers is the same, the absolute value (the number without the sign) of each number is added and the sum holds the same sign.

2. If the signs of the numbers are different, determine the absolute value of the positive numbers, then find the absolute value of the negative numbers. Once you have completed this step, subtract the sum of positive numbers from the sum of negative numbers. The difference carries the same sign as the sign of the largest absolute value.

$$(+3) + (-7) + (+5) + (-11) = \underline{\quad}$$

- The absolute value of all positive numbers is

$$(+3) + (+5) = 3 + 5$$
$$= 8$$

- The absolute value of all negative numbers is

$$(-7) + (-11) = 7 + 11$$
$$= 18$$

- The difference between the absolute value of all positive numbers and all negative numbers is

$$18 - 8 = 10$$

- The sign of the sum is always the same as the sign of the sum with the highest absolute value. In this example, the absolute value of all negative numbers is larger than the absolute value of all positive numbers, so the sum is -10.

$$(+3) + (-7) + (+5) + (-11) = -10$$

Another example of adding numbers with unlike signs is

$$(+3) + (+7) + (-5) + (+11) =$$

- The absolute value of all positive numbers is

$$(+7) + (+11) = 7 + 11$$
$$= 18$$

- The absolute value of all negative numbers is

$$(-3) + (-5) = 3 + 5$$
$$= 8$$

- The difference between the absolute value of all positive numbers and all negative numbers is

$$18 - 8 = 10$$

- The sign of the sum is always the same as the sign of the sum with the highest absolute value. In this example, the absolute value of all positive numbers is larger than the absolute value of all negative numbers, so the sum is +10 or just 10.

$$(-3) + (+7) + (-5) + (+11) = 10$$

Notice in these two examples that all numbers with like signs are grouped together. Next, the absolute value for all positive and negative numbers is determined. Then the difference between the absolute values is computed. Finally, the sign of the sum is determined by the numbers with the greatest absolute value.

Subtracting Signed Numbers

Subtraction is the opposite operation of addition. Yet each subtraction problem can be converted into an addition problem when a few changes are made. To make a subtraction problem into an addition problem, change the minus (−) sign to a plus (+) sign, and change the sign of the number being subtracted to its opposite sign. For example, $7 - 3$ can be changed into an addition problem by changing the minus sign (−) into a plus sign (+), and changing the 3 into a −3.

$$(+7) - (+3) = 4$$

$$(+7) + (-3) = 4$$

Any subtraction problem can be solved by three basic steps:

1. Change all subtraction signs to addition signs.
2. Change the sign of each number being subtracted (the number that follows the original subtraction sign) to its opposite sign.
3. Follow the procedures for adding signed numbers.

   - If the signs of the numbers are all the same (either all positive or all negative values), add the absolute values of each number and use the same sign for the sum.
   - If the signs of the numbers are different, determine the absolute value of all the positive numbers, then find the absolute value of all the negative numbers. Once you have determined the absolute values of the positive and negative numbers, find the difference between the two absolute values. The sum (answer) carries the same sign as the sign with the greatest absolute value.

For example, using these three basic steps to solve the following problem, the following calculations are needed:

$(+5) - (-6) - (-2) - (-1) = \underline{\quad}$

$(+5) + (+6) + (+2) + (+1) = \underline{\quad}$ (Change − signs to + signs and change the sign of the numbers being subtracted)

$5 + 6 + 2 + 1 = 14$ (Add the numbers with like signs)

Another example that illustrates how to subtract signed numbers is:

$(-6) - (+5) - (-2) - (-1) = \underline{\quad}$

$(-6) + (-5) + (+2) + (+1) = \underline{\quad}$ (Change − signs to + signs and change the sign of the numbers being subtracted)

$5 + 6 + = 11$ and $2 + 1 = 3$ (Add numbers with like signs)

$11 - 3 = 8$ (Find the difference between the + and − values)

$(-6) - (+5) - (-2) - (-1) = -8$ (The sign of the sum is the same sign as the sum of the greatest absolute value)

One word of caution: *You can only change the sign of the numbers that follow a subtraction sign, and only minus signs are changed to plus signs.* Problems may call for the addition and subtraction of signed numbers. So it is important to remember this rule. For example:

$$(+2) - (-4) + (-3) - (+1) =$$

$$(+2) + (+4) + (-3) + (-1) =$$

$$(+2) + (+4) = 6 \quad \text{and} \quad (-3) + (-1) = -4$$

$$6 - 4 = 2$$

Notice in this example that *only* the subtraction (−) signs were changed to addition (+) signs and only the signs of the numbers that followed the subtraction (−) signs were changed to compute the sum.

This completes the review of adding and subtracting signed numbers.

REVIEW QUESTIONS

1. Given the following statistical tools, which one reveals more information?
   (a) Precontrol charts   **(b)** Control charts

2. What needs to be controlled in a process?
   (a) Quality   **(b)** Variation

3. True or false? Processes operating in control have no variation.

4. Normal distribution is used to illustrate _____ cause variation.

5. _____ cause variation can be eliminated.

6. Normal distribution describes ____% of the variation in the process.

7. Variation that exceeds normal distribution is due to _____ causes.

8. Classify the following causes of variation as "common" or "special."
   (a)   Broken machine   **(c)**   Improper adjustments
   (b)   Machines used in the process   **(d)**   Materials from one lot
   (e)   Methods used in the process   **(g)**   Various departments
   (f)   Power failure   **(h)**   Computer breakdown

9. When all the points fall within the UCL and LCL, the process is _____.

10. If a point exceeds the UCL or LCL, the process is _____.

11. If patterns are formed within the UCL and LCL, the process is _____.

12. The UCL is equivalent to ___ standard deviations.

13. The LCL is equivalent to ___ standard deviations.

14. The central line is equivalent to the process ____.

15. Given the following, indicate whether it is variable or attribute data.
    (a)   10 units are defective
    (b)   67 nm, 87 nm, 37 nm
    (c)   1.0 in, 1.5 in., 2.1 in.
    (d)   14 out of 16 pieces failed inspection
    (e)   Items that can be measured
    (f)   Items that are counted

16. List the steps required to construct a control chart.

17. When variable control charts are used, how many samples should be collected per subgroup?

18. If an item is measurable, but reliable and accurate testing devices are not available, what type of control chart should be used?

19. Should samples be selected at the same time each hour?

20. Why is random sampling important?

21. Add the following numbers.
    (a) $-16 + -4 + 5 + 7$
    (b) $3 + -2 + 0 + 1$
    (c) $-17 + 12 + -25 + -6$
    (d) $-24 + 13 + -6 + 7$

22. Subtract the following numbers.
    (a) $2 - (-4)$
    (b) $-3 - 7$
    (c) $-37 - (-53)$
    (d) $-9 - (-6)$

23. $2 - (-4) + (-3) - 1 =$

24. $6 - (-2) - 7 - (-4) =$

25. $(-6) - (+5) - (-2) - (-1) =$

Chapter 9

Variable Control Charts

In Chapter 8, control charts were introduced along with a brief review of adding and subtracting signed numbers. In this chapter you will learn how to construct and analyze variable control charts. These charts are frequently used to monitor and analyze variation in measurable data.

INSTRUCTIONAL OBJECTIVES

When you have completed this chapter, you will be able to:

- Identify and define the conditions for using an $X-R$ control chart.
- Construct an $X-R$ control chart.
- Analyze and interpret an $X-R$ control chart.
- Compute the capability ratio using the $X-R$ control chart.

LEARNING ACTIVITY

9A: VARIABLE CONTROL CHARTS

Variable control charts are used to monitor and control the variation in processes that produce measurable data. Measurable data in any process can be expressed numerically in terms of length of time, magnitude, weight, size, hardness, diameter, dimension, and so on. The most widely used variable control chart is the average and range chart, known more commonly as the $\bar{X}-R$ (pronounced "ex-bar R") chart.

The $\bar{X}-R$ chart is slightly different from other control charts because it combines two separate charts into one chart. The top chart measures the average value or *mean.* The bottom chart measures the process variation in terms of the range. In effect, the $\bar{X}-R$ chart measures two things:

1. The X chart measures the variation that exists *between* the samples.
2. The R chart measures the variation that exists *within* the samples.

By analyzing both the average and the range, you can determine critical information on the variation occurring within the process. The $X-R$ chart can be used to answer vital questions concerning the operation of any process that produces measurable data. For instance, the $X-R$ chart enables you to determine whether or not:

*   The process is properly centered
*   The process variation is acceptable
*   The variation is due to common or special causes
*   A special cause is operating within the process
*   The process is operating in control and capable

Steps for Constructing an *X–R* Chart

For the purpose of this discussion, a working example will follow each step used to construct an $X-R$ chart. The example will demonstrate the practical application of each step.

Step 1: Prepare a Legend. Completely fill in all of the necessary information to describe the process and the data collected for the control chart. The working example in this unit addresses the roughing operation on the outside diameter of a shaft. Although this is a manufacturing example, the same steps can be applied to any administrative task producing measurable data, such as the length of time to do a certain task, response time, and so on.

Step 2: Collect and Record Sample Data. Based on the preliminary steps required to construct the $\bar{X}-R$ chart, collect the data needed to monitor and analyze the process. The decisions made prior to selecting samples from the process should address the following:

*   The characteristics to be measured
*   The testing or gaging instruments required
*   The control chart to be used
*   The sample size to be selected from the process or lot
*   When the samples are to be selected from the process or lot
*   The methods used to select the samples from the process

Once this information has been defined, you can collect and record the individual measurements for each sample subgroup. The following decisions were made on the process used in our working example.

Characteristics to Be Measured: The most critical quality characteristic for this particular process is the outside diameter of the shaft in the roughing operation.

Testing Devices and Gages: An air gage is used to measure the outside diameter of shafts. These gages are accurate and dependable.

Selection of the Appropriate Control Chart: Since the critical characteristic of the part is measurable and requires precise control, the $X-R$ control chart will be used.

Sample Size: Four consecutive samples randomly selected from the process will provide the information needed for this process.

Timing of Collecting the Samples: Four consecutive samples will be randomly selected from the process at various times during the hour for each hour of production.

Method of Sampling: The method of sample selection will be to randomly select four samples that have been produced under the same conditions (i.e., same operator, same machine, same lot of materials, etc.).

At 7:00 a.m., four consecutive samples were randomly selected, measured, and recorded from the shaft grinder machine. At various times throughout each hour of the day, four additional samples were selected, measured, and recorded on the $X-R$ control chart. At the end of the day, the sample shown in Figure 9-1 had been collected, measured, and recorded.

VARIABLES CONTROL CHART ($\bar{X}$ & R)

PART NO. 999 76   CHART NO. 1

PART NAME (PRODUCT) MOTOR SHAFT		OPERATION (PROCESS) OUTSIDE DIAMETER - ROUGHING OPERATION				SPECIFICATION LIMITS .910" — .930		
OPERATOR S. SMITH #0823	MACHINE SHAFT GRINDER		GAGE AIR GAGE		UNIT OF MEASURE .0001"		ZERO EQUALS N/A	

DATE		12/1							
TIME		7:00	8:10	9:20	10:30	11:40	12:50	13:00	14:10
SAMPLE MEASUREMENTS	1	.920	.918	.918	.924	.919	.920	.920	.924
	2	.921	.919	.920	.921	.920	.921	.922	.920
	3	.922	.920	.922	.919	.919	.921	.920	.921
	4	.921	.919	.920	.920	.918	.922	.918	.922
	5								
SUM									
AVERAGE, $\bar{X}$									
RANGE, R									
NOTES									

Figure 9-1

Step 3: Compute the Sum, Average, and Range for Each Subgroup.

(a) Add the measurements in each subgroup. Indicate the sum of each subgroup in the column labeled "sum."

(b) Compute the *average* value (X) of each subgroup. To compute the average, divide the sum by the number of samples. The formula used to compute the average value is

$$\overline{X} = \frac{X_1 + X_2 + X_3 + X_4 + X_5 + \cdots + X_n}{n} \quad \text{or} \quad \overline{X} = \frac{\Sigma X}{n}$$

Once the average has been computed, insert the value in the column labeled "average" for each subgroup.

(c) Compute the *range* (R) of each subgroup by subtracting the smallest value from the largest value in each subgroup:

$$\text{largest value} - \text{smallest value} = \text{range}$$

Once the range has been computed, insert the value in the column labeled "range" for each subgroup (Figure 9-2).

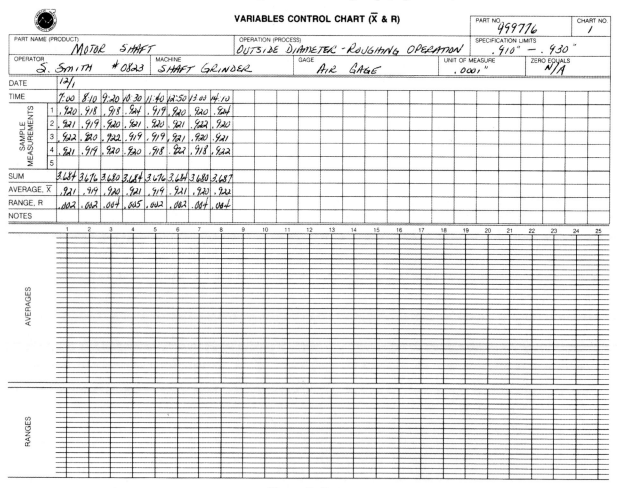

Figure 9–2

Step 4: Plot Each Average and Range Value onto the Chart. For each sub-group, plot the average (X) on the top graph and the range (R) on the bottom chart. This is illustrated in Figure 9-3. Before the control limits can be computed,

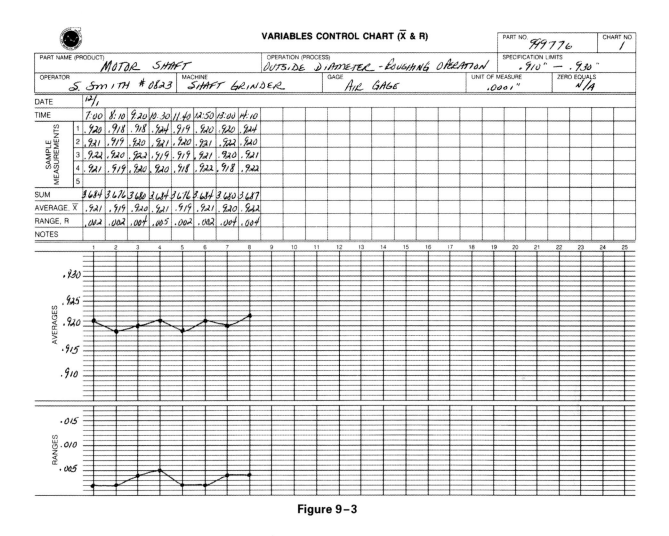

Figure 9–3

25 subgroups are needed. To meet this requirement, additional samples were collected, measured, and recorded. Using the worksheet in the back of this book, you can practice this step by computing the sum, average, and range for the remaining subgroups. Round all values to three decimal places. Remember to round the last number up when it is 5 or more. Otherwise, the last number remains the same. Figure 9-4 contains examples on rounding. Then plot the averages and ranges on the graph.

Once the sum, average, and range have been computed for each subgroup, the control limits are calculated. The control chart contains three control limits: the upper control limit (UCL), the central line (CL) or grand average, and the lower control limit (LCL).

Sums	*Averages*
3.684*0* = 3.684	.921*0* = .921
3.684*1* = 3.684	.921*1* = .921
3.684*2* = 3.684	.921*2* = .921
3.684*3* = 3.684	.921*3* = .921
3.684*4* = 3.684	.921*4* = .921
3.684*5* = 3.685	.921*5* = .922
3.684*6* = 3.685	.921*6* = .922
3.684*7* = 3.685	.921*7* = .922
3.684*8* = 3.685	.921*8* = .922
3.684*9* = 3.685	.921*9* = .922
3.685*0* = 3.685	.922*0* = .922

Figure 9–4

Step 5: Compute the Central Line (CL) or Grand Average ($\overline{\overline{X}}$).

The *central line* is the *grand average* ($\overline{\overline{X}}$). The grand average is the average value of all the subgroup averages. The formula used to compute the central line or grand average is

$$\overline{\overline{X}} = \frac{\Sigma \overline{X}}{k} \qquad \text{or} \qquad \overline{\overline{X}} = \frac{\overline{X}_1 + \overline{X}_2 + \overline{X}_3 + \overline{X}_4 + X_n}{k}$$

where $\overline{\overline{X}}$ = average of all subgroup averages or the grand average
   $\overline{X}$ = average of each individual sample group
   k = total number of sample *groups*
   Σ is the capital Greek letter sigma, meaning "the sum of."

To compute the grand average, add the average of each subgroup. Then divide the sum of all averages by the number of subgroups. The grand average ($\overline{\overline{X}}$) for the example used throughout this activity is computed as

$$\overline{\overline{X}} = \frac{\Sigma \overline{X}}{k}$$
$$= \frac{22.985}{25}$$
$$= .9194$$
$$= .919 \quad \text{(rounded to three decimal places)}$$

Once you have computed the grand average, draw a horizontal line on the average graph at the point corresponding to the grand average's value (Figure 9-5). This is the central line for the average chart.

VARIABLES CONTROL CHART ($\bar{X}$ & R)

| | PART NO. 999 776 | CHART NO. 1 |

| PART NAME (PRODUCT) MOTOR SHAFT | OPERATION (PROCESS) OUTSIDE DIAMETER - ROUGHING OPERATION | SPECIFICATION LIMITS .910" — .930" |
| OPERATOR S. SMITH | MACHINE SHAFT GRINDER | GAGE AIR GAGE | UNIT OF MEASURE .0001" | ZERO EQUALS N/A |

DATE	12/1								12/2								12/3								12/4
TIME	7:00	8:10	9:20	10:30	11:40	12:50	13:00	14:10	7:10	8:20	9:30	10:40	11:50	13:00	14:10	15:20	7:20	8:30	9:40	10:50	12:00	13:20	14:30	15:40	7:30
1	.920	.918	.918	.924	.919	.920	.920	.924	.915	.912	.920	.919	.918	.915	.919	.915	.915	.917	.925	.927	.923	.920	.914	.918	.926
2	.921	.919	.920	.921	.920	.921	.922	.920	.920	.915	.919	.912	.920	.913	.920	.916	.925	.918	.920	.924	.922	.923	.910	.920	.924
3	.922	.920	.922	.919	.919	.921	.920	.921	.918	.913	.923	.913	.918	.910	.915	.920	.926	.920	.919	.922	.922	.921	.915	.926	.913
4	.921	.919	.920	.920	.918	.922	.918	.922	.920	.914	.916	.915	.916	.912	.911	.921	.928	.921	.915	.920	.925	.923	.920	.930	.918
5																									
SUM	3.684	3.676	3.680	3.684	3.676	3.684	3.680	3.687	3.673	3.654	3.678	3.659	3.672	3.650	3.665	3.672	3.694	3.676	3.679	3.693	3.692	3.687	3.659	3.694	3.681
AVERAGE, $\bar{X}$	.921	.919	.920	.921	.919	.921	.920	.922	.918	.914	.920	.915	.918	.913	.916	.918	.924	.919	.920	.923	.923	.922	.915	.924	.920
RANGE, R	.002	.002	.004	.005	.002	.002	.004	.004	.005	.003	.007	.007	.004	.005	.009	.006	.013	.004	.010	.007	.003	.003	.010	.012	.013
NOTES																									

Figure 9–5

Step 6: Compute the Average Range ($\bar{R}$). The average range represents the average value of the ranges for all subgroups. The following formula is used to compute the average range:

$$\bar{R} = \frac{\Sigma R}{k} \qquad \text{or} \qquad \bar{R} = \frac{R_1 + R_2 + R_3 + R_4 + R_n}{k}$$

where $\bar{R}$ = average of all range values; Σ = the sum of; R = range of each subgroup; k = total number of subgroups

To compute the average range, add each range and divide the sum by the number of subgroups. The average range in this example is computed as follows:

$$\bar{R} = \frac{R}{k}$$
$$= \frac{.146}{25}$$
$$= .00584$$
$$= .006 \quad \text{(rounded to three decimal places)}$$

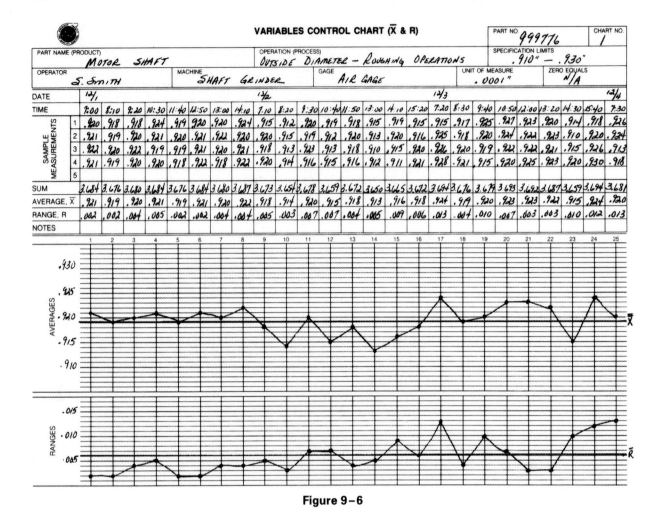

VARIABLES CONTROL CHART (X̄ & R)

PART NO. *999776* — CHART NO. *1*

PART NAME (PRODUCT): *MOTOR SHAFT*
OPERATION (PROCESS): *OUTSIDE DIAMETER — ROUGHING OPERATIONS*
SPECIFICATION LIMITS: *.910" — .930"*
OPERATOR: *S. SMITH*
MACHINE: *SHAFT GRINDER*
GAGE: *AIR GAGE*
UNIT OF MEASURE: *.0001"*
ZERO EQUALS: *N/A*

Figure 9–6

Once the average range has been computed, a horizontal line is drawn on the second graph indicating the computed value (Figure 9-6).

Step 7: Compute the Upper Control Limit for the Average Chart. The upper control limit (UCL_x) represents +3 standard deviations from the central line (grand average). The UCL_x indicates the upper limit of values that can occur when the process is in control (Figure 9-7).

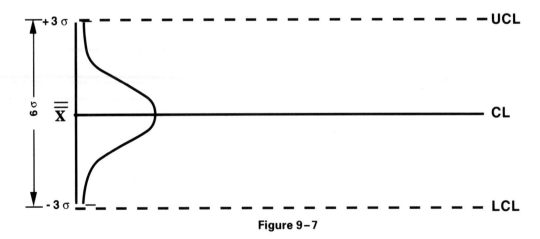

Figure 9–7

The formula used to calculate the upper control limit (UCL$_x$) is:

$$UCL_X = \bar{\bar{X}} + (A_2 \times \bar{R})$$

This formula may look Greek at first glance, but essentially it states that the upper control limit for the average chart (UCL$_x$) is equal to the grand average ($\bar{\bar{X}}$) plus the value of the population's standard deviation, reduced in proportion to the number of subgroups (A_2), multiplied by the average range value ($\bar{R}$).

Most of the values required in this equation have already been computed:

$$\bar{\bar{X}} = .919$$

$$A_2 = \text{unknown}$$

$$\bar{R} = .006$$

To solve this equation, insert the known values into the equation:

$$UCL_X = \bar{\bar{X}} + (A_2 \times \bar{R})$$
$$= .919 + (A_2 \times .006)$$

Now all that remains to be identified is the value of A_2. No complicated calculations are required to compute the value of A_2. The table located on the back of the control chart contains the values for the control limit factors.

In the "factors for control limits" table (Figure 9-8), the first column (n) indicates the number of samples in each subgroup. To determine the value of A_2, locate the number of samples in each subgroup in the first column. The corresponding value of A_2 is located in the next column. Since there are four samples in each subgroup, the corresponding A_2 value is .73.

n	A_2	D_4	d_2	A_M
2	1.88	3.27	1.128	.78
3	1.02	2.57	1.693	.75
4	.73	2.28	2.059	.73
5	.58	2.11	2.326	.71
6	.48	2.00	2.534	.70

Figure 9-8   Factors for control limits.

Once the value of A_2 has been determined, insert the value into the formula.

$$UCL_X = .919 + (A_2 \times .006)$$
$$= .919 + (.73 \times .006)$$

To compute this formula, multiply the values in parentheses ( ), and add the remaining values.

$$UCL_X = .919 + (.73 \times .006)$$
$$= .919 + .00438$$
$$= .919 + .004 \quad \text{(rounded)}$$
$$= .923$$

The value for the UCL_X is .923. Once the UCL_X has been computed, a dashed horizontal line is drawn on the average chart indicating this value (Figure 9-9).

VARIABLES CONTROL CHART ($\bar{X}$ & R)

PART NO. 999776   CHART NO. 1

PART NAME (PRODUCT): MOTOR SHAFT

OPERATION (PROCESS): OUTSIDE DIAMETER – ROUGHING OPERATIONS

SPECIFICATION LIMITS: .910" – .930"

OPERATOR: S. SMITH   MACHINE: SHAFT GRINDER   GAGE: AIR GAGE   UNIT OF MEASURE: .0001"   ZERO EQUALS: N/A

DATE	12/1							12/2							12/3						12/4				
TIME	7:00	8:10	9:20	10:30	11:40	12:50	13:00	14:10	7:10	8:20	9:30	10:40	11:50	13:00	14:10	15:20	7:20	8:30	9:40	10:50	12:00	13:20	14:30	15:40	7:30
SAMPLE 1	.920	.918	.918	.924	.919	.920	.920	.924	.915	.912	.920	.919	.918	.915	.919	.915	.915	.917	.925	.927	.923	.920	.914	.918	.926
2	.921	.919	.920	.921	.920	.921	.922	.920	.920	.915	.919	.912	.920	.913	.920	.916	.925	.918	.920	.924	.922	.923	.910	.920	.924
3	.922	.920	.922	.919	.919	.921	.920	.921	.918	.913	.923	.913	.918	.910	.915	.920	.926	.920	.919	.922	.922	.921	.915	.926	.913
4	.921	.919	.920	.920	.918	.922	.918	.922	.920	.914	.916	.915	.916	.912	.911	.921	.928	.921	.915	.920	.925	.923	.920	.930	.918
5																									
SUM	3.684	3.676	3.680	3.684	3.676	3.684	3.680	3.687	3.673	3.654	3.678	3.659	3.672	3.650	3.665	3.672	3.694	3.676	3.679	3.693	3.692	3.687	3.659	3.694	3.681
AVERAGE, $\bar{X}$	.921	.919	.920	.921	.919	.921	.920	.922	.918	.914	.920	.915	.918	.913	.916	.918	.924	.919	.920	.923	.923	.922	.915	.924	.920
RANGE, R	.002	.002	.004	.005	.002	.002	.004	.004	.005	.003	.007	.007	.004	.005	.009	.006	.013	.004	.010	.007	.003	.003	.010	.012	.013
NOTES																									

Figure 9–9

Step 8: Compute the Lower Control Limit for the Average Chart.

The lower control limit (LCL_X) represents -3 standard deviations from the central line (grand average). The LCL_X indicates the lower limit of values that can occur when the process is in control. The LCL_X has also been reduced in direct proportion to the number of samples used to estimate the value of -3 standard deviations for the entire population. The formula used to calculate the lower control limit is

$$UCL_X = \bar{\bar{X}} - (A_2 \times \bar{R})$$

The upper and lower control limit formulas are very similar. The only difference is that the value of $(A_2 \times \bar{R})$ is added to the grand average in the UCL, whereas the value of $(A_2 \times \bar{R})$ is subtracted from the grand average in the LCL.

$$UCL_X = X + (A_2 \times \bar{R})$$

$$LCL_X = X - (A_2 \times \bar{R})$$

Given this, you can insert the same values into the formula.

$$UCL_X = .919 + (.73 \times .006)$$

$$
\begin{aligned}
LCL_X &= .919 - (.73 \times .006) \\
&= .919 - .00438 \\
&= .919 - .004 \quad \text{(rounded)} \\
&= .915
\end{aligned}
$$

The value for the LCL_X is .915. Once this value has been computed, a dashed horizontal line is drawn on the control chart indicating this value (Figure 9-10).

Step 9: Compute the Upper Control Limit for the Range Chart. The upper control limit (UCL_R) for the range chart (R) represents +3 standard deviations from the range's central line. The UCL_R indicates the upper limit of values that

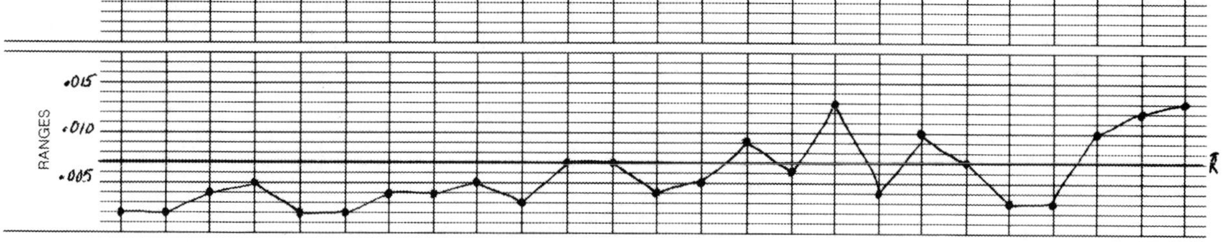

Figure 9-10

can occur when the process is in control. The formula for the upper control limit for the range chart is

$$\text{UCL}_R = D_4 \times R$$

To solve this equation, insert the known values.

$$\text{UCL}_R = D_4 \times R$$
$$= D_4 \times .006$$

To complete the formula, the value of D_4 needs to be determined. This value can be found in the table on the back of the control chart, entitled "Factors for Control Limits" (Figure 9-8, page 141). First, locate the number of samples in each subgroup. Then go across two columns to locate the corresponding D_4 value.

In our working example there are four samples per subgroup. Using the table on the back of the control chart, the value of D_4 is 2.28. To compute this formula, insert the D_4 value and multiply the two values.

$$\text{UCL}_R = D_4 \times .006$$
$$= 2.28 \times .006$$
$$= .01368$$
$$= .014 \quad \text{(rounded)}$$

Now that the UCL_R has been computed, a line can be drawn on the range chart to indicate this value (Figure 9-11).

In most cases, the maximum number of samples per subgroup in the $X–R$ control chart is 5. Given this, the lower control limit for the range chart is 0. Since variation below the number 0 serves no purpose, it is generally not included on the chart.

The control limits on the control chart indicate the process's common-cause variation. The average chart illustrates the variation *between* sample averages; the range chart illustrates the variation *within* the samples selected from the process (Figure 9-12). All points that fall within the control limits represent variation that is due to common or natural causes. Points that exceed the control limits indicate that a special or assignable cause of variation is operating in the process.

9B: ANALYZING AND INTERPRETING THE $\overline{X}–R$ CONTROL CHART

Once the $\overline{X}–R$ control chart has been constructed, the process can be analyzed. This chart is used to determine two critical aspects of process control:

1. Is the process in control?
2. Is the process capable of repeatedly meeting the requirements?

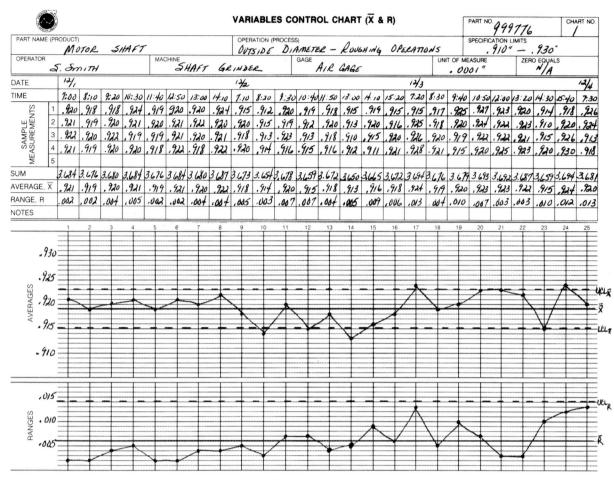

Figure 9–11

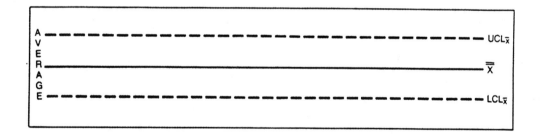

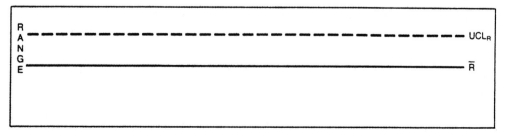

Figure 9–12

In Control. Two conditions are necessary to determine if the process is in control:

1. All points fall within the control limits.
2. No pattern is formed by the points within the control limits.

The first condition can be easily determined by examining the points on the average and range charts. The upper and lower control limits indicate the levels of common-cause variation in the process. Any point that exceeds these limits indicates that a special or assignable cause of variation may be present. These causes can be identified, corrected, and eliminated.

When all of the points plotted on the control chart are within the UCL and LCL lines (Figure 9-13), the variation in the process is due to common or natural

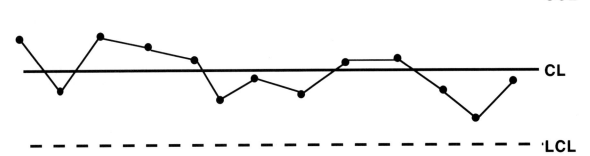

Figure 9-13 Process operating in control; variation is due to common causes.

causes. Common-cause variation represents natural process variation. This level of variation can only be reduced by changing the process.

Whenever a point exceeds these limits, however (Figure 9-14), the special or assignable cause of variation should be eliminated in order to restore common-cause variation.

The second condition that must be satisfied is to ensure that no patterns are formed by the points within the control limit lines. Patterns indicate that an abnormal condition is operating within the process. Patterns can also serve as warning signs that detect changes in variation. The basic difference between points outside the control limits and patterns formed within the control limits is only a

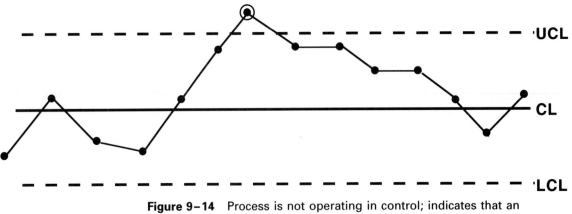

Figure 9-14 Process is not operating in control; indicates that an assignable cause is present.

matter of degrees. Points outside the control limits indicate that a special cause of variation *is* present, whereas the patterns formed by the points within the control limits indicate that a problem *may* exist and that one should monitor the process closely. There are several basic patterns that can occur within any given process. These patterns are called *runs, trends, cycles, jumps,* and *hugging.*

Runs. A *run* is a series of consecutive points that fall on one side of the central line (Figure 9-15). A run typically indicates that a change has occurred in the average value or the process variation. Whenever a run occurs, the process should be closely monitored to offset any problems arising within the process.

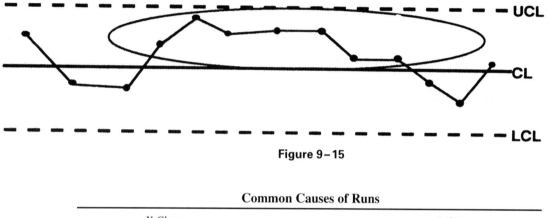

Figure 9–15

Common Causes of Runs

X Chart	R Chart
• Changes in material	• New person or operator
• Changes in methods	• New machines/equipment
• Changes in setup	• Different supplier
• Changes in personnel	• Different material
• New machines/equipment	• Inadequate maintenance

Trends. *Trends* are formed when a series of consecutive points continue to rise or fall in one direction (Figure 9-16). When a series of seven or more consecutive points continues to rise or fall, an abnormal condition is operating within the process.

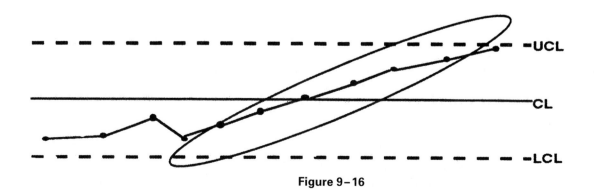

Figure 9–16

Common Causes of Trends

X Chart	R Chart
• Machine deterioration	• Changes in personnel skills
• Fatigue levels	• Fatigue levels
• Tool/equipment wear	• Change in material quality
• Changes in personnel	• Tool/equipment wear
• New machines/equipment	• Inadequate maintenance

Cycles.   *Cycles* are a series of points that display a similar or repeated pattern over equal intervals of time (Figure 9-17). There is no hard-and-fast rule used to detect a cycle on a control chart. However, critical analysis is required to identify any continuous or recurring cycles.

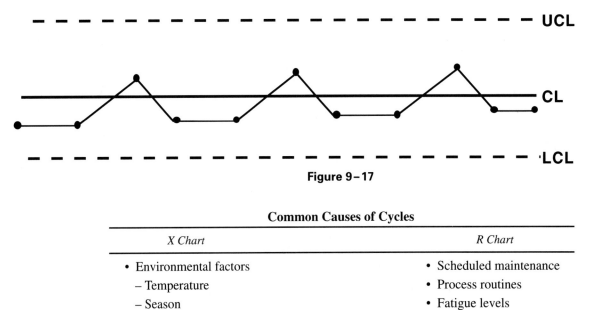

Figure 9–17

Common Causes of Cycles

X Chart	R Chart
• Environmental factors	• Scheduled maintenance
– Temperature	• Process routines
– Season	• Fatigue levels
– Humidity	• Tool/equipment wear
• Regular job rotation	

Jumps.   *Jumps* occur when there is a tremendous shift between two consecutive points (Figure 9-18).

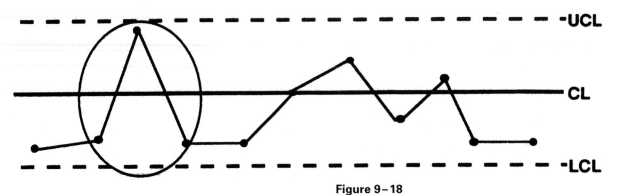

Figure 9–18

Common Causes of Jumps

X Chart	R Chart
• Changes in materials	• Change in materials
• New personnel	• Change in process/routines
• New machines/equipment	• New personnel
• Method or process change	• New tools/equipment
• Instrument changes	

Hugging. *Hugging* is a pattern that occurs when the points remain close to the central line (Figure 9-19) or the control limit lines (Figure 9-20).

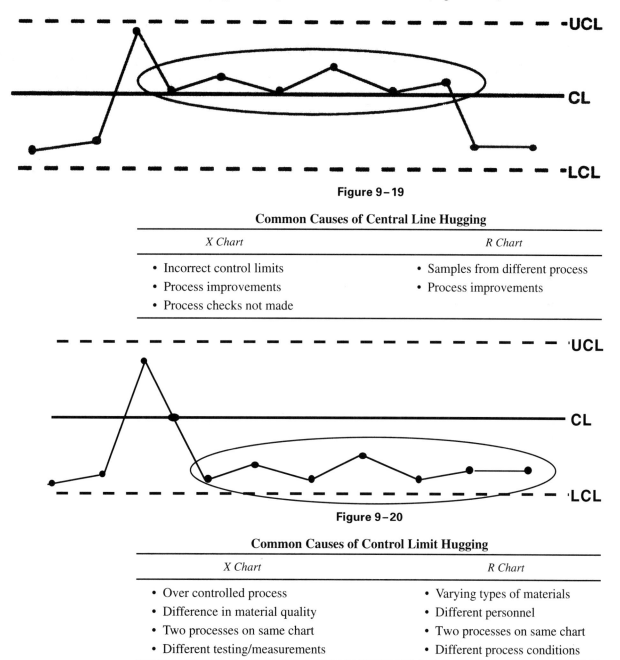

Figure 9-19

Common Causes of Central Line Hugging

X Chart	R Chart
• Incorrect control limits	• Samples from different process
• Process improvements	• Process improvements
• Process checks not made	

Figure 9-20

Common Causes of Control Limit Hugging

X Chart	R Chart
• Over controlled process	• Varying types of materials
• Difference in material quality	• Different personnel
• Two processes on same chart	• Two processes on same chart
• Different testing/measurements	• Different process conditions

In summary, a process is in control when the following conditions are met:

1. No points exceed the upper or lower control limits.
2. No patterns are formed by the points within the control limit lines.

Points that exceed the control limits indicate a special or assignable cause of variation. Patterns formed by points within the control limits indicate that a special or assignable cause of variation *may* be present.

Is the Process Capable?   Once the process is in control, the second aspect of process control can be determined: Is the process capable? *Capability* refers to the process's ability, repeatedly, to meet the stated requirements. As noted earlier, a process can be operating in control but not be capable of meeting the requirements repeatedly. To ensure statistical control over the process, it must be in control *and* capable.

A quick test can be conducted to determine the capability of any given process. Recalling the capability ratio formula, you learned that the capability of a process in control is equal to 6 standard deviations ($\pm 3\sigma$). Therefore, to determine the capability of any process, the value of 6 standard deviations needs to be identified. The following formula is used to determine this value:

$$\text{capability} = 6\left(\frac{\bar{R}}{d_2}\right)$$

$\bar{R}/d_2$ represents 1 standard deviation—and multiplied by 6 equals 6 standard deviations.

It is important to point out that this formula can only be used to compute the capability ratio of a process when the range chart is in control. To compute this formula, you need to translate it into meaningful terms. The value of $\bar{R}$ was computed when the control limit lines were calculated for the control chart. The value for d_2 can be found in the table labeled "Factors for Control Limits" on the back of the control chart (see Figure 9-8, page 141).

To translate this formula, insert the values for $\bar{R}$ and d_2. Once the formula has been translated, divide the values contained within the parentheses ( ), then multiply that value by 6.

$$6\left(\frac{\bar{R}}{d_2}\right) = 6 \text{ standard deviations for the process}$$

Once the value of 6 standard deviations has been determined, the capability ratio can be computed.

$$\text{Capability ratio} = \frac{6 \text{ standard deviations}}{\text{specification spread}}$$

To compute the capability ratio, the value of 6 standard deviations is divided by the value of the specification spread or process tolerance (USL – LSL). The process is capable if the capability ratio is less than 1. (Remember that *ideally,* the capability ratio should be .75 or less.)

Once the process is in control and capable, the control chart can be used to continuously monitor and control variation in the process. Provided that no points exceed the control limit lines and that no patterns are formed by the points within the control limit lines, 99.73% of the output produced by the process will be within the stated requirements. If any point exceeds the control limits or form patterns, the process should be investigated to identify, correct, and eliminate any special causes of variation. If any changes or improvements are made in the process, the control limits need to be recomputed and adjusted to reflect the new levels of variation in the process.

Given the information necessary to analyze and interpret control charts, let's review these points, using the control chart that was constructed throughout this unit (Figure 9-11).

1. Is This Process in control?

- Do any points exceed the control limit lines?   Yes. Two of the points on the average chart exceed the upper control limit (UCL$_x$), and two of the points exceed the lower control limit (LCL$_x$). The points that exceed the control limits indicate that a special or assignable cause of variation is operating in the process. This may be due to any variation due to any of the following conditions.

  - Broken tools/equipment
  - Environment changes
    - Temperature
    - Humidity
    - Lighting

  - Machine wear
  - Various personnel
  - Poor quality of materials
  - Improper adjustments
  - Tool/equipment wear

  To eliminate a special or assignable cause of variation, the cause must be identified and corrected. Once this has been done, the process variation can be brought back into control.

- Are any patterns formed by the points within the control limit lines?
  Runs: Do seven or more consecutive points fall on one side of the central line?   Yes. The first eight points on the control chart lie above the central line. Although this condition does not indicate that an assignable cause is present, it serves as a warning that a change is occurring in the process. If the process had been investigated when the run first became apparent, perhaps the special cause of variation could have been detected earlier.
  Trends: Do seven or more consecutive points rise or fall in one direction?   No.

Cycles :   Do any points form repeated patterns over time?   No.

Jumps: Is there a tremendous shift between consecutive points?   Yes. A large shift occurs between the 23rd and 24th points on the control chart. This jump could be a warning sign of additional problems operating in the process.

Hugging: Do consecutive points lie close to the central line or control limit lines?   No.

2. Is the Process Capable?   To determine if this process is capable, the value of 6 standard deviations (normal curve) needs to be computed. Since the range chart is in control, the following formula can be used to compute this value:

$$6\left(\frac{R}{d_2}\right) = 6 \text{ standard deviations for the process}$$

The value of $\bar{R}$ computed previously for the control limits was .006. The value of d_2 can be found in the "Factors for Control Limits" table on the back of the control chart (see Figure 9-8, page 141). The d_2 value for subgroups of 4 is 2.059. To compute the value of 6 standard deviations for this process, insert the known values into the formula.

$$6\left(\frac{\bar{R}}{d_2}\right) = 6\left(\frac{.006}{2.059}\right)$$

Then, divide the values within the ( ):

$$.006 \div 2.059 = .0029$$

The value of .0029 represents 1 standard deviation. To determine the value of 6 standard deviations, multiply this value by 6:

$$6 \times .0029 = .0174$$
$$= .017$$

The value of 6 standard deviations for this process is .017. Now the capability ratio can be computed using the following formula:

$$\text{capability ratio} = \frac{6 \text{ standard deviations}}{\text{specification spread}}$$
$$= \frac{.017}{.930 - .910}$$
$$= \frac{.017}{.020}$$
$$= .85$$

The capability ratio is .85. Therefore, the process is capable of meeting the requirements repeatedly, since the capability ratio is less than 1.

As a result of this analysis, the process is not in control, yet it is capable. To improve the process, the assignable cause of variation needs to be identified and eliminated. Once this occurs, statistical control over the process can be resumed.

One final point should be made about the $X-R$ control chart. The average (X) chart enables you to control the variation that occurs "between" sample subgroups. This represents the variation occurring over a longer period of time compared to the variation exhibited in the range (R) chart. The range (R) chart enables you to determine the amount of variation occurring "within" the sample subgroups. This represents the variation occurring in the process during a shorter period of time.

REVIEW QUESTIONS

1. An $\bar{X}-R$ control chart contains two charts. The top chart measures _____ and the bottom chart measures _____ of samples.

2. What two critical process characteristics are measured via the control chart?

3. Match the following patterns.

   _____ Seven or more consecutive points that
   (a) Runs   continue to rise/fall in one direction
   (b) Trends   _____ A tremendous shift between points
   (c) Cycle   _____ Seven or more consecutive points on
       one side of the central line
   (d) Jump   _____ Points displaying a similar pattern

4. If a process has an $\bar{R}$ of .02, a tolerance of .050, and there are four samples per subgroup, what is the capability ratio?

5. Given the information in Question 4, is this process capable? _____

6. Construct a control chart for the following data.

Subgroup 1:	195	201	194	201	205	Subgroup 14:	199	199	197	204	202
Subgroup 2:	204	190	199	195	202	Subgroup 15:	189	199	205	197	199
Subgroup 3:	195	197	205	201	195	Subgroup 16:	198	196	199	205	197
Subgroup 4:	211	198	193	199	204	Subgroup 17:	198	201	201	206	206
Subgroup 5:	204	193	197	200	194	Subgroup 18:	206	200	190	202	196
Subgroup 6:	200	202	195	200	107	Subgroup 19:	197	198	198	195	201
Subgroup 7:	196	198	197	196	196	Subgroup 20:	196	199	197	198	204
Subgroup 8:	201	197	206	207	197	Subgroup 21:	196	207	203	193	197
Subgroup 9:	200	202	204	192	201	Subgroup 22:	202	202	206	209	202
Subgroup 10:	203	201	209	192	198	Subgroup 23:	200	213	196	193	199
Subgroup 11:	195	198	196	204	201	Subgroup 24:	204	192	198	205	199
Subgroup 12:	193	203	197	198	201	Subgroup 25:	199	201	194	205	207
Subgroup 13:	200	206	208	199	200						

7. Given the information on the control chart constructed above, answer the following questions.
   (a) Is the process in control?
   (b) Are there any patterns formed by the points within the control limits?
   (c) The process requirements are 180–220. Is this process capable?

8. Construct a control chart for the following data.

Subgroup 1:	−5	0	12	4	−11	Subgroup 14:	−10	−6	−20	−7	−7
Subgroup 2:	20	3	8	-6	−20	Subgroup 15:	−18	6	17	−6	6
Subgroup 3:	−5	13	−5	−1	−7	Subgroup 16:	−10	8	13	3	−4
Subgroup 4:	−2	8	13	13	8	Subgroup 17:	10	−8	−16	−22	−4
Subgroup 5:	9	5	−5	−4	−10	Subgroup 18:	16	2	0	9	13

9. Given the information on the control chart constructed above, answer the following questions.
   (a) Is the process in control?
   (b) Based on this, what type(s) of causes are operating in the process?
   (c) The process requirements are ±23. Is this process capable?

Chapter 10

Attribute Control Charts

As mentioned earlier, two basic types of control charts are commonly used to monitor, analyze, and control process variation: variable and attribute control charts. In Chapter 9 a variable control chart (X–R) was used to analyze the process variation of measurable data. This chapter focuses on the use of attribute control charts.

INSTRUCTIONAL OBJECTIVES

When you have completed this chapter, you will be able to:

- Identify the use of attribute control charts.
- Define the difference between defects and defectives.
- Construct and analyze a p and an np control chart.
- Construct and analyze a c and a u control chart.

LEARNING ACTIVITIES

_____10A: Introduction to Attribute Control Charts
_____10B: p and np Control Charts
_____10C: c and u Control Charts
_____10D: Control Chart Summary

10A: INTRODUCTION TO ATTRIBUTE CONTROL CHARTS

Attribute control charts are used to analyze process variation of countable data. Countable data can be used when the process does not produce measurable data or when measurable data are difficult to obtain. Attribute control charts are used when the output produced is:

- Measured with go/no-go gages
- Inspected for conformance or nonconformance
- Inspected for the number of defects or defectives
- Inspected for the percentage of defects or defectives

Attribute control charts can also be used for processes that produce measurable data when any of the following conditions exist:

- Accurate and reliable measurement instruments are not available.
- The measurement of samples is too time consuming or impractical.
- More than one characteristic of the process needs to be analyzed.

Attribute control charts are based on the same theories as variable control charts. The basic difference between these two charts is that attribute control charts analyze the characteristics of the process output in terms of being acceptable/not acceptable, conforming/nonconforming, go/no-go, and so on, whereas variable control charts analyze the measurable differences in a specific characteristic of the process. Given this, attribute control charts are less sensitive in detecting the changes or problems occurring in the process. To compensate for this, more samples are needed to analyze process variation when attribute control charts are used.

There are four primary attribute control charts (Figure 10-1):

1. *p Charts:* the fraction or percentage of defective parts
2. *np Charts:* the number of defective parts
3. *c Charts:* the number of defects per unit
4. *u Charts:* the average number of defects per unit

p and *np* control charts are used to determine the number of *defectives. c* and *u* control charts are used to determine the number of *defects.*

- A *defective* is any item that fails to conform to *one or more* quality characteristics, specifications, or requirements.

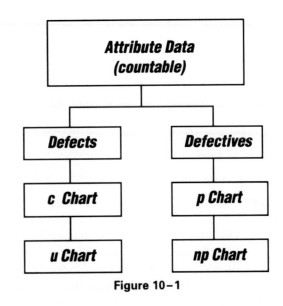

Figure 10-1

- A *defect,* on the other hand, is an item's failure to conform to *one specific* quality characteristic, specification, or requirement.

In effect, a defective item may contain one or more defects. A defective item is often classified as a *nonconforming* item, and a defect is a *nonconformity.*

10B: *p* AND *np* CONTROL CHARTS

The *p* and *np* control charts are used to determine the defective items produced by a given process. Although both charts are used for defectives, two basic differences exist:

1. The *p* control chart determines the *fraction* or *percentage* of defectives, whereas the *np* control chart determines the *number* of defectives.

2. The *p* control chart can be used to determine the fraction or percentage of defectives when the number of samples per subgroup is constant or when the number of samples per subgroup varies.
   The *np* control chart should be used to determine the number of defectives *only* when the number of samples per subgroup remains constant.

p and *np* control charts can be used to determine the number of items that fail to conform to one or more quality characteristic and provided that they can be classified as acceptable or not acceptable.

Constructing a *p* Control Chart

Step 1: Collect Data.   To collect an appropriate amount of data for a *p* control chart, 20 to 25 subgroups are needed. Each subgroup should contain a minimum of 50 individual samples. Once a subgroup has been collected and inspected, the following information should be recorded on the control chart:

- Date
- Number of samples inspected
- Number of defectives
- Total number of defectives

Once again, a working example will be used to illustrate how each step is applied. The *p* chart in Figure 10-2 contains the data that will be used throughout this unit. Although the *p* chart can be used for sample sizes that vary, it is recommended that constant sample sizes are used whenever possible to reduce the amount of work required to compute the control limits for the *p* chart. Whenever the number of samples per subgroup varies, the control limits must be recomputed for each subgroup. If the sample size per subgroup remains constant, the control limits only need to be computed once.

ATTRIBUTE CONTROL CHART (P AND NP)

| DEPT. BILLING | ITEM CUSTOMER INVOICES | OPERATION 70 |

DATE JULY	1	2	3	4	5	6	7	8	9	10	11	12	13	14	15	16	17	18	19	20						
No. Pieces Inspected	50	50	50	50	50	50	50	50	50	50	50	50	50	50	50	50	50	50	50	50						

Number Defective	Percent Defective

TYPE OF DEFECT																										
1. MISCODED	1	3	3	3	1	1	1	2	1	4	0	0	2	0	2	3	2	1	4	3						
2. WRONG PRICE	0	3	2	2	3	2	1	0	3	2	2	1	1	1	2	2	2	0	2	3						
3.																										
4.																										
5.																										
6.																										
Total Number Defective	1	6	5	5	4	3	2	2	4	6	2	1	3	1	4	5	4	1	6	6						
Percent Defective																										

Figure 10–2

Step 2: Compute the Percentage of Defectives (p).

The following formula is used to compute the percentage of defectives.

$$\text{Percent defective } (p) = \frac{\text{total number of defectives per subgroup } (np)}{\text{total number of samples within the subgroup}}$$

or

$$p = \frac{np}{n}$$

np/n expresses the fraction of defectives. To express the number of defectives as a percentage, divide np by n and multiply that number by 100. For example, in the first subgroup, 50 samples were inspected and the total number of defectives was 1. To compute the percentage of defectives, the following calculations are needed:

$$p = \frac{1}{50}$$
$$= .02$$
$$= .02\,(100)$$
$$= 2\% \quad \text{(expressed as a percentage)}$$

The percentage of defectives has already been computed for the first 10 subgroups. Now, compute the percentage of defectives for the remaining subgroups. When you have completed this activity, check your answers against the ones on the *p* control chart in Figure 10-3.

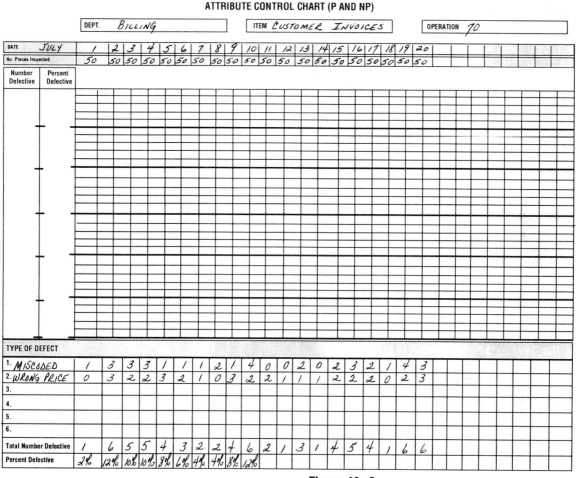

ATTRIBUTE CONTROL CHART (P AND NP)

DEPT. *BILLING* ITEM *CUSTOMER INVOICES* OPERATION *70*

DATE *JULY*	1	2	3	4	5	6	7	8	9	10	11	12	13	14	15	16	17	18	19	20							
No. Pieces Inspected	50	50	50	50	50	50	50	50	50	50	50	50	50	50	50	50	50	50	50	50							

TYPE OF DEFECT

	1	2	3	4	5	6	7	8	9	10	11	12	13	14	15	16	17	18	19	20
1. MISCODED	1	3	3	3	1	1	1	2	1	4	0	0	2	0	2	3	2	1	4	3
2. WRONG PRICE	0	3	2	2	3	2	1	0	3	2	2	1	1	1	2	2	2	0	2	3
3.																				
4.																				
5.																				
6.																				
Total Number Defective	1	6	5	5	4	3	2	2	4	6	2	1	3	1	4	5	4	1	6	6
Percent Defective	2%	12%	10%	10%	8%	6%	4%	4%	8%	12%										

Figure 10-3

Step 3: Plot the Percentage of Defectives on the Chart. Once the percentage of defectives has been computed for each subgroup, plot the points on the graph of the control chart (Figure 10-4).

Step 4: Compute the Average Percentage of Defectives ($\overline{p}$). The *average percentage of defectives* is computed by adding the number of defectives in each subgroup. Then divide the sum by the number of samples inspected.

$$\text{Average percentage of defectives } \overline{p} = \frac{\text{total number of defectives } (np)}{\text{total number of samples } (\Sigma n)}$$

or

$$\overline{p} = \frac{\Sigma np}{\Sigma n}$$

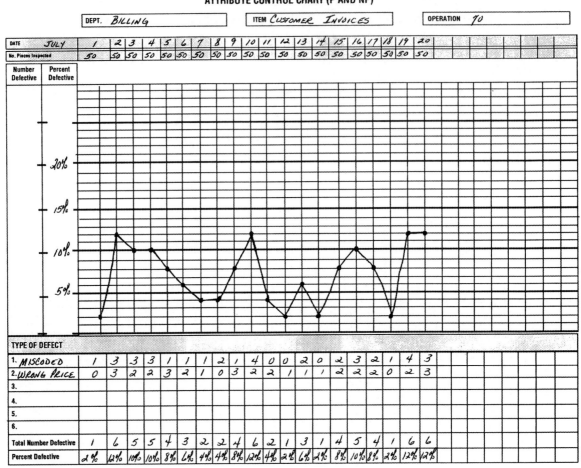

ATTRIBUTE CONTROL CHART (P AND NP)

| DEPT. *BILLING* | | ITEM *CUSTOMER INVOICES* | | OPERATION *70* |

DATE *JULY*	1	2	3	4	5	6	7	8	9	10	11	12	13	14	15	16	17	18	19	20							
No. Pieces Inspected	50	50	50	50	50	50	50	50	50	50	50	50	50	50	50	50	50	50	50	50							

TYPE OF DEFECT

	1	2	3	4	5	6	7	8	9	10	11	12	13	14	15	16	17	18	19	20
1. *MISCODED*	1	3	3	3	1	1	1	2	1	4	0	0	2	0	2	3	2	1	4	3
2. *WRONG PRICE*	0	3	2	2	3	2	1	0	3	2	2	1	1	1	2	2	2	0	2	3
3.																				
4.																				
5.																				
6.																				
Total Number Defective	1	6	5	5	4	3	2	2	4	6	2	1	3	1	4	5	4	1	6	6
Percent Defective	2%	12%	10%	10%	8%	6%	4%	4%	8%	12%	4%	2%	6%	2%	8%	10%	8%	2%	12%	12%

Figure 10-4

In the working example, there were a total of 71 defectives and 1000 samples were inspected. The average percentage of defectives is computed as follows:

$$\bar{p} = \frac{71}{1000}$$
$$= .071$$
$$= .071(100)$$
$$= 7.1\% \quad \text{(expressed as a percentage)}$$

The central line for the *p* control chart is 7.1% (Figure 10-5).

Step 5: Compute the Upper and Lower Control Limits. The upper and lower control limits for the *p* control chart are two dashed straight lines when the number of samples per subgroup remains constant. When the number of samples per subgroup varies, the upper and lower control limits need to be computed each time the number of samples per subgroup changes. When this occurs, the control limits are not two straight dashed lines, as illustrated in Figure 10-6.

ATTRIBUTE CONTROL CHART (P AND NP)

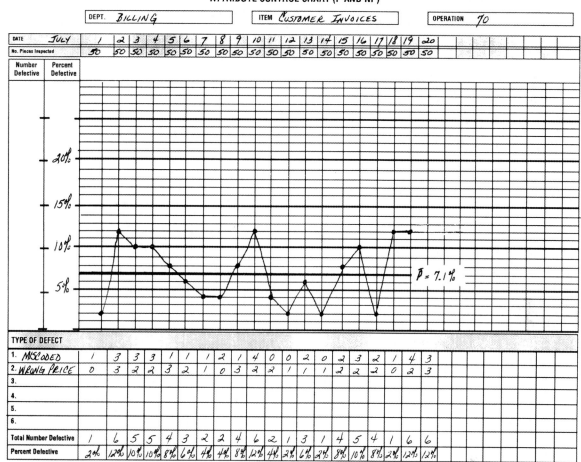

| DEPT. | BILLING | ITEM | CUSTOMER INVOICES | OPERATION | 70 |

DATE	JULY	1	2	3	4	5	6	7	8	9	10	11	12	13	14	15	16	17	18	19	20									
No. Pieces Inspected		50	50	50	50	50	50	50	50	50	50	50	50	50	50	50	50	50	50	50	50									

$\bar{p} = 7.1\%$

TYPE OF DEFECT

		1	2	3	4	5	6	7	8	9	10	11	12	13	14	15	16	17	18	19	20
1.	MISCODED	1	3	3	3	1	1	1	2	1	4	0	0	2	0	2	3	2	1	4	3
2.	WRONG PRICE	0	3	2	2	3	2	1	0	3	2	2	1	1	1	2	2	2	0	2	3
3.																					
4.																					
5.																					
6.																					
Total Number Defective		1	6	5	5	4	3	2	2	4	6	2	1	3	1	4	5	4	1	6	6
Percent Defective		2%	12%	10%	10%	8%	6%	4%	4%	8%	12%	4%	2%	6%	2%	8%	10%	8%	2%	12%	12%

Figure 10–5

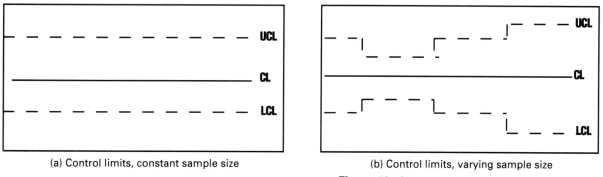

(a) Control limits, constant sample size   (b) Control limits, varying sample size

Figure 10–6

The following formula is used to compute the upper control limit (UCL) for the *p* control chart.

$$\mathrm{UCL}_p = \bar{p} + 3\sqrt{\frac{p(1-\bar{p})}{n}}$$

where $\bar{p}$ = average percentage of defectives

n = number of samples within the subgroup

To translate this formula using the data from our example, the value of $\bar{p}$, computed in Step 4, is .071 and n is 50.

$$UCL_p = .071 + 3\sqrt{\frac{.071(1 - .071)}{50}}$$

To compute the UCL_p, the following order of operations is required:

1. Compute the numbers contained in parentheses ( ).

$$UCL_p = .071 + 3\sqrt{\frac{.071(1 - .071)}{50}}$$

$$UCL_p = .071 + 3\sqrt{\frac{.071(0.929)}{50}}$$

2. Simplify the numerator by multiplying the two values.

$$UCL_p = .071 + 3\sqrt{\frac{.071(0.929)}{50}}$$

$$UCL_p = .071 + 3\sqrt{\frac{.0659}{50}}$$

3. Simplify the operation under the $\sqrt{}$ by dividing the numerator (the number on top) by the denominator (the number on the bottom).

$$UCL_p = .071 + 3\sqrt{\frac{.0659}{50}}$$

$$UCL_p = .071 + 3\sqrt{.0013}$$

4. Find the square root for the value under the $\sqrt{}$. To determine the square root for any value, enter the number under the $\sqrt{}$ in your calculator and depress the $\sqrt{}$ key.

$$UCL_p = .071 + 3\sqrt{.0013}$$

$$UCL_p = .071 + 3(.036)$$

5. Multiply the two numbers together.

$$UCL_p = .071 + 3(.036)$$

$$= .108$$

6. Add the two remaining values.

$$UCL_p = .071 + .108$$
$$= .179$$
$$= .18 \quad \text{(rounded)}$$

The value for the UCL_p can be expressed as 18% by multiplying the decimal value of 0.18 by 100.

The formula used to compute the LCL_p is almost identical to the UCL_p formula. The only difference is that the average *percentage of defectives* (the value of *p*) is subtracted from the balance of the formula rather than added.

$$UCL_p = \bar{p} + 3\sqrt{\frac{\bar{p}(1-\bar{p})}{n}} \qquad LCL_p = \bar{p} - 3\sqrt{\frac{\bar{p}(1-\bar{p})}{n}}$$

Given the similarities between these two formulas, the values in the UCL_p formula can be used to compute the LCL_p.

$$UCL_p = .071 + .108$$

$$LCL_p = .071 - .108$$

Since these two formulas are so similar, all that is required to compute the LCL_p is to subtract the two values.

$$LCL_p = .071 - .108$$
$$= -.037$$
$$= -.037 \times 100$$
$$= -3.7\%$$

Whenever the LCL_p is a negative value, it is not entered on the control chart because defectives cannot be expressed as a negative number.

Step 6: Draw the Control Limit Lines on the Chart. Once the values for the control limits have been computed, they are drawn onto the chart to indicate the boundaries of the normal distribution. Remember that a process's normal distribution represents common-cause variation. This level of variation is expected to occur in the process when it is operating in control.

- The UCL_p represents +3 standard deviations from the mean.
- The central line represents the mean.
- The LCL_p represents −3 standard deviations from the mean.

With this information, the control chart can be used to monitor and analyze the variation in the process. That is, you can determine if the process is in control and capable of repeatedly meeting the requirements (Figure 10-7). The following

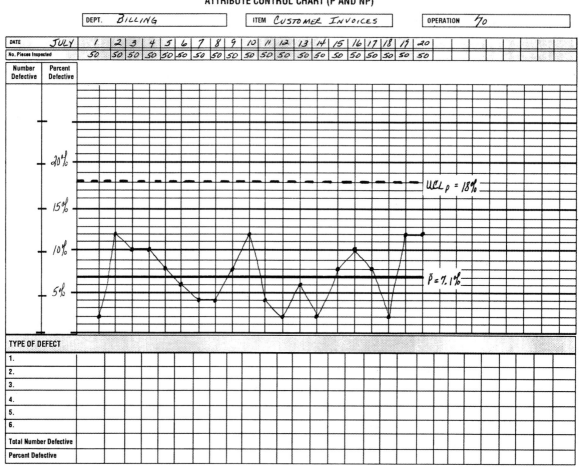

Figure 10–7

control limits were computed for our working example:

$$\text{UCL}_p = 18\%$$

$$\text{CL or } \bar{p} = 7.1\%$$

$$\text{LCL}_p = -3.7\% \quad \text{(since this is a negative value, it is not included on the control chart)}$$

Analyzing the *p* Control Chart

To determine if the process is operating in control, two conditions must be satisfied:

1. No points exceed the upper or lower control limit lines.
2. No patterns are formed by the points within the control limits.

If any point exceeds the UCL or LCL, a special or assignable cause of variation is operating in the process. When this occurs, the process should be investigated to determine the cause and correct the problem. Once the problem has been corrected, common-cause variation will be restored. That is, all of the points plotted on the control chart will be within the UCL and LCL lines.

A process can also be out of control when the points within the control limits form a pattern. A pattern may be any one of the following conditions:

- *Runs:* seven or more consecutive points on one side of the central line

- *Trends:* seven or more consecutive points that progress in one direction

- *Cycles:* points that display similar trends or patterns over time

- *Hugging:* series of points close to the central line or control limits

Whenever a pattern is formed by the points within the control limits, it usually indicates that an abnormal condition is beginning to occur in the process. Under these circumstances the process should be closely monitored and analyzed to prevent any condition that may force the process output beyond its level of common-cause variation.

Once the process's common-cause variation is stable, the capability of the process can be determined. When an attribute control chart is used, capability is determined by comparing the defectives actually produced to the desired levels or goals established for the process. If the defectives actually produced exceed the desired levels or goals, actions should be taken to reduce the number of defectives produced by the process. If, on the other hand, the defectives produced are within the required levels or goals, the control chart can be used to monitor and control the process on an ongoing basis.

In analyzing the *p* control chart in this unit, all of the points fall within the established control limits and no apparent patterns are formed by the points within the control limits. Therefore, it can be concluded that the process in this example is operating in control. The second part of the analysis is to determine if the process capability is capable. That is, is the process output within acceptable limits? If the goal is to hold the average percentage of defectives below 10%, this process would be operating at an acceptable level, since the average percentage of defectives *is* 7.1%. However, if the goal is to hold the average percentage of defectives below 5%, this process would not be capable of operating within the acceptable or desired levels.

In summary, the control limits indicate the extent of common-cause variation in the process. Common-cause variation *cannot* be entirely eliminated; however, actions can be taken to improve the process in order to reduce the amount of common-cause variation. Special or assignable causes of variation can be identified, corrected, and entirely eliminated. The *p* control chart is a valuable tool used to monitor, analyze, control, and improve the variation in process's producing countable data.

Special Considerations

The number of samples per subgroup in this example was constant. There may be times, however, when the number of samples per subgroup varies. This may occur when 100% inspection is necessary and the number of items produced varies. Under these circumstances, the control limits need to be computed each time the number of samples per subgroup changes. Figure 10-8 illustrates the control limits for varying sample sizes.

ATTRIBUTE CONTROL CHART (P AND NP)

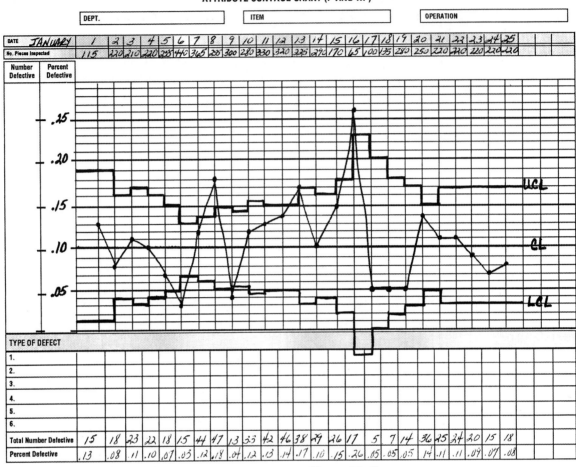

Figure 10-8

The *np* control chart is very similar to the *p* control chart. Both control charts are used to identify the defectives in the process. There are two basic differences between *p* and *np* control charts:

1. The *p* control chart expresses defectives as a percentage and the *np* control chart expresses defectives as a whole number.
2. The *p* control chart can be used when the number of samples per subgroup is constant or when the number varies. The *np* control chart should be used only when the number of samples per subgroup remains constant.

Constructing an *np* Control Chart

The basic steps involved in constructing the *np* control chart are very similar to those required for the *p* control chart. Given the similarities between these two charts, a brief review of the steps will be provided to highlight the differences.

Step 1: Collect Data.   To obtain an accurate picture of the defectives produced by the process, a minimum of 50 samples per subgroup is needed. Each subgroup must contain the *same* number of samples and approximately 20 to 25 subgroups are required for the *np* control chart.

Once the samples for the subgroup have been collected and examined, the data are recorded on the *np* control chart. Then the total number of defectives in each subgroup is plotted on the graph portion of the chart.

Step 2: Compute the Average Number of Defectives ($n\bar{p}$). The *np* control chart is used to determine the average number of defectives in each subgroup, *not* the percentage of defectives. To compute the average number of defectives for all subgroups, add the number of defectives in each subgroup. Then divide the sum of defectives by the number of subgroups.

$$\text{Average number of defectives } (n\bar{p}) = \frac{\text{total number of defectives } (np)}{\text{total number of subgroups } (k)}$$

or

$$n\bar{p} = \frac{np}{k}$$

The average number of defectives is the central line on the *np* control chart.

Using the data on the *np* control chart in Figure 10-9, the average number of

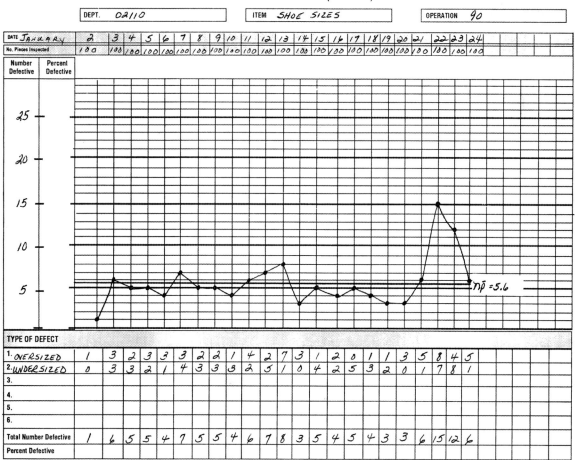

Figure 10–9

defectives is computed as follows:

$$n\bar{p} = \frac{\Sigma np}{k}$$

$$= \frac{129}{23}$$

$$= 5.6$$

Step 3: Compute the Control Limits (UCL_{np} and LCL_{np}). The formula used to compute the upper control limit is

$$UCL_{np} = n\bar{p} + 3\sqrt{n\bar{p}(1-\bar{p})}$$

where $n\bar{p}$ = average number of defectives for all subgroups
$\quad\quad \bar{p}$ = average percentage of defectives for all subgroups

In this formula, the values of both $\bar{p}$ and $n\bar{p}$ are used. The value of $n\bar{p}$ was computed in Step 2 as 5.6.

The formula used to compute the value of $\bar{p}$ is:

$$\text{average percentage of defectives } (\bar{p}) = \frac{\text{total number of defectives } (np)}{\text{total number of samples } (\Sigma n)}$$

or

$$\bar{p} = \frac{\Sigma np}{\Sigma n}$$

Once these values have been computed, they are inserted into the formula.

$$n\bar{p} = \frac{\text{total number of defectives}}{\text{total number of subgroups}}$$

$$= \frac{129}{23}$$

$$= 5.6$$

$$\bar{p} = \frac{\text{total number of defectives}}{\text{total number of samples}}$$

$$= \frac{129}{2300}$$

$$= .056$$

Given these two values, the UCL_{np} formula can be translated as follows:

$$UCL_{np} = n\bar{p} + 3\sqrt{n\bar{p}(1-\bar{p})}$$
$$= 5.6 + 3\sqrt{5.6(1-.056)}$$

Once the formula has been translated, the following operations are required:

1. Compute the number in parentheses ( ).

$$UCL_{np} = 5.6 + 3\sqrt{5.6(1-.056)}$$
$$= 5.6 + 3\sqrt{5.6(.944)}$$

2. Simplify the operation under the $\sqrt{}$ sign by multiplying the values.

$$UCL_{np} = 5.6 + 3\sqrt{5.6(.944)}$$
$$= 5.6 + 3\sqrt{5.286}$$

3. Compute the square root of the value under the $\sqrt{}$.

$$UCL_{np} = 5.6 + 3\sqrt{5.286}$$
$$= 5.6 + 3(2.299)$$

4. Multiply the two values.

$$UCL_{np} = 5.6 + 3(2.299)$$
$$= 5.6 + 6.9$$

5. Add the remaining values.

$$UCL_{np} = 5.6 + 6.9$$
$$= 12.5$$

Now the LCL_{np} needs to be computed. Here again, the two control limit formulas are very similar. The only difference is the average (central line) and standard deviation (upper or lower control limits) values are added in the UCL formula and subtracted in the LCL formula.

$$UCL_{np} = n\bar{p} + 3\sqrt{n\bar{p}(1-\bar{p})} \qquad LCL_{np} = n\bar{p} - 3\sqrt{n\bar{p}(1-\bar{p})}$$

Given these similarities, the values used to compute the UCL_{np} can be inserted into the LCL_{np} formula and subtracted.

$$UCL_{np} = 5.6 + 6.9$$
$$LCL_{np} = 5.6 - 6.9$$
$$= -1.3$$

Since the LCL_{np} is a negative value, it is not included on the control chart.

Step 4: Draw the Control Limit Lines on the Chart. The control limit lines represent the common-cause variation in the process. The UCL indicates +3 standard deviations and the UCL indicates −3 standard deviations. After the control limit lines have been drawn on the graph (Figure 10-10), the process can be analyzed to determine if it is in control and capable.

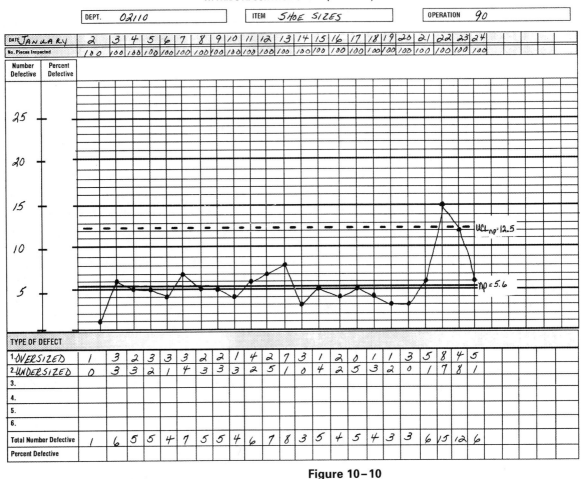

Figure 10–10

Analyzing the *np* Control Chart

The most obvious condition on this *np* control chart shown is that one point exceeds the upper control limit. Any point outside the control limits indicates that a special or assignable cause is operating in the process. Whenever this occurs, the process should be investigated to identify and correct the cause of the problem. Whenever corrective actions are taken to solve a problem in the process, the control limits need to be recomputed. If the problem is solved, the value outside the control limits should be omitted. If the problem has not been corrected, the value outside the control limits should be included until the problem has been corrected.

Another, less obvious condition exists in this *np* control chart. A run occurred just before the point exceeded the upper control limit. Patterns indicate that an abnormal condition is occurring in the process and usually serve as a *warning* that an out of control condition is about to occur. If patterns are spotted early in the process, a number of problems can be prevented.

The second condition that needs to be determined is the process capability. That is, is the process capable of repeatedly meeting the requirements? Since the *np* control chart is used to determine the number of defectives, the only way to determine this is to compare the defectives actually produced by the process to the desired number or level of defectives that are acceptable. For example, if the maximum number of defectives allowed is 5 out of 100 samples, the process used in our working example would not be operating at an acceptable level. If, on the other hand, the goal was to keep the defectives under 20 for every 100 samples inspected, this process is capable of operating at the desired level of performance.

10C: *c* AND *u* CONTROL CHARTS

In the previous units, *p* and *np* control charts were described as the attribute control charts used to determine the defectives in a given process. Defectives are items that have one or more defects. The *p* and *np* control charts are extremely useful tools to analyze items that are classified as accepted–rejected, good–bad, go/no-go, defective–nondefective, and so on. *p* and *np* control charts are frequently used for relatively simple items with a limited number of quality characteristics. There are times, however, when the items are too complex to be classified simply as defective or nondefective. For example, a car or complex order form may contain multiple defects. Yet it would be improper to classify the entire car or order as a defective. In these instances, *c* and *u* control charts are used to determine the specific defects in the items produced. A defect is defined as *each instance* an item fails to conform to a single quality characteristic.

To further clarify the difference between defectives and defects, a defective is an item that fails to conform to one or more quality characteristics. A defect is *each instance* that an item fails to conform to a single quality characteristic. In effect, a defective item may contain one or more defects.

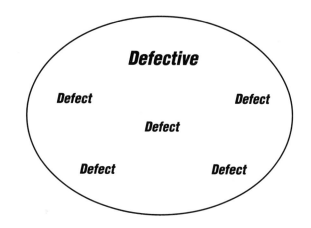

The *c* and *u* control charts are used to determine the defects per item or items produced by a given process. The *c* control chart is used to determine the *number of defects* in one item, or a fixed number of items. The *u* control chart is used to determine the *average defects* per item or items. The *u* control chart can be used when the number of samples per subgroup remains constant or varies. The *c* chart can be used only when the number of samples per subgroup remains constant.

Constructing a *c* Control Chart

Step 1: Collect Data. A sufficient amount of data needs to be collected to construct a *c* control chart. The number of samples per subgroup should remain constant and 20 to 25 subgroups are required before the control limits are computed. The samples for each subgroup must come from only *one* source (i.e., unit, article, item, lot, batch, bin, etc.). In many cases, only one sample is in a subgroup. However, this control chart is not limited to one sample per subgroup. When more than one sample is in a subgroup, the total number of defects in all samples is recorded as if it were a single item or sample.

Once samples are selected and inspected, the data are recorded on the control chart (Figure 10-11). Once again, a working example will follow each step to illustrate its application.

Step 2: Compute the Average Number of Defects. The average number of defects is computed by adding the total number of defects in all subgroups and dividing that sum by the number of subgroups.

ATTRIBUTE CONTROL CHART (C AND U)

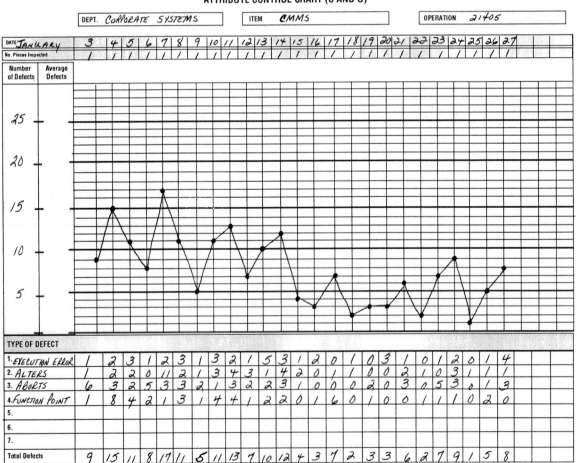

Figure 10-11

$$\text{Average number of defects } (\bar{c}) = \frac{\text{total number of defects } (c)}{\text{total number of subgroups } (k)}$$

or

$$\bar{c} = \frac{\Sigma c}{k}$$

For the *c* control chart in this example, the average number of defects is computed as follows:

$$\bar{c} = \frac{189}{25}$$

$$= 7.56$$

The average number of defects is the central line on the control chart.

Step 3: Compute the Upper and Lower Control Limits.   The following formulas are used to compute the control limits:

$$\text{UCL}_c = \bar{c} + 3\sqrt{\bar{c}} \qquad \text{LCL}_c = \bar{c} - 3\sqrt{\bar{c}}$$

To compute the UCL_c and LCL_c, translate the formula by inserting the known values into the formula.

The value of $\bar{c}$ was computed in step 2. Therefore, the formula can be translated as follows:

$$\text{UCL}_c = \bar{c} + 3\sqrt{\bar{c}} \qquad \text{LCL}_c = \bar{c} - 3\sqrt{\bar{c}}$$
$$\text{UCL}_c = 7.56 + 3\sqrt{7.56} \qquad \text{LCL}_c = 7.56 - 3\sqrt{7.56}$$

To compute the UCL and LCL values for the *c* control chart, the following order of operations needs to be calculated.

1.   Determine the square root for the value contained under the $\sqrt{}$ sign.

$$\text{UCL}_c = 7.56 + 3\sqrt{7.56} \qquad \text{LCL}_c = 7.56 - 3\sqrt{7.56}$$
$$\text{UCL}_c = 7.56 + 3(2.749) \qquad \text{LCL}_c = 7.56 - 3(2.749)$$

2.   Multiply the two values.

$$\text{UCL}_c = 7.56 + 3(2.749) \qquad \text{LCL}_c = 7.56 - 3(2.749)$$
$$= 7.56 + 8.247 \qquad = 7.56 - 8.247$$

3.   Add the values for the UCL_c and subtract for the LCL_c .

$$UCL_c = 7.56 + 8.247 \qquad LCL_c = 7.56 - 8.247$$
$$= 15.8 \qquad\qquad\qquad = -.687$$

Anytime the lower control limit is a negative value, it is generally omitted from the control chart.

Step 4: Draw the Control Limit Lines on the Control Chart.   The control limits establish the normal distribution of common-cause variation. The UCL_c is equivalent to $+3$ standard deviations away from the mean, the central line is the mean, and the LCL_c is equivalent to -3 standard deviations from the mean.

Once the control lines are drawn on the graph (Figure 10-12), the process can be analyzed in order to determine if it is in control and capable. Using the data in our working example, the control limits are:

$$UCL_c = 15.8$$

$$CL \text{ or } \bar{c} = 7.56$$

$$LCL_c = .687$$

(The LCL will not appear on the chart, as it is a negative value.)

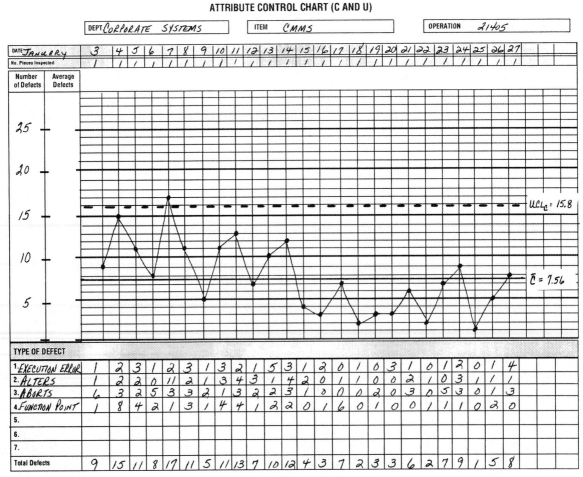

Figure 10-12

This control chart indicates that the process is not operating in control, as one point exceeds the UCL and a run and possible cycle are formed by the points within the control limits. The special or assignable causes of variation need to be identified, corrected, and eliminated in order to bring this process into statistical control. Once the common-cause variation is stable, a comparison can be made between the defects produced and the goals or requirements for the process. If the defects fall within an acceptable range, the process is capable. If the defects exceed the requirements, the process is not capable of repeatedly producing items that meet the requirements.

Constructing a *u* Control Chart

The *c* and *u* control charts are very similar. Both charts are used to determine the *defects*. The *u* control chart, however, is more sensitive to changes in process variation as it identifies the *average* defects per subgroup.

To demonstrate how control charts are constructed for subgroups with varying samples, this working example contains three different subgroup sizes.

Step 1: Collect Data. There is no set number of samples required per subgroup. However, 20 to 25 subgroups are required before the control limits are computed. Figure 10-13 contains the data that will be used to illustrate the application of each step in this unit.

ATTRIBUTE CONTROL CHART (P AND NP)

DEPT. *FINAL INSPECTION*   ITEM *PACKAGING*   OPERATION *09110*

DATE June	3	4	5	6	7	8	9	10	11	12	13	14	15	16	18	19	20	21	22
No. Pieces Inspected	10	10	10	10	10	10	10	20	20	20	20	20	20	15	15	15	15	15	15

TYPE OF DEFECT

1. BLISTERS	3	7	2	5	10	5	3	11	7	3	5	9	4	10	9	5	4	5	7	5
2. PITTED	5	5	7	5	4	4	7	6	7	7	6	7	7	6	6	10	7	4	6	6
3. BURNS	7	6	7	9	3	2	6	6	9	5	5	7	6	8	7	6	5	8	9	4
4. SCRATCHED	6	5	2	3	8	6	8	7	4	17	5	6	4	6	7	7	4	6	4	6
5.																				
6.																				
Total Number Defective	21	23	18	22	25	17	24	30	27	32	21	28	21	30	29	28	20	23	26	21
Percent Defective																				

Figure 10-13

Step 2: Compute the Average Defects for Each Subgroup. To compute the average number of defects per subgroup, add the number of defects in the subgroup and divide the sum by the number of samples.

$$\text{Average number of defects } (u) = \frac{\text{total number of defects per subgroup } (c)}{\text{total number of samples per subgroup } (n)}$$

or

$$u = \frac{c}{n}$$

Once the average number of defects has been computed for the subgroup, plot the value on the control chart (Figure 10-14). The average number of defects has been computed and plotted for the first 15 sample groups. Compute the average number of defects for the remaining subgroups, and plot the values onto the following control chart.

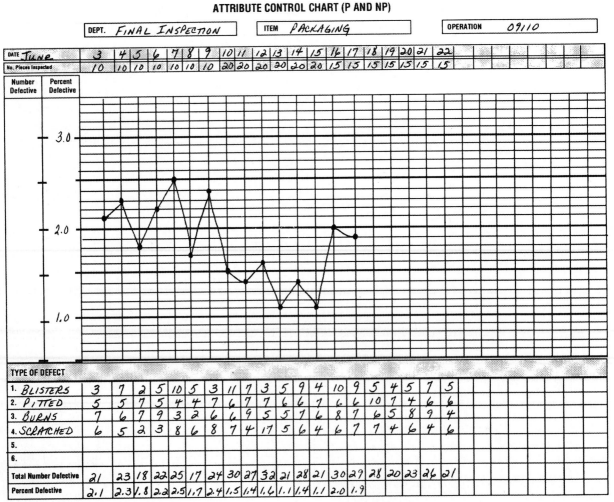

Figure 10–14

REMEMBER: The number of samples per subgroup varies, so be careful to divide the defects by the number of samples in each subgroup.

Step 3: Compute the Grand Average of Defects.   To compute the grand average, add all the defects in each subgroup and divide that sum by the total number of samples.

$$\text{Grand average for all subgroups } (\bar{u}) = \frac{\text{sum of defects } (\Sigma c)}{\text{sum of samples } (\Sigma n)}$$

or

$$u = \frac{\Sigma c}{\Sigma n}$$

In our working example, there are 486 defects and 295 samples were inspected. The grand average of defects is computed as follows:

$$\bar{u} = \frac{486}{295}$$
$$= 1.65$$

The grand average is the central line on the *u* control charts.

Step 4: Compute the Upper and Lower Control Limits.   The upper and lower control limits are computed only once when the numbers of samples in each subgroup remains constant. When the number of samples per subgroup varies, the control limits need to be recomputed each time the number of samples per subgroup changes.

The following formulas are used to compute the upper and lower control limits:

$$\text{UCL}_u = \bar{u} + 3\sqrt{\frac{\bar{u}}{n}} \qquad \text{LCL}_u = \bar{u} - 3\sqrt{\frac{\bar{u}}{n}}$$

In this formula,

- $\bar{u}$ is the grand average of defects.
- *n* is the total number of samples in the subgroup.

To compute the upper and lower control limits, the first thing that needs to be done is to translate the formula into more meaningful terms. This is done by inserting the known values into the formula.

Since this control chart contains varying number of samples per subgroup, the control limits need to be computed each time the number of samples per subgroup changes. The formula for the upper and lower control limits for the first seven subgroups can be translated as follows:

$$\text{UCL}_u = \bar{u} + 3\sqrt{\frac{\bar{u}}{n}} \qquad \text{LCL}_u = \bar{u} - 3\sqrt{\frac{\bar{u}}{n}}$$

$$\text{UCL}_u = 1.65 + 3\sqrt{\frac{1.65}{10}} \qquad \text{LCL}_u = 1.65 - 3\sqrt{\frac{1.65}{10}}$$

Once the formulas have been translated, the following operations are conducted to compute the value.

1. Compute the operation under the $\sqrt{}$ sign.
2. Find the square root for the value under the $\sqrt{}$ sign.
3. Multiply the values to the right of the $+$ or $-$ sign.
4. Add the remaining values to compute the UCL and subtract them to compute the LCL.

The UCL and LCL for the first seven subgroups is computed as follows:

$$\begin{aligned}
\text{UCL}_u &= 1.65 + 3\sqrt{\frac{1.65}{10}} & \text{LCL}_u &= 1.65 - 3\sqrt{\frac{1.65}{10}} \\
&= 1.65 + 3\sqrt{.165} & &= 1.65 - 3\sqrt{.165} \\
&= 1.65 + 3(.406) & &= 1.65 - 3(.406) \\
&= 1.65 + 1.218 & &= 1.65 - 1.218 \\
&= 2.87 & &= .432
\end{aligned}$$

Once the first set of control limits have been computed, draw them on the chart (Figure 10-15).

Now that the control limits for the first seven subgroups have been computed, compute the limits for the remaining subgroups. Remember to recompute the control limits each time the number of samples per subgroup changes. When you have completed this exercise, check your answers with the ones that follow. The control limits for the remaining subgroups were computed as follows:

Sample Sizes of 20:

$$\text{UCL}_u = \bar{u} + 3\sqrt{\frac{\bar{u}}{n}} \qquad \text{LCL}_u = \bar{u} - 3\sqrt{\frac{\bar{u}}{n}}$$

$$\begin{aligned}
\text{UCL}_u &= 1.65 + 3\sqrt{\frac{1.65}{20}} & \text{LCL}_u &= 1.65 - 3\sqrt{\frac{1.65}{20}} \\
&= 1.65 + 3\sqrt{.0825} & &= 1.65 - 3\sqrt{.0825} \\
&= 1.65 + 3(.287) & &= 1.65 - 3(.287) \\
&= 1.65 + .861 & &= .1.65 - .861 \\
&= 2.5 & &= .789 \quad \text{or} \quad .8
\end{aligned}$$

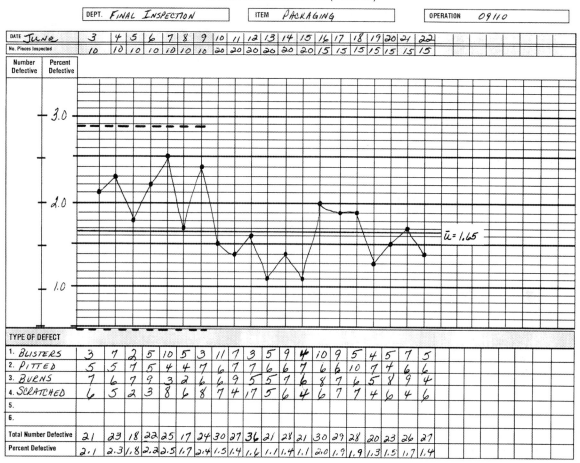

Figure 10–15

Sample Sizes of 15:

$$\text{UCL}_u = \bar{u} + 3\sqrt{\frac{\bar{u}}{n}} \qquad \text{LCL}_u = \bar{u} - 3\sqrt{\frac{\bar{u}}{n}}$$

$$\text{UCL}_u = 1.65 + 3\sqrt{\frac{1.65}{15}} \qquad \text{LCL}_u = 1.65 - 3\sqrt{\frac{1.65}{15}}$$

$$= 1.65 + 3\sqrt{.11} \qquad\qquad = 1.65 - 3\sqrt{.11}$$

$$= 1.65 + 3(.33) \qquad\qquad = 1.65 - 3(.33)$$

$$= 1.65 + .99 \qquad\qquad = 1.65 - .99$$

$$= 2.64 \qquad\qquad = .66 \quad \text{or} \quad .7$$

Now that all of the control limits have been computed, they can be plotted onto the *u* control chart (Figure 10-16). Then the chart can be analyzed to determine if the process is operating in control and is capable of meeting the requirements repeatedly.

Is the Process in Control?   Reviewing this control chart, all of the points fall within the control limits; however, a run is formed by the first seven points on the graph. Remember, a run occurs when seven or more consecutive

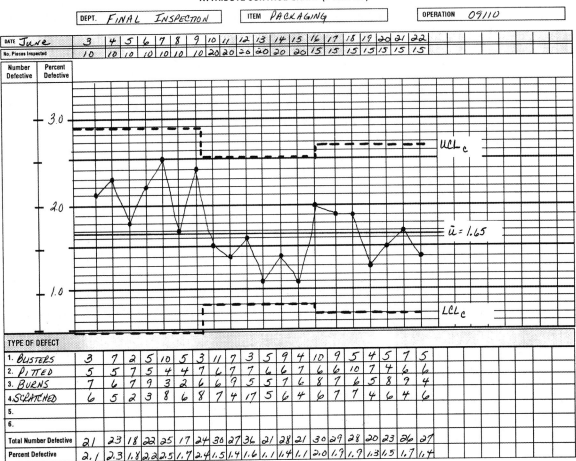

Figure 10–16

points fall on one side of the central line. A pattern generally serves as an early warning sign that a change or problem may be occurring in the process. Whenever this occurs, the process should be closely monitored to ensure that abnormal conditions are quickly detected and eliminated.

Is the Process Capable? When an attribute control chart is used, the only way to determine if the process is capable is to compare the process's performance to the requirements. The grand average of defects in the previous u control chart is 1.65. The grand average can be compared to the goals or requirements established for the process. If the grand average is less than the maximum number of acceptable defects, the process is capable of meeting the requirements. On the other hand, if the grand average is greater than the maximum number of acceptable defects, the process is not capable of meeting the requirements. Whenever this occurs, the process should be investigated to determine what can be done to improve the quality of output produced.

10D: CONTROL CHART SUMMARY

Any process can be described as a series of repeated events conducted to produce a product or service. The behavior of all processes is influenced by a variety of factors. These factors are commonly classified into five basic categories: *people, materials, methods, machines,* and *environment.* When these factors are combined, the output produced by process varies. To improve the quality of the items produced by any given process, the process itself must be improved. One of the tools commonly used to improve process quality is the *control chart* (Figures 10-17 and 10-18). The *control chart* separates the causes of variation into two basic categories: common and special or assignable causes of variation.

Common causes of variation describe the differences that occur in the items produced by the process that are due to natural or normal events. Although common causes of variation cannot be eliminated from operating within the process, the amount of variation can be reduced by the actions taken to improve the overall process. Common causes of variation should be monitored and controlled continuously to ensure that the process is operating in a stable and predictable manner.

Special or *assignable* causes of variation describe the differences that occur in the items produced by the process that are due to unnatural or abnormal events. In most cases, whenever a special or an assignable cause of variation is operating within the process, it forces the process to produce parts that exceed the stable or predictable levels of variation that have been established for the process.

The *control chart* graphically illustrates the quality of items produced by the process. The points that fall within the established control limits represent the variation that is due to common causes. When all of the points on a control chart fall within the established control limits, the process is operating within statistical *control,* and no corrective actions need to be taken. The points that exceed the established control limits represent the variation that is due to special or assignable causes. Any point that exceeds the established control limits indicates that the process is no longer operating in a stable or predictable manner. Whenever this occurs, corrective actions should be taken to identify and remove the special or assignable causes of variation operating within the process.

The control chart provides valuable information on output produced by the process over a period of time. Additionally, the statistical limits on the control chart act as guidelines to indicate when corrective actions are needed and when the process should be left alone. In effect, the control chart is simply a tool that can be used to guide your quality improvement efforts.

CONSTRUCTING A CONTROL CHART

1. Define the focus of the control chart.
2. Collect sample data.
3. Plot the samples on the control chart.
4. Calculate and plot the control limits on the control chart.
5. Determine if the process is in control and capable of meeting the requirements.
6. Correct the conditions within the process to improve the control and capability of the process.
7. Recalculate the control limits whenever a change has been made to correct or improve the performance of the overall process.

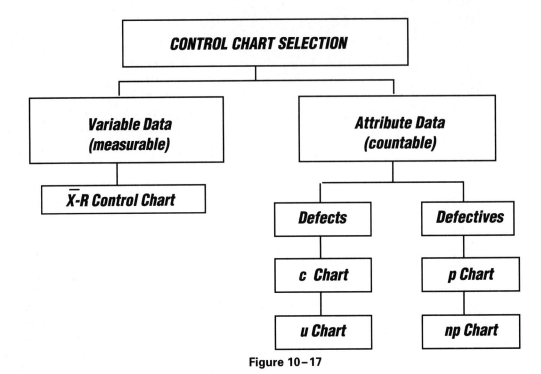

Figure 10–17

Measurable Data	Defectives	Defects

Measurable Data

$\bar{X}$–R Control Charts

$\bar{X}$ control chart is for sample averages.
$\bar{X}$ is the grand average for each sample.
$\bar{\bar{X}}$ is the grand average for all sample averages.

$$\bar{X} = \frac{\Sigma X}{n}$$

$$\bar{\bar{X}} = \frac{\Sigma \bar{X}}{k}$$

$$UCL_{\bar{X}} = \bar{\bar{X}} + A_2(\bar{R})$$

$$LCL_{\bar{X}} = \bar{\bar{X}} + A_2(\bar{R})$$

R control chart is for sample ranges.
R is the range for each sample.
$\bar{R}$ is the average range for all sample groups.

$$R = \text{largest} - \text{smallest value}$$

$$\bar{R} = \frac{\Sigma R}{k}$$

$$UCL_R = D_4(\bar{R})$$

$$LCL_R = D_3(\bar{R})$$

Defectives

p Control Charts

p control chart is for the fraction or percentage of defectives.

$$\bar{p} = \frac{\text{total number of defectives } (np)}{\text{total number of items inspected } (\Sigma n)}$$

$$UCL_p = \bar{p} + 3\sqrt{\frac{\bar{p}(1-\bar{p})}{n}}$$

$$LCL_p = \bar{p} - 3\sqrt{\frac{\bar{p}(1-\bar{p})}{n}}$$

Can be used when sample size remains constant or varies.

np Control Charts

np control chart is for the number of defectives.

$$n\bar{p} = \frac{\text{total number of defectives } (np)}{\text{total number of sample groups } (k)}$$

$$UCL_{np} = n\bar{p} + 3\sqrt{n\bar{p}(1-\bar{p})}$$

$$LCL_{np} = n\bar{p} - 3\sqrt{n\bar{p}(1-\bar{p})}$$

where $\bar{p} = \dfrac{\text{total number of defectives } (np)}{\text{total number of items inspected } (n)}$

Can be used only when sample size remains constant.

Defects

u Control Charts

u control chart is for the average number of defects.

$$\bar{u} = \frac{\text{total number of defects } (c)}{\text{total number of items inspected } (\Sigma n)}$$

$$UCL_u = \bar{u} + 3\sqrt{\frac{\bar{u}}{n}}$$

$$LCL_u = \bar{u} - 3\sqrt{\frac{\bar{u}}{n}}$$

Can be used when sample size remains constant or varies.

c Control Charts

c control chart is for the number of defects.

$$\bar{c} = \frac{\text{total number of defects } (c)}{\text{total number of sample groups } (k)}$$

$$UCL_c = \bar{c} + 3\sqrt{\bar{c}}$$

$$LCL_c = \bar{c} - 3\sqrt{\bar{c}}$$

Can be used only when sample size remains constant.

(k = total number of sample groups and n = total number of samples)

Figure 10–18 Factors for Control Charts.

REVIEW QUESTIONS

1. Attribute control charts are used to analyze processes that produce ____data.

2. Match the following charts and data.

   (a) p Control charts   ____ Average defects
   (b) np Control charts   ____ Number of defects
   (c) c Control charts   ____ Percent defective
   (d) u Control charts   ____ Number of defectives

3. Fifty samples per subgroup were collected from the systems development group and the total number of defectives were identified for each subgroup.

Subgroup	1:	4	Subgroup	11:	3
Subgroup	2:	3	Subgroup	12:	2
Subgroup	3:	2	Subgroup	13:	5
Subgroup	4:	6	Subgroup	14:	2
Subgroup	5:	3	Subgroup	15:	2
Subgroup	6:	1	Subgroup	16:	1
Subgroup	7:	3	Subgroup	17:	3
Subgroup	8:	2	Subgroup	18:	2
Subgroup	9:	9	Subgroup	19:	1
Subgroup	10:	5	Subgroup	20:	3

   Construct a p control chart.

4. Given the p control chart constructed in Question 3, answer the following questions.
   (a) Is the process operating in control?
   (b) What actions need to be taken to improve the process?
   (c) If the department's goal was to produce zero defects, is this process capable?

5. Fifty samples per subgroup were collected from the systems development group and the total number of defectives were identified for each subgroup.

Subgroup	1:	4	Subgroup	11:	3
Subgroup	2:	3	Subgroup	12:	2
Subgroup	3:	2	Subgroup	13:	5
Subgroup	4:	6	Subgroup	14:	2
Subgroup	5:	3	Subgroup	15:	2
Subgroup	6:	1	Subgroup	16:	1
Subgroup	7:	3	Subgroup	17:	3
Subgroup	8:	2	Subgroup	18:	2
Subgroup	9:	9	Subgroup	19:	1
Subgroup	10:	5	Subgroup	20:	3

   Construct an np control chart.

6. Given the p control chart constructed in Question 5, answer the following:
   (a) Is the process operating in control?
   (b) What actions need to be taken to improve the process, if any?
   (c) If the department's goal was to produce an average of 2 defectives, is this process capable?

7. One sample was inspected per subgroup and the total number of defects were identified for each subgroup.

Subgroup 1:	9	Subgroup 10:	7	Subgroup 19:	6
Subgroup 2:	15	Subgroup 11:	10	Subgroup 20:	2
Subgroup 3:	10	Subgroup 12:	14	Subgroup 21:	7
Subgroup 4:	8	Subgroup 13:	4	Subgroup 22:	9
Subgroup 5:	17	Subgroup 14:	3	Subgroup 23:	4
Subgroup 6:	11	Subgroup 15:	7	Subgroup 24:	5
Subgroup 7:	5	Subgroup 16:	6	Subgroup 25:	8
Subgroup 8:	11	Subgroup 17:	3		
Subgroup 9:	13	Subgroup 18:	5		

Construct a *c* control chart.

8. Given the *u* control chart constructed in Question 7, answer the following:
   (a) Is the process operating in control?
   (b) What actions need to be taken to improve the process?
   (c) If the department's goal is to hold the number of defects to 5.0, is this process capable?

9. Various samples were inspected per subgroup. The following number of samples and defects per subgroup were collected.

17 Samples per Subgroup		10 Samples per Subgroup		12 Samples per Subgroup	
Subgroup 1:	39	Subgroup 11:	21	Subgroup 21:	27
Subgroup 2:	30	Subgroup 12:	23	Subgroup 22:	28
Subgroup 3:	26	Subgroup 13:	18	Subgroup 23:	21
Subgroup 4:	42	Subgroup 14:	22	Subgroup 24:	18
Subgroup 5:	31	Subgroup 15:	26	Subgroup 25:	20
Subgroup 6:	35	Subgroup 16:	25		
Subgroup 7:	37	Subgroup 17:	17		
Subgroup 8:	32	Subgroup 18:	24		
Subgroup 9:	27	Subgroup 19:	30		
Subgroup 10:	30	Subgroup 20:	32		

Construct a *u* control chart.

10. Given the *u* control chart constructed in Question 9, answer the following:
    (a) Is the process operating in control?
    (b) If the departments goal is to hold the number of defects to 2.0 or less, is this process capable?

Chapter 11

Determining the Cause

Up to this point, you have learned how control charts can be used to determine two important characteristics of a process:

1. Is the process in control?
2. Is the process capable?

Yet the control chart does not identify the *cause* of problems in the process. To improve the process and the quality of its output, the control chart needs to be analyzed to determine the *cause* of problems in the process. Once the causes have been identified, corrective action can be taken to eliminate problems and improve the process.

Two tools are commonly used to determine the cause of problems occurring in the process: cause-and-effect diagrams and scatter diagrams. These tools are discussed throughout this chapter.

INSTRUCTIONAL OBJECTIVES

When you have completed this chapter, you will be able to:

- Define the difference between simple and complex cause-and-effect relationships.
- Identify various causes of variation.
- Construct and analyze cause-and-effect diagrams.
- Construct and analyze a scatter diagram.
- Describe the effects of patterns used to describe relationships.
- Test the extent of two items using the median method.

LEARNING ACTIVITIES

_____11A: Cause-and-Effect Diagrams
_____11B: Scatter Diagrams

11A: CAUSE-AND-EFFECT DIAGRAMS

Before any particular problem can be solved, the cause of the problem needs to be determined. The causes of any particular problem may be simple or complex.

Simple		Complex	
Cause	*Effect*	*Causes*	*Effect*
• Water on the floor	• Someone slips and falls	• Tool wear • Improper adjustment • Bad lot of material	• Defective unit

In effect, a problem can be defined as the net effect of a particular cause or a group of related causes:

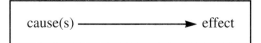

cause(s) —————————→ effect

Many quality problems are the result of complex causes. Once a problem has been identified in a process, the potential causes need to be determined before any corrective actions are taken.

The *cause-and-effect diagram* (Figure 11-1) is one of the tools that can be used to identify all of the potential causes. The cause-and-effect diagram is also used to describe the relationship between the various causes and the effect (problem) on the process. The left side of the diagram lists the primary causes of variation. This half of the diagram is the *cause* side. The right side of the diagram lists the problem or quality characteristic to be improved. This half of the diagram is the *effect* side. The major purpose of the cause-and-effect diagram is to identify the relationships that exist between each of the various causes and to determine their overall effect on the problem.

The cause-and-effect diagram is also referred to as the *fishbone diagram* or *Ishikawa diagram*. The term "fishbone" is used because the chart resembles a

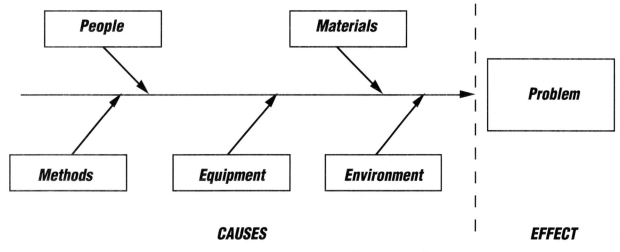

Figure 11-1   Cause-and-effect diagram.

fishbone (Figure 11-2). The term "Ishikawa diagram" is due to Dr. Ishikawa's extensive use of the diagram in solving complex problems in Japan.

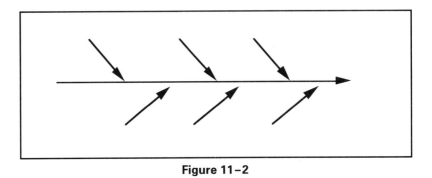

Figure 11–2

As you have learned, all things vary. That is, each item differs to some degree from the others produced by the process. These differences are the result of various causes in the process. Causes of variation can be categorized as *common* or *assignable*.

Common causes of variation result from normal events operating within the process. Common causes cannot be eliminated entirely, but their effect on the quality of items produced can be controlled. *Assignable* causes, on the other hand, are the result of abnormal or unnatural events in the process. Assignable causes can be detected, corrected, and eliminated.

As you have seen, common causes of variation are usually grouped into five major categories: people, equipment, methods, materials, and environment. A brief review of the variation that occurs from these factors is provided below.

> *People.* Since every person is unique, individual performance and perceptions vary from one person to the next. Even when established procedures are used to perform a specific task, no two people perform tasks in the exact same manner. Given this, variation occurs as a result of the people involved in the process.
>
> *Equipment.* The performance of equipment and tools used in processes changes daily. These changes are due to mechanical functions, machine wear, and so on. Variation naturally occurs as a result of equipment, tools, and so on.
>
> *Methods.* On the surface, methods of operation appear to be fairly consistent. Yet, in reality, differences exist. These differences may occur between shifts, supervisors, pressures, location, and so on. The methods used in a process are based on interpretation. Various interpretations of methods affect the variation in the process.
>
> *Materials.* The basic composition and measurements of raw materials vary. In addition, the materials delivered by various suppliers also vary. Therefore, the materials used in any process vary to some degree.
>
> *Environment.* The events that naturally make up the environment, such as the organizational culture, management, humidity, temperature, pollution, and so on, all affect the variation in the process.

When these factors are combined in a process, a certain level of variation will occur in the process. These causes of variation are referred to as *common-cause variation.* Common-cause variation cannot be entirely eliminated.

In addition to common-cause variation in the process, *assignable* causes may also be present. Assignable causes of variation are the result of abnormal or unnatural events. Any factor outside the realm of a *common* cause can be defined as an *assignable* cause.

The following examples describe a few assignable causes of variation.

Environmental factors such as an air-conditioner breakdown, doors left open in the winter, power outages, or abnormally high levels of pollution are abnormal events. Environmental factors can also be a change in management style, direction, and so on: that is, events which are not considered to be common, everyday occurrences. These events are classified as *special* or *assignable* causes of variation.

Measurement devices or gages are designed to perform a specific task. When these items are not accurate or reliable, items cannot be inspected or measured with the precision or accuracy originally intended. The inaccuracy or lack of reliability in the measurement devices or gages used in the process can be classified as an assignable cause of variation.

Equipment and tools are designed to help people accomplish asks. When these items are broken, worn out, or malfunctioning, excess variation will occur. Variation resulting from these types of events can be identified and eliminated, making this an assignable cause of variation in the process.

An adequate amount of *time* must be allocated to perform tasks properly. Whenever an attempt is made to condense or reduce the amount of time normally required to do a job or perform a given task, variation in the process increases. This additional level of variation is classified as an assignable cause of variation.

For the most part, both *common* and *assignable* causes of variation are present in all processes. These combined levels of variation directly affect the quality of the items produced by the process. The higher the level of variation, the poorer the quality of items produced by the process. To improve quality, the variation in the process must be carefully monitored and controlled. Any *assignable* cause of variation should be eliminated and common-cause variation can be reduced by improving the process continuously. The fundamental purpose of statistical process control is to control the causes of variation in the process in order to improve the quality of items produced.

The cause-and-effect diagram can be used to identify the causes of variation in the process. This information allows you to identify the major causes of variation that can be controlled or eliminated. The net effect of these efforts will enable you to reduce variation in the process and improve quality.

Constructing a Basic Cause-and-Effect Diagram

Step 1: Identify a Problem or Quality Characteristic. Single out *one* problem or quality characteristic in the process. If no real problem is apparent, select one of the *critical* quality characteristics. Once a specific problem or quality characteristic has been identified, draw a box on the right side of the paper and write the problem or quality characteristic in the box.

If more than one problem or quality characteristic has been identified, construct a separate cause-and-effect diagram for each problem.

Step 2: Draw a Line Pointing to the Problem Identified.   After one problem has been identified, draw a line pointing to the problem, defect, or quality characteristic that requires improvement. (Constructing a cause-and-effect diagram is like drawing a tree. The line drawn in this step is comparable to the trunk of the tree.)

Step 3: Determine the Major Causes of the Problem or Variation.   Identify the *major* causes of the problem that has been identified and list each *major* cause in a box around the main line. Then draw an arrow pointing toward the main line. These lines form the branches of the tree trunk created in Step 2.

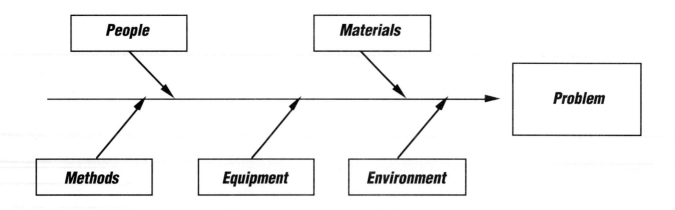

Step 4: Determine the Minor Causes of the Problem or Variation.   *Minor* causes are the causes associated with each major cause. Isolate each major cause and determine all of the factors that contribute to each major cause. Then list each minor cause around the major cause and draw an arrow pointing to the major cause. These arrows become the twigs of the branches constructed in Step 3.

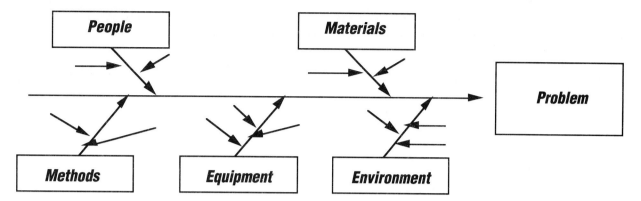

Step 5: Identify the Subcauses for Each Minor Cause.   The primary purpose of the cause-and-effect diagram is to illustrate the interactions between the various causes of variation in a given process. Therefore, it is necessary to break each cause down, in a step-by-step fashion, from the most major to the most minor aspects of each cause. For example, if equipment is listed as a major cause, a specific piece of equipment could be listed as a minor cause; the condition of the equipment could be a *subcause;* and the measurements or characteristics produced by the equipment could be yet another subcause. List all of the subcauses around the minor cause and draw an arrow from the subcause to the minor cause to illustrate their relationship.

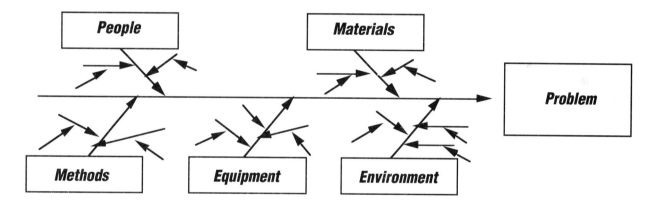

Step 6: Review the Cause-and-Effect Diagram.   When you review the cause-and-effect diagram, be sure that all of the items contributing to the problem have been identified. If no other causes or contributions to the problem or the variation in the process can be determined, the cause-and-effect diagram is complete.

One sure method of accomplishing this is to start out by asking why the problem exists, or how did the defect or problem occur. Then each time an item is discovered, write it down and repeat the question again for each item identified. When no other items can be identified, all of the possible causes have been determined.

Application

For example, let's say that you want to solve an on-going problem with the coffee served at the office. The problem is that the coffee tastes bad. Therefore, the first step in constructing a cause-and-effect diagram is to list the problem on the *effect* side of the diagram. Then, draw a line pointing to the problem.

After the main line has been drawn, the major causes are identified. In most cases, the primary categories of common-cause variation are listed as the major causes. These categories are people, materials, equipment, methods, measurements, and the environment. To identify the major causes of the problem, start out by asking the question, "What makes the coffee taste bad?" Once a major cause has been identified, list it in a box around the main line.

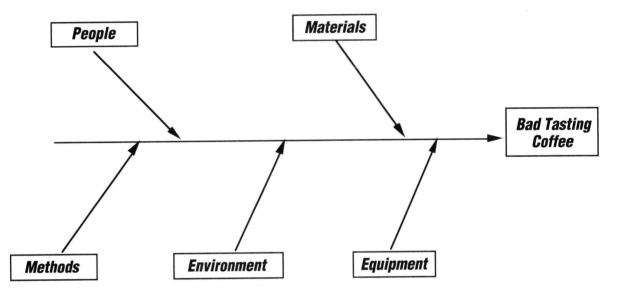

Once all of the major causes have been identified, probe each major cause to determine the minor causes that contribute or relate to that particular cause. This can be done by asking, "Why or how does this major cause contribute to the problem?" Using the cause-and-effect diagram in this unit, you can ask:

- How does the *machine* affect the taste of the coffee?
- What *methods* are used to create the bad-tasting coffee?
- What *materials* could create bad-tasting coffee?
- How do *people* affect the taste of the coffee?
- Does the *environment* affect the taste of the coffee?

The answers to each of these questions are classified as a minor cause of the problem in question. Once a minor cause has been identified, list it under its associated major cause (Figure 11-3).

After all of the minor causes have been listed, probe each cause to identify the factors contributing to each minor cause listed on the chart. The factors identified in this step are subcauses (Figure 11-4). To identify all possible subcauses, continue to ask what factors are associated with or contribute to the minor cause in question.

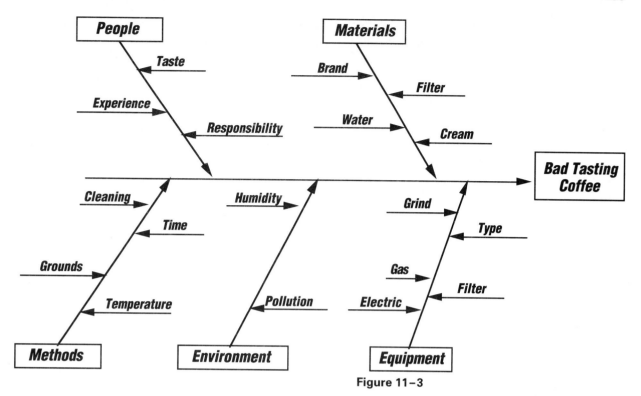

Figure 11-3

It is extremely important to identify *all* possible causes contributing to the problem. In many cases, the obvious causes are merely *symptoms* of the real cause. To effectively solve any problem, the real cause needs to be identified. The cause-and-effect diagram is essentially a tool that is used to probe a problem by breaking each major cause into smaller and smaller aspects in order to uncover the real causes of the problem.

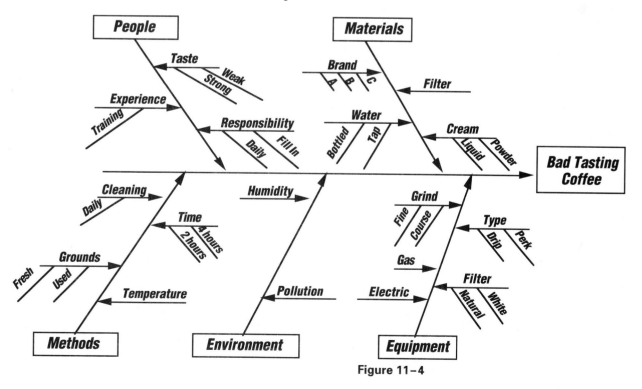

Figure 11-4

The final step in constructing a cause-and-effect diagram is to review all the items listed. During this review, make sure that all possible factors contributing to the problem have been identified. This can be done by asking: "In what way could this particular factor cause the problem in question?" When no additional causes can be added to the diagram, the cause-and-effect diagram is complete.

The primary purpose of constructing a cause-and-effect diagram is to illustrate the various causes and the relationships that impact quality. Once the cause-and-effect diagram has been completed, the appropriate solutions can be determined. Analyzing all potential causes allows you to uncover the *real* or *root* cause of the problem.

Types of Cause-and-Effect Diagrams

There are three basic methods used to construct a cause-and-effect diagram: dispersion analysis, production process classification, and cause enumeration.

Dispersion Analysis

The *dispersion analysis method* is similar to the method just described. This method is based on continuously asking what causes a specific problem or defect to occur. In short, this method provides a thorough analysis of the dispersion or variation in a given process. By breaking each cause down into smaller components, the *root cause* of the problem can be uncovered. To use this method effectively, *all* the potential causes of the problem must be identified. In many cases, the obvious or major causes are only symptoms. The real cause is often found in the smallest of causes.

Process Analysis

The *process analysis method* is also referred to as a process flow diagram. This method outlines each step of the process in a logical manner. Once the process steps are outlined, the causes affecting the process are inserted on the diagram where they are likely to occur in the process. Essentially, this method traces the actual flow of the process and lists the various causes affecting the process along the way (Figure 11-5).

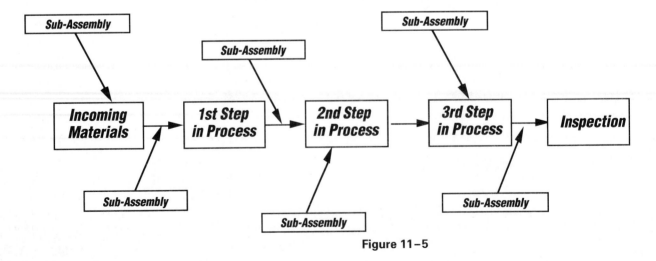

Figure 11-5

The major advantage of this method is that all causes are organized into the logical process sequence. As a result, the diagram is easier to construct and understand. The disadvantage of this method is that it is difficult to illustrate certain causes that repeatedly occur in the process or problems that are due to more than one cause.

Cause Enumeration

The *cause enumeration method* is the most basic type of cause-and-effect diagram. The cause enumeration diagram is very similar to the dispersion analysis method but is constructed differently. To construct a cause-and-effect diagram using this method, all of the possible causes affecting the process or the factors contributing to the given problem are listed. Once all of the causes have been listed, they are organized into categories to illustrate the *major, minor,* and *subcauses* affecting the process or problem. After the causes are organized, the actual cause-and-effect diagram is constructed.

The cause enumeration method utilizes "brainstorming" techniques. Brainstorming sessions involve a group of people who volunteer information on all of the possible events that can occur in a given situation. It is important that all of the suggestions or ideas generated during the brainstorming sessions are considered with an open mind.

The primary advantage of this method is there is no limit to the number of factors suggested. The disadvantage is that a great deal of information is obtained and it may be difficult to organize and classify. Given this, it is difficult to illustrate the relationships that exist between various causes and the overall effect on the diagram itself.

Any of the methods described in this unit can be used to construct a cause-and-effect diagram. The cause-and-effect diagram is a tool commonly used to identify and sort the potential causes of a particular problem. Once all of the causes have been identified, the most probable or likely causes can be identified and corrective actions can be taken. A few important points to remember in constructing a cause-and-effect diagram are:

Participation. Everyone involved in the process or problem-solving effort should be encouraged to actively participate in the discussion or construction of the cause-and-effect diagram. This is a critical point because each person has a different perspective. Given this, a more comprehensive diagram can be constructed if all members actively participate in the process.

Idea Generation. The more ideas (causes) that are generated by the group, the more effective the diagram will be. Listing only one or two causes of a particular problem is not an effective way to solve any problem. In cases where only a few causes are listed, the *symptoms* of the problem are actually addressed, not the root cause.

Free Thought Process. There is a saying that "one could not see the forest for the trees." This holds true for problem solving as well. Often those who are closest to the problem have a more difficult time defining the causes clearly. Given this, it is better to encourage free and open communication among all group members. Criticism or embarrassing remarks should not be allowed during group discussions.

Exhaust All Possible Causes.   Prior to making any decisions or taking any corrective actions, all possible causes should be exhausted thoroughly. Any actions taken prior to this tend to be a short-term quick fix, not a long-term solution.

Vote.   Once all of the possible causes have been exhausted, everyone should vote on the most important causes. Then the most important causes can be addressed first.

The use of a cause-and-effect diagram to solve quality-related problems can offer many benefits. Cause-and-effect diagrams can be a vehicle to:

- Identify the important causes of variation affecting quality
- Direct the problem-solving process
- Readily define the major solutions needed
- Describe the relationship between the various causes of a particular problem and its overall effect on the entire process

11B: SCATTER DIAGRAMS

As you learned in the preceding unit, cause-and-effect diagrams are used to identify the various causes of problems. The cause-and-effect diagram divides the causes into general categories *(people, materials, methods, equipment, measurements, environment,* etc.) and illustrates the relationships that exist. Yet the cause-and-effect diagram does not define the *extent* or *degree* of these relationships. When the extent of the relationship needs to be examined, the scatter diagram is used.

For example, let's say that after a cause-and-effect diagram had been constructed, five causes were determined to be the most probable or likely causes of the problem. To isolate the most likely cause of the problem, a scatter diagram could be used to determine the *extent* or the *degree* of the relationship that exists between the various causes and the effect. Given this, the scatter diagram can be used to sort out the most important cause(s) of the problem. Scatter diagrams enable you to solve quality problems more effectively because the *extent* or *degree* of the relationships can readily be defined.

A few examples of the various relationships that can be studied with the aid of a scatter diagram are listed below.

Cause	*Effect*
• Cycle time	• Size variation
• Grinding wheel grit	• Surface finish
• Temperature change	• Expansion/contraction
• Vehicle speed	• Fuel economy
• Cutting speed	• Length of parts
• Processing time	• Number of errors

In effect, the cause-and-effect diagram lists all possible causes contributing to a given problem, and the scatter diagram studies the extent of the relationship that exists between a specific cause and effect or two or more causes.

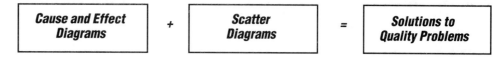

The solution to quality-related problems requires a thorough analysis of the most probable causes identified in the cause-and-effect diagram. This analysis enables you to determine which causes are directly related to the problem or process. The scatter diagram simplifies your problem-solving efforts and enables you to improve the process.

Relationships are commonly divided into two categories: *cause* and *effect*, or one *cause* and another *cause.*

Type	*Example*
• Cause and effect	• Raw materials and product hardness • Process time and ordering errors
• Cause and cause	• Raw materials and moisture content • Process time and clerk experience

Due to the complexity of many problems, it is important to classify the potential causes into two categories: causes that affect quality directly and those that *do not* affect quality directly. Once all of the causes have been sorted, the relationship of causes that affect quality directly can be examined and appropriate corrective actions can be taken.

Constructing a Scatter Diagram

The scatter diagram is the tool commonly used to examine causal relationships. To examine this, data need to be collected on the areas under investigation.

Step 1: Select Two Items to Be Studied. Identify two items where the extent or degree of the relationship needs to be studied. These items may be:

- *Cause* and *effect*
- One *cause* and another *cause*
- One *cause* and two other *causes*

To demonstrate the steps that are needed to construct a scatter diagram in a more thorough manner, a working example will follow each step.

Example: Let's say that you are interested in examining the relationship that exists between *speed* and variation in the *length* of items produced. To construct a scatter diagram, data need to be collected on both items: speed and the length of the items produced.

Step 2: Collect and Record the Data. Approximately 50 to 100 groups of *paired data* (data collected for the two items selected in Step 1) should be collected from one group or population to determine accurately the relationship that exists between two items.

Example: Fifty samples were selected and the data shown in Figure 11-6 were recorded.

Sample	Speed	Length	Sample	Speed	Length	Sample	Speed	Length	Sample	Speed	Length
1	65	72	14	71	71	27	85	85	40	95	88
2	65	71	15	71	72	28	85	84	41	97	93
3	65	71	16	75	74	29	85	83	42	97	95
4	65	69	17	75	73	30	85	86	43	97	97
5	65	72	18	75	78	31	88	86	44	97	96
6	68	71	19	75	76	32	88	87	45	97	95
7	68	71	20	75	75	33	88	88	46	100	97
8	68	72	21	77	80	34	88	85	47	100	93
9	68	70	22	77	81	35	88	84	48	100	96
10	68	73	23	77	81	36	95	87	49	100	95
11	71	70	24	77	82	37	95	90	50	100	94
12	71	77	25	77	79	38	95	92			
13	71	73	26	85	84	39	95	91			

Figure 11-6

Step 3: Draw the Axes for the Scatter Diagram. One of the items under investigation will be listed on the vertical axis, and the other item on the horizontal axis. Draw and label each axis (Figure 11-7). The data should be arranged in increasing values on both axes. The smaller values on the horizontal axis are listed from left to right. The smaller values on the vertical axis are listed from the bottom up.

Step 4: Plot Each Set of Paired Data onto the Graph. To plot each set of paired data onto the graph, simply locate the first value on the horizontal or *x*

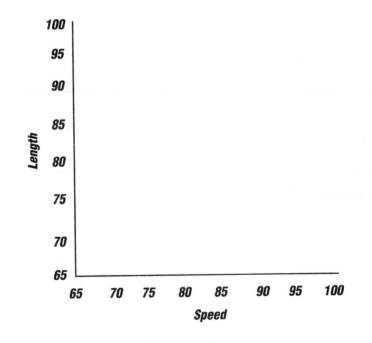

Figure 11-7

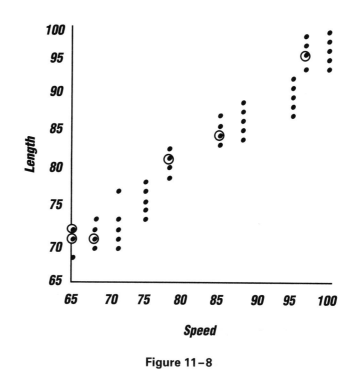

Figure 11–8

axis. From that point, locate the second value on the vertical or y axis by moving your pen up the graph until you have reached the value on the y axis. Plot the point on the graph where the values of the x and y axes intersect (Figure 11-8). The circled points represent a repetition in the intersection of values. One circle is drawn around a point each time the intersection is repeated. If three sets of paired data were repeated, the point would have two circles.

When the number of intersections is frequent, this method becomes increasingly difficult to construct and interpret. When situations like this occur, it is better to construct a frequency table.

Once all of the data have been plotted onto the scatter diagram, it can be analyzed to determine the extent of the relationship between the two items. If a strong relationship exists, the change in one of the items will automatically cause a change in the other. If a strong relationship does not exist, the change in one item will not change or affect the other item. The interpretation of the scatter diagram can lead you to the corrective actions required to improve the process.

Five basic relationships can be detected on a scatter diagram.

1. A positive relationship exists.
2. A positive relationship may be present.
3. No relationship exists.
4. A negative relationship exists.
5. A negative relationship may be present.

A *positive relationship* (Figure 11-9) indicates that as the item on the *x* axis increases, the item on the *y* axis also increases, and vice versa. Therefore, if the value of the item plotted on the *x* axis is reduced, the item on the *y* axis is reduced automatically. For example, if the scatter diagram displayed a *positive* relationship between speed and length, as the value of speed decreases, the value of the length will also decrease. Conversely, as the value of the speed increases, the value of the length will also increase.

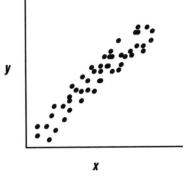

Figure 11-9 Positive relationship.

A *positive relationship* may be present when the points on the graph (Figure 11-10) have a wider spread than the one shown in Figure 11-9. The wider spread implies that a definite positive relationship does not exist. However, this pattern indicates that one *may* exist. That is, as the value of the item on the *x* axis increases, the value of the item on the *y* axis increases somewhat. Whenever this occurs it may indicate that other causes are affecting the relationship between the items plotted on the *x* and *y* axes. When a scatter diagram indicates that a positive relationship *may* exist, *x* and *y* are not *directly* dependent on each other.

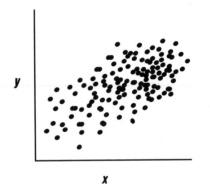

Figure 11-10 A positive relationship may be present.

When no definite pattern or relationship can be detected between the items plotted on the *x* and *y* axes (Figure 11-11), it indicates that *no relationship exists* between the two items. That is, one item *does not* affect the other item. As a result, a change in the value of *y* will have no effect on the value of *x*, and vice versa.

A *negative relationship* between two items is the opposite of the positive relationship. A negative relationship means that as the values on one of the axes in-

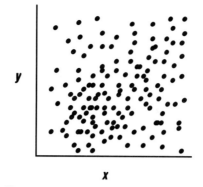

Figure 11–11   No relationship exists.

crease, the values on the other axis decrease (Figure 11-12). For example, if a negative relationship existed between length and speed, it would indicate that as the value of speed increases, the value of the length decreases. Conversely, as speed decreases, the length increases.

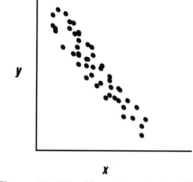

Figure 11–12   Negative relationship.

A negative relationship may be present when the points on the graph (Figure 11-13) have a wider spread than the one shown in Figure 11-12. This wider spread implies that although a definite negative relationship does not exist, the pattern indicates that one *may* be present. That is, as the values on one of the axes increase, the values on the other axis will decrease somewhat. Essentially, this means that a *direct* relationship between the two items does not exist and that other causes may be affecting the relationship of the items.

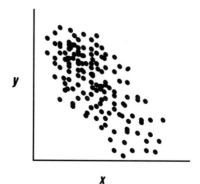

Figure 11–13   A negative relationship may be present.

The five basic patterns just described are the most common. However, two additional patterns may occur, although their occurrence is very rare. These two patterns are *peaks* and *troughs*.

Whenever a *peak* is formed on a scatter diagram (Figure 11-14), divide the diagram in half. The area on the left is treated as a positive relationship, and the area on the right is treated as a negative relationship.

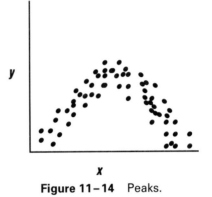

Figure 11-14   Peaks.

Whenever a *trough* is formed on a scatter diagram (Figure 11-15), divide the diagram in half. The area on the left is treated as a negative relationship and the area on the right is treated as a positive relationship.

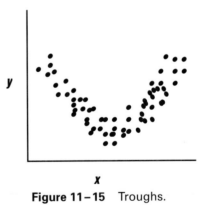

Figure 11-15   Troughs.

Testing the Relationship

Once the relationship between the data has been identified, the relationship can be tested to determine its extent. There are several methods used to test the extent of a relationship; however, only one will be discussed in this unit. The testing method most commonly used is called the *median method*. The median method is used to analyze the extent of the relationship that exists between two sets of data.

Step 1: Determine the Median Value for Both Items.   The *median* is the *middlemost* value of the data. To locate the median value for an *even* number of data, add the two middlemost values and divide the sum by 2. To locate the median value for an *odd* number of data, simply locate the middlemost value in the data.

Example: Using the scatter diagram introduced in the beginning of this unit, the following calculations are needed to compute the median values for the data plotted on the *x* and *y* axes (see Figure 11-16). The *x* axis contains an even number of data. To compute the median value, the two middlemost values are added together and divided by 2.

$$80 + 85 = 165$$

$$165 \div 2 = 82.5$$

The median value for the *x* axis is 82.5.

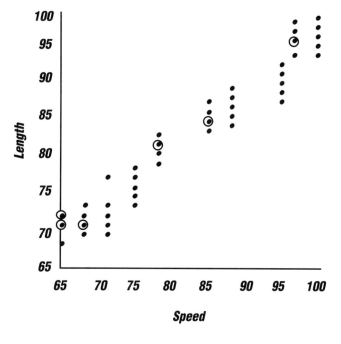

Figure 11–16

Next, the median value for the *y* axis is computed. The *y* axis also contains an *even* number of data; therefore, the same procedure can be used to compute the median value for the *y* axis.

$$80 + 85 = 165$$

$$165 \div 2 = 82.5$$

The *median* value for the *y* axis is 82.5.

Another method of determining the median value for each axis is to locate the value on the axis where half of the points are on one side of the value and half of the points are on the other side.

Step 2: Draw the Median Lines on the Scatter Diagram.   Locate point 82.5 (the median value for the *x* axis) on the *x* axis, and draw a vertical line through

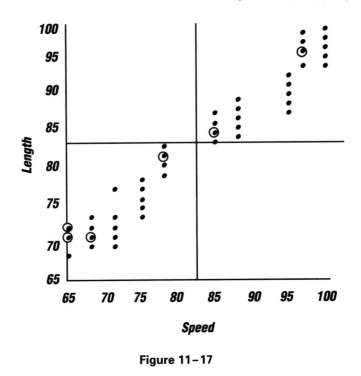

Figure 11–17

the scatter diagram. Then locate point 82.5 (the median value for the *y* axis) on the *y* axis and draw a horizontal line through the scatter diagram (Figure 11-17).

Step 3: Label Each Quadrant.   The scatter diagram is divided into four sections called *quadrants*. Each quadrant is labeled I, II, III, and IV in a counter-clockwise manner starting at the upper right-hand corner (Figure 11-18).

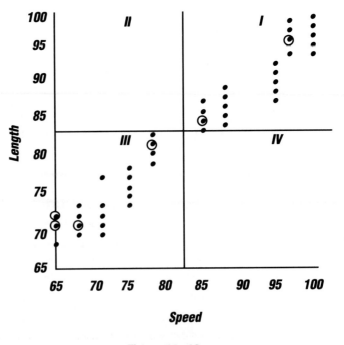

Figure 11–18

Step 4: Count the Points in Each Quadrant.

Quadrant	Points
I	25
II	0
III	25
IV	0
Total:	50

Step 5: Count All Points and Points in Quadrants II and IV. To complete this step, add all of the points contained in each of the quadrants. Whenever a point falls on a line, the point is subtracted from the total. For example, if there were a total of 50 points on the scatter diagram and 3 of the points fell on the dividing lines, the total number of points would be $50 - 3 = 47$. Once the total has been determined, add the points in quadrants II and IV. In our example, there are 50 points and 0 in quadrants II and IV.

Step 6: Compare the Points with the Limits on the Table. Referring to the sign test table in Figure 11-19, locate the value of N (the total number of points contained in the scatter diagram). Then compare the number of points in quadrants II and IV with those listed under the "limits" column for the corresponding value of N.

- Whenever the total number of points in quadrants II and IV are less than the "limits" listed in the sign test table, a *positive relationship does,* in fact, exist between the two items on the scatter diagram.

N	Limit of Points for II + IV	N	Limit of Points for II + IV
20	5	42	14
21	5	44	15
22	5	46	15
23	6	48	16
24	6	50	17
25	7	52	18
26	7	54	19
27	7	56	20
28	8	58	21
29	8	60	21
30	9	62	22
32	9	64	23
34	10	66	24
36	11	68	25
38	12	70	26
40	13		

Figure 11-19 Sign test table.

- When the total number of points in quadrants II and IV is greater than the "limits" listed on the sign test table for the value of *N*, the test indicates that a positive relationship does not exist between the two items on the scatter diagram.

In the scatter diagram example, the value of *N* is 50 and the number of points in quadrants II and IV is 0. Using the sign test table (Figure 11-19), the limit of points in II and IV when *N* = 50 is 17. Since 0 is less than 17, the test indicates that a positive relationship does exist between the two items on the scatter diagram.

Testing the relationship between the items on the scatter diagram provides stronger evidence of the relationship. Whenever a positive relationship exists between the items, the corrective actions taken on one of the items automatically affects the other item on the scatter diagram. The scatter diagram can also be used to illustrate the causes that are directly related to the problem and those that are not.

One additional comment regarding the construction and use of scatter diagrams should be mentioned before concluding this unit. There are times when the relationship between two items is not readily apparent in the actual process, but is more apparent under experimental conditions. Therefore, the data that are observed in the actual process may indicate that a relationship does not exist. However, further analysis should be conducted under experimental conditions before these conclusions can be drawn. Figure 11-20 illustrates this point.

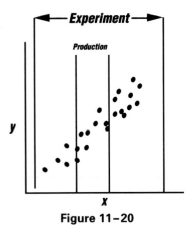

Figure 11-20

REVIEW QUESTIONS

1. Indicate whether the following cause(s) and effect are simple or complex.
   (a) Battery drained/electrical shortage = car stops
   (b) Out of gas = car stops
   (c) Improper setup and requirements, gage drifting = parts exceed specs
   (d) New equipment, temporary personnel = service delays

2. Consider the following event: A car stops running and the driver discovers that the car is out of gas. Yet, after more gas is added, the car still does not run. What has been addressed?
   (a) Symptom   (b) Cause

3. One method commonly used to determine all possible causes of a problem is the _____.

4. The left side of the cause-and-effect diagram lists _____. The right side is known as the _____ side.

5. List the five primary common causes of variation.

6. True or false? More than one problem or quality characteristic can be used in a cause-and-effect diagram?

7. Outline the steps required to construct a cause-and-effect diagram.

8. Construct a cause-and-effect diagram for poor gas mileage.

9. The _____ is a tool used to study various cause-and-effect relationships.

10. Given the following data, construct a scatter diagram. Then test the relationship using the median method.

Overtime	Number of Errors	Overtime	Number of Errors
3	5	6	7
1	8	5	7
5	6	5	8
4	4	4	3
8	9	6	9
5	3	4	6
2	4	1	1
7	10	7	8
1	2	5	3
3	3	7	7

11. Classify each scatter diagram.

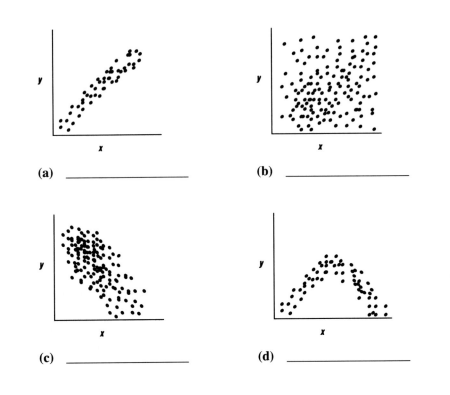

(a) _____   (b) _____

(c) _____   (d) _____

12. If a positive relationship exists, a change in one item will automatically _____ the other item.

13. If a negative relationship exists, as one item increases the other item _____.

14. If no relationship exists, a change in one _____ affects the other.

15. How would you treat a peak relationship?

Chapter 12

Continuous Process Improvement

Throughout this book you have learned the essential elements of basic statistical process control. You have also learned that massive changes are taking place in the global market. Today, consumers have a wide variety of choices and there are many organizations throughout the world that are willing to do whatever it takes to provide high-quality products and service at competitive prices. Competing in today's global environment depends largely on our ability to adapt to rapidly changing market conditions, to meet newly emerging challenges head-on, and to provide high-quality goods and services at competitive prices.

Historical ways of doing business created excessive waste and high costs. These factors have hindered our ability to compete in the areas of quality, productivity, and price. To improve this situation, waste must be eliminated and sound investments need to be made in technology and human resource development. These improvements will enable us to make better use of the productive resources (inputs) required to produce products and services (outputs) that satisfy customers and provide value.

One of the primary ways to accomplish this task is to improve quality. Quality improvement ultimately leads to less rework, fewer mistakes and delays, and makes better use of productive resources. As this occurs, the cost of producing goods and services declines. Reduced costs enhances an organization's ability to compete in areas of quality and price.

Across the board, executives agree that:

1. Quality improvement is a survival issue.
2. Neither government, industry, nor academia can do it alone.
3. We must all work together to seek continuous process improvement in everything we do.

In short, quality improvement is critical in today's fiercely competitive global market. Quality improvement in everything we do will lead the way to greater demand, more jobs, and prosperity for all.

Quality improvement is a customer-driven process. Customers want high-quality products and services that meet their specific needs at a cost that represents value. To be successful we must build processes that produce high-quality goods and services at competitive prices. A *process* is the blending of interdependent resources to provide the products or services that meet customer needs (Figure 12-1). The key to continuous quality improvement is to understand what customers want (voice of the customer) and what the process produces (voice of the process). With this information, everyone can continuously seek ways to ensure that the voice of the process matches the voice of the customer. Once we have achieved this, we continually need to develop ways to exceed their expectations.

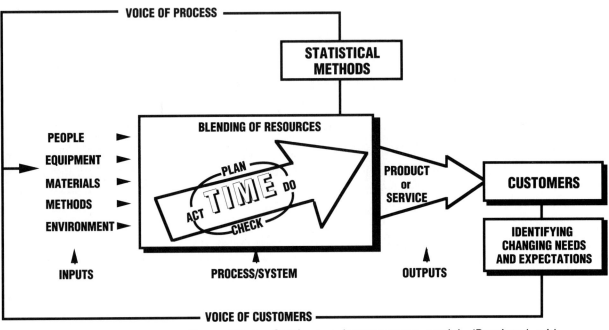

Figure 12–1   Continuous improvement model. (Reprinted with permission from Ford Motor Company © 1990.)

Continuous process improvement in all aspects of the organization is absolutely essential to providing world-class products and services that meet and exceed customer satisfaction at competitive prices. Over the years, tremendous improvements have been made in the area of manufacturing. Yet unlimited potential exists for improvements in nonmanufacturing areas. All areas within the organization contain opportunities for continuous improvement. Whether you produce products, develop computer systems, provide customer service, perform administrative functions, and so on, continuous process improvement is critical.

Virtually everything that is done can be described in terms of a process or a system. It is vitally important to view *all* work as a process, define the customer requirements, outline each step in the process, understand the variation produced, and compare the voice of the process to the voice of the customers. With this information, you can more effectively manage and improve the process.

A sound understanding of variability is critically important in any improvement effort. The statistical methods introduced throughout this book will enable you to base decisions on timely, accurate, and factual data. Statistical methods provide the facts you need to determine how a process has performed in the past, how it is currently performing, or how to predict its future performance. Therefore, statistical techniques and tools provide a *basis for taking action* to improve the overall performance of a process (Figure 12-2).

Through the use of statistical tehcniques, you can evaluate a process's ability to consistently produce output that is *on target* and *within the stated requirements*. To accomplish this, three things need to be determined:

1. Is the process in control?
2. Is the process properly centered?
3. Is the process capable?

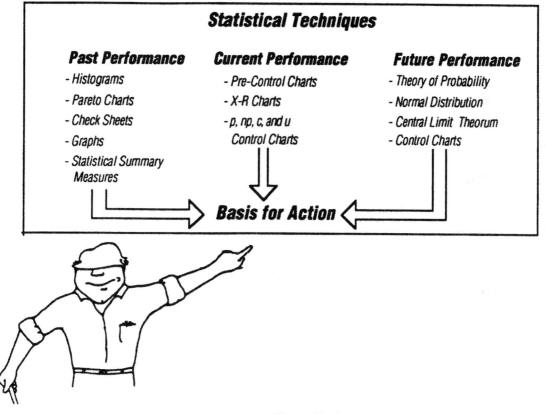

Figure 12–2

When a process is in control, only common-cause variation is operating. Under these conditions, the process will perform in a stable and predictable manner. Common-cause variation in a process will continue to be distributed within the control limits until a change is made to the process or a special cause of variation appears.

When a process is in control, you can confidently predict the output over the course of time. One of the primary tools used to determine the state of statistical control is the control chart.

The control chart shown in Figure 12-3 illustrates the amount of natural variation in the process that is due to common causes. The upper control limit (UCL), central line (CL), and lower control limit (LCL) represent the boundaries of variation that can be expected to occur within the process. The central line

(CL) can be used to compare the process mean to the midpoint of the requirements or specifications. Once these two items have been achieved, the process is operating within statistical control. At that point, you can determine the capability of the process.

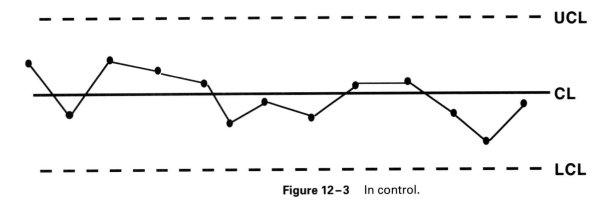

Figure 12–3   In control.

Process capability is a statistical measure of the common-cause variation operating within the process compared to the requirements or specifications. Generally speaking, a short-term capability study is conducted, followed by a long-term capability study (see Figure 12-4).

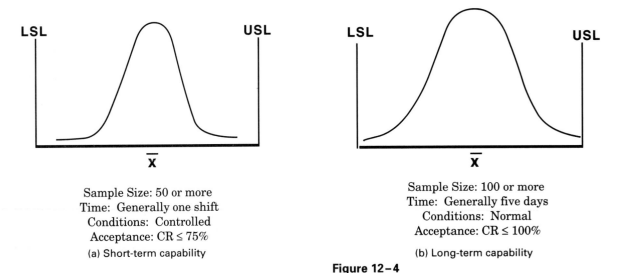

Sample Size: 50 or more
Time: Generally one shift
Conditions: Controlled
Acceptance: CR ≤ 75%

(a) Short-term capability

Sample Size: 100 or more
Time: Generally five days
Conditions: Normal
Acceptance: CR ≤ 100%

(b) Long-term capability

Figure 12–4

Once the long-term common-cause variation has been established, efforts can be taken to improve the process continuously by reducing common-cause variation (Figure 12-5).

Throughout this book, you have learned the statistical methods needed to define problems; set priorities; analyze the past, present, and future performance of a process; and determine causes and relationships. These statistical methods provide the facts you need to continually improve quality. Continuous quality improvement, however, requires more than statistical methods: It requires a new way of thinking. Everything we do needs to be viewed as a process or system

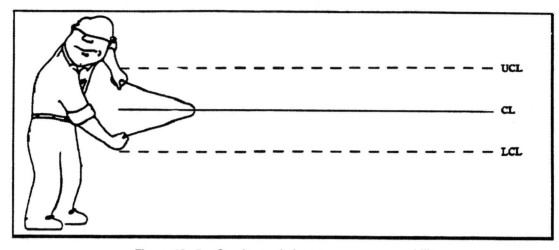

Figure 12-5   Continuously improve process capability.

(Figure 12-6). From this viewpoint, you can outline the steps involved in the process, understand the variation produced, compare the variation in the process to the customer's requirements, and endlessly seek ways to improve the process and reduce variation. In short, we are in a competitive race with no finish line. Regardless of how well we are doing today, our competitors are constantly seeking ways to improve and our customers will continue to expect more. Through a united effort of teamwork, cooperation and continuous process improvement, we will meet these challenges successfully.

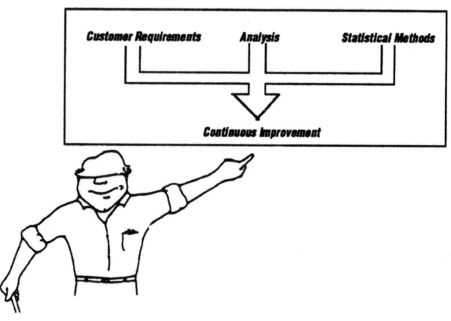

Figure 12-6

Glossary

Assignable causes: Those causes of variation that are not considered to be normal or common causes. Assignable causes of variation can be identified, corrected, and eliminated from operating within a process.

Attribute data: Data that are countable: for example, data that are classified as good/bad, accepted/rejected, defective/nondefective, and so on.

Average: "Sum" of all values in a group divided by the number of values. The average is also called the mean ($\bar{X}$).

Capability: Maximum amount or inherent variation of a process. This is also referred to as the process's normal distribution (the value of 6σ).

Capability ratio: Ratio of the process capability to the design tolerance or specification spread. The *ideal* capability ratio should be .75 or less to maintain an acceptable level of statistical process control.

Cause-and-effect diagram: Method of analyzing the potential sources or causes of variation. This is often used to identify and determine the possible causes for problems.

Chance-cause system: Various factors contributing to the amount of variation contained in any given process.

Characteristic: Property or trait that distinguishes one item from similar items.

Common causes: Natural causes of variation that can be expected to occur in any process that cannot be changed or eliminated unless the process itself is changed.

Consecutive selection: Selection method that is often used for machine-dominant operations whereby several items in a row are selected from a population.

Control (as applied to "process"): Condition that monitors, analyzes, and maintains the amount of variation contained in any given process to that which is due strictly to common or natural causes of variation.

Control chart: Graphic chart with control limits and plotted values of some statistical measure for a series of samples or subgroups, over a period of time.

Control limits: Limits on a control chart that serve as a guide and a basis for action to the inherent variation (normal distribution) of the plotted statistic.

Controlled process (in control): Process in which all, or nearly all, of the plotted statistics fall within the established control limits. A process that repeats itself in a predictable manner.

Critical defect: Defects that could result in hazardous or unsafe conditions for the person using or maintaining the product, or could result in a functional failure.

Data: Facts (numerically expressed) used as a basis for decisions and conclusions.

Defect: Each instance that any item or unit fails to meet or conform to a single quality characteristic or standard imposed on it.

Defective: Unit that fails to conform to the stated quality standards, making the *entire* unit unacceptable. A defective may contain one or more defects.

Distribution: Frequency of *all* possible results.

Fishbone diagram: *See* Cause-and-effect diagram.

Fraction rejected: Ratio of defective pieces to the total number of all pieces inspected, usually expressed as a decimal.

Histogram: Pictorial display that illustrates the characteristics of a mass of data.

Inspection lot: Specific quantity of similar units offered for inspection and acceptance at one time.

Ishikawa diagram: *See* Cause-and-effect diagrams.

Item: Single member of an inspection lot, usually, though not necessarily, a single article or unit.

Lot: *See* Inspection lot.

Mean: Arithmetical "average" that is computed by dividing the sum of all samples by the number of samples. Also called the average value and expressed symbolically as $\bar{X}$.

Median: "Middlemost" value contained in a group of data such that half the values are above and half are below it.

Mode: "Most frequently occurring" value in a group of samples.

Nonconformance: Any item or group of items that do not meet the established quality standards or specifications.

Normal distribution: Natural distribution of all values that can occur when a process is operating in control. Also referred to as the normal or bell-shaped curve.

One hundred percent inspection: Inspection of *all* items in the inspection lot.

Out of control (as applied to a process): Amount of variation that exceeds the limits of its normal distribution that can be identified and attributed to a special or assignable cause.

Pareto chart: Bar chart used to define problems and set priorities by listing the various problems or causes of a particular problem according to their frequency of occurrence.

Percent defective: Ratio of defective pieces to the total number of pieces inspected, multiplied by 100.

Population: Entire group of items from which data or samples are drawn.

Probability: Chance or likelihood that some future or unknown event will (or will not) occur, usually expressed as a number between 0 and 1.

Process: Operation or a series of operations that are combined to produce a change (i.e., a part, product, unit, etc.).

Process capability: Measure of the inherent or natural variation of a process. The normal distribution (6σ) of any given process.

Random sample or *selection:* Selection of an item from a population such that each has an equal chance of being selected.

Range: Difference between the largest and smallest values in a sample which indicates the spread or dispersion in the data.

Sample: Group of items taken from a population (the entire lot) which is used to make decisions and draw conclusions about the population.

Sampling inspection: Evaluation of the quality of material by inspecting only a portion of the material.

Sigma (σ):   Greek letter used to denote standard deviation.

Specification limits: Limits of the tolerance within which a process should run if its product is to be made according to design.

Standard deviation: Measure of the dispersion (scatter or spread) of a set of data or values around its mean.

Statistic: Numerical data that summarize a group or series of events.

Statistical process control: Method of mathematically analyzing process results to determine if the process is behaving predictably. Satisfactory control:

- $\bar{X}$-*R Control charts:* A process is operating in satisfactory control with respect to a measurable quality characteristic if all, or nearly all, of the points are plotted within the control limits and are randomly distributed around the mean or central line (CL); and all, or nearly all, of the points are within the stated specifications.
- *p, np, c, and u Control charts:* A process is operating within satifactory control if all of the points are plotted within the control limits and the overall average (central line) is less than or equal to the maximum number of defects that is considered to be acceptable or satisfactory.

Statistics: Mathematical method of analyzing masses of numerical data.

Subgroup: Collection of individual pieces from a common source, possessing a similar set of quality characteristics from which a random sample is selected.

Three-sigma limits: Calculated limits based on observed data. The validity of these limits is based on the assumption that the data were selected from a "normal" or nearly normal distribution.

Tolerance: Allowable design deviation from a nominal value. The specification limits define the total allowable tolerance.

Unit: One of a number of similar items, objects, pieces, etc.

Upper and lower control limits (UCL and LCL):   These values are calculated limits, each 3σ distant from the mean or central line, and between which 99.73% of the individual values or items from a normal distribution will fall.

Variability: Normal scatter or dispersion within any group of data.

Variable data: Data that are measurable. That is, one can measure the precise characteristic of a given item.

Variation: Full pattern of variability in the data.

Variation limits: Limits of a process distribution which include about 99.73% of all possible results. "Variation limits" is actually another name for ± 3 standard deviations.

Appendix

Symbols and Formulas

DEFINITION OF *SPC* SYMBOLS

X	Value of an individual measurement or a single observation
$\bar{X}$	Mean or average value of all values for a group of samples
$\bar{\bar{X}}$	Grand average of all averages for a group of samples
R	Range, which measures the amount of dispersion or scatter contained in a group of samples
$\bar{R}$	Average range of all ranges for a group of samples
c	Number of defects per sample or unit
$\bar{c}$	Average number of defects per sample or unit inspected
np	Number of defectives in a sample group
$\overline{np}$	Average number of defectives for all sample groups
p	Fraction or percentage of defectives contained in a sample group
$\bar{p}$	Average fraction or percentage of defectives for all sample groups
u	Average number of defects per sample (a sample in this case may be a unit or a group of units)
$\bar{u}$	Average number of defects for all sample groups
UCL	Upper control limit (equivalent to $+3\sigma$)
CL	Central line (equivalent to the mean or average value)
LCL	Lower control limit (equivalent to -3σ)
USL	Upper specification limit
LSL	Lower specification limit
Σ	Symbol used to indicate "the sum of"
k	Total number of sample groups or subgroups
n	Number of individual sample measurements or observations contained in a sample group
N	Total number of sample measurements or observations contained in a population
σ	Standard deviation, which measures the amount of dispersion or scatter contained in a group of samples; referred to as sigma
$\bar{\sigma}$	Average standard deviation for a group of samples that can be used to estimate the value of the population's standard deviation
$+3\sigma$	Three standard deviations to the right of the mean (positive)
-3σ	Three standard deviations to the left of the mean (negative)

MATHEMATICAL SYMBOLS

Symbols	Definition	Operation	Example
+	Plus	Add	$2 + 2 = 4$
−	Minus	Subtract	$2 - 2 = 0$
×	Times	Multiply	$2 \times 3 = 6$
·	Times	Multiply	$2 \cdot 3 = 6$
$2(X)$	Times	Multiply	$2(3) = 6$
$2A$	Times	Multiply	$2 \times$ the value of A
÷	Divided by	Divide	$6 \div 2 = 3$
/	Divided by	Divide	$6/2 = 3$
$\dfrac{a}{b}$	a divided by b	Divide	$\dfrac{6}{3} = 6 \div 3$ $= 2$
( )	The quantity	Compute operation in ( ) first	$2(1 + 2) = 2\,(3)$ $= 6$
X^2	Squared	Square	$3^2 = 3 \times 3$ $= 9$
$\sqrt{\ }$	Square root	Take root of	$\sqrt{9} = 3$
Σ	The sum of	Add all values	ΣX, when $x = 7,9,10$ $= 7 + 9 + 10$ $= 26$

FORMULAS

Variation analysis

$$\overline{X} = \frac{\Sigma X}{n}$$

$$R = X_{\text{largest}} - X_{\text{smallest}}$$

$$\sigma = \sqrt{\frac{\Sigma(X - \overline{X})^2}{n - 1}}$$

$$\sigma_{\overline{X} - R} = \frac{\overline{R}}{d_2}$$

$$\sigma_c = \sqrt{\overline{c}}$$

$$\sigma_p = \sqrt{\frac{\overline{p}(1 - \overline{p})}{n}}$$

$$\sigma_{n\overline{p}} = \sqrt{np(1 - \overline{p})}$$

$$\sigma_u = \sqrt{\frac{u}{n}}$$

$$\text{Capability} = 6 \text{ standard deviations } (6\sigma)$$

$$\text{Capability ratio} = \frac{\text{capability}}{\text{spec. spread}} = \frac{6\sigma}{\text{USL} - \text{LSL}}$$

$$\text{UCL} = +3\sigma \text{ plus the value of the mean}$$

$$\text{LCL} = -3\sigma \text{ plus the value of the mean}$$

Variable Control Charts

$$\overline{X} = \frac{\Sigma X}{n}$$

$$R = X_{\text{largest}} - X_{\text{smallest}}$$

$$\overline{\overline{X}} = \frac{\Sigma \overline{X}}{k}$$

$$\text{UCL}_{\overline{X}} = \overline{\overline{X}} + A_2 \overline{R}$$

$$\text{LCL}_{\overline{X}} = \overline{\overline{X}} - A_2 \overline{R}$$

$$\overline{R} = \frac{\Sigma R}{k}$$

$$\text{UCL}_R = D_4 \overline{R}$$

$$\text{LCL}_R = D_3 \overline{R}$$

$$\text{Capability ratio} = \frac{6(\overline{R}/d_2)}{\text{spec. spread}}$$

Attribute Control Charts

Defectives (Unit Is Either Good or Bad)
p Control Chart *(Percent Defective)*

$$p = \frac{\text{number defective } (np)}{\text{number of samples } (n)}$$

$$\overline{p} = \frac{\text{total number of defectives } (\Sigma np)}{\text{total number of samples inspected } (\Sigma n)}$$

$$\text{UCL}_p = \overline{p} + 3\sqrt{\frac{\overline{p}(1-\overline{p})}{n}}$$

$$\text{LCL}_p = \overline{p} - 3\sqrt{\frac{\overline{p}(1-\overline{p})}{n}}$$

- Sample sizes may vary or remain constant.
- Process capability is defined as the central line $(\overline{p})$ when the process is operating in control.

np Control Chart *(Number Defective)*

$$np = \text{number defective in the sample}$$

$$n\bar{p} = \frac{\text{total number of defectives } (\Sigma np)}{\text{total number of sample groups } (k)}$$

$$\text{UCL}_p = n\bar{p} + 3\sqrt{n\bar{p}(1-\bar{p})}$$

$$\text{LCL}_{np} = n\bar{p} - 3\sqrt{n\bar{p}(1-\bar{p})}$$

- Sample size must be constant.
- Process capability is defined as the central line $(n\bar{p})$ when the process is operating in control.

Defects (Unit Can Have Multiple Problems)

c Control Chart *(Number of Defects)*

$$c = \text{number of defects}$$

$$\bar{c} = \frac{\text{total number of defects } (c)}{\text{total number of sample groups } (k)}$$

$$\text{UCL}_c = \bar{c} + 3\sqrt{\bar{c}}$$

$$\text{LCL}_c = \bar{c} - 3\sqrt{\bar{c}}$$

- Sample size must be constant.
- Process capability is defined as the central line $(\bar{c})$ when the process is operating in control.

u Control Chart *(Average Number of Defects)*

$$u = \frac{\text{number of defects } (c)}{\text{number of samples } (n)}$$

$$\bar{u} = \frac{\text{total number of defects } (\Sigma c)}{\text{total number of samples inspected } (\Sigma n)}$$

$$\text{UCL}_u = \bar{u} + 3\sqrt{\frac{\bar{u}}{n}}$$

$$\text{LCL}_u = \bar{u} - 3\sqrt{\frac{\bar{u}}{n}}$$

- Sample size must be constant.
- Process capability is defined as the central line $(\bar{u})$ when the process is operating in control.

VARIABLES CONTROL CHART (X̄ & R)

PART NAME (PRODUCT): MOTOR SHAFT	PART NO. 999776
OPERATION (PROCESS): OUTSIDE DIAMETER	CHART NO. 1
	SPECIFICATION LIMITS .910" – .930"
OPERATOR: S. SMITH	
MACHINE: SHAFT GRINDER #0823	UNIT OF MEASURE .0001"
GAGE: AIR GAGE	ZERO EQUALS N/A

DATE: 12/1, 12/2, 12/3, 12/4

TIME	7:00	8:10	9:20	10:30	11:40	12:50	1:00	2:10	7:10	8:20	9:30	10:40	11:50	12:00	1:10	2:20	7:20	8:30	9:46	10:50	11:00	12:10	1:20	2:30	7:30
1	.920	.918	.918	.924	.919	.920	.920	.924	.915	.915	.920	.919	.918	.915	.919	.915	.915	.917	.925	.927	.923	.920	.914	.918	.926
2	.921	.919	.920	.921	.920	.921	.922	.920	.920	.916	.919	.912	.920	.913	.920	.916	.925	.918	.920	.924	.922	.923	.910	.920	.924
3	.922	.920	.922	.919	.919	.921	.920	.921	.918	.913	.923	.913	.918	.910	.915	.920	.924	.920	.919	.922	.922	.921	.915	.926	.913
4	.921	.919	.920	.920	.918	.922	.918	.922	.920	.914	.916	.915	.916	.912	.911	.921	.928	.921	.915	.920	.225	.923	.920	.930	.918
5																									
SUM	3.684	3.676	3.680	3.684	3.676	3.684	3.680	3.687																	
AVERAGE, X̄	.921	.919	.920	.921	.919	.921	.920	.922																	
RANGE, R	.002	.002	.004	.005	.002	.002	.004	.004																	
NOTES																									

AVERAGES scale: .930, .925, .920, .915, .910

RANGES scale: .015, .010, .005

CALCULATION WORK SHEET

CONTROL LIMITS

SUBGROUPS
INCLUDED _____   _____

$\bar{\bar{R}} = \dfrac{\Sigma R}{k}$ = _____ = _____ =

$\bar{\bar{X}} = \dfrac{\Sigma \bar{X}}{k}$ = _____ = _____ =

OR

$\bar{X}'$ (MIDSPEC. OR STD.) = _____ =

$A_2\bar{R}$ =   x   = _____   x   = _____

$UCL_{\bar{X}} = \bar{\bar{X}} + A_2\bar{R}$ =   =

$LCL_{\bar{X}} = \bar{\bar{X}} - A_2\bar{R}$ =   =

$UCL_R = D_4\bar{R}$ =   x   =   x   =

LIMITS FOR INDIVIDUALS

COMPARE WITH SPECIFICATION OR
TOLERANCE LIMITS

$\bar{\bar{X}}$ =

$\dfrac{3}{d_2}\bar{R}$ =   x   = _____

$UL_x = \bar{\bar{X}} + \dfrac{3}{d_2}\bar{R}$ =

$LL_x = \bar{\bar{X}} - \dfrac{3}{d_2}\bar{R}$ =

US =

LS = _____

$US - LS$ =

$6\sigma = \dfrac{6}{d_2}\bar{R}$ =

MODIFIED CONTROL LIMITS FOR AVERAGES

BASED ON SPECIFICATION LIMITS AND PROCESS CAPABILITY.
APPLICABLE ONLY IF: $US - LS > 6\sigma$.

US = LS =

$A_M\bar{R}$ =   x   = _____ $A_M\bar{R}$ = _____

$URL_{\bar{X}} = US - A_M\bar{R}$ = $LRL_{\bar{X}} = LS + A_M\bar{R}$ =

FACTORS FOR CONTROL LIMITS

n	A_2	D_4	d_2	$\dfrac{3}{d_2}$	A_M
2	1.880	3.268	1.128	2.659	0.779
3	1.023	2.574	1.693	1.772	0.749
4	0.729	2.282	2.059	1.457	0.728
5	0.577	2.114	2.326	1.290	0.713
6	0.483	2.004	2.534	1.184	0.701

VARIABLES CONTROL CHART (X̄ & R)

PART NAME (PRODUCT)	MOTOR SHAFT		
OPERATION (PROCESS)	OUTSIDE DIAMETER		
PART NO.	999776		
SPECIFICATION LIMITS	.910" – .930"		
CHART NO.	1		
OPERATOR	S. SMITH #0823		
MACHINE	SHAFT GRINDER		
GAGE	AIR GAGE		
UNIT OF MEASURE	.0001"		
ZERO EQUALS	N/A		

DATE	12/1								12/2								12/3								12/4
TIME	7:00	8:10	9:20	10:30	11:40	12:50	1:00	2:10	7:10	8:20	9:30	10:40	11:50	12:00	1:10	2:20	7:20	8:30	9:40	10:50	11:00	12:10	1:20	2:30	7:30
Sample 1	.920	.918	.913	.924	.919	.920	.920	.924	.915	.912	.920	.919	.918	.915	.919	.915	.915	.917	.925	.927	.923	.920	.914	.918	.918
Sample 2	.921	.919	.920	.921	.920	.921	.922	.920	.920	.915	.919	.912	.920	.913	.920	.916	.925	.918	.920	.924	.922	.923	.910	.920	.926
Sample 3	.922	.920	.922	.919	.919	.921	.920	.918	.918	.913	.923	.918	.918	.910	.915	.920	.926	.920	.919	.922	.922	.921	.915	.926	.913
Sample 4	.921	.919	.920	.920	.918	.922	.918	.922	.920	.914	.916	.916	.916	.912	.911	.921	.928	.921	.915	.920	.925	.923	.910	.930	.918
Sample 5																									
SUM	3.694	3.676	3.680	3.684	3.676	3.684	3.680	3.687																	
AVERAGE, X̄	.921	.919	.920	.921	.919	.921	.920	.922																	
RANGE, R	.002	.002	.005	.004	.002	.002	.004	.004																	
NOTES																									

AVERAGES

.930
.925
.920
.915
.910

RANGES

.015
.010
.005

CALCULATION WORK SHEET

CONTROL LIMITS

SUBGROUPS
INCLUDED _____   _____

$\bar{R} = \dfrac{\Sigma R}{k} =$ _____ = _____ =

$\bar{\bar{X}} = \dfrac{\Sigma \bar{X}}{k} =$ _____ = _____ =

OR

$\bar{X}'$ (MIDSPEC. OR STD.) = _____ = _____

$A_2\bar{R} =$ ____ x ____ = _____ x = _____

$UCL_{\bar{X}} = \bar{\bar{X}} + A_2\bar{R} =$ _____ = _____

$LCL_{\bar{X}} = \bar{\bar{X}} - A_2\bar{R} =$ _____ = _____

$UCL_R = D_4\bar{R} =$ ____ x ____ = ____ x ____ =

LIMITS FOR INDIVIDUALS

COMPARE WITH SPECIFICATION OR
TOLERANCE LIMITS

$\bar{\bar{X}}$ = _____

$\dfrac{3}{d_2}\bar{R} =$ ____ x ____ = _____

$UL_x = \bar{\bar{X}} + \dfrac{3}{d_2}\bar{R} =$ _____

$LL_x = \bar{\bar{X}} - \dfrac{3}{d_2}\bar{R} =$ _____

US = _____

LS = _____

US − LS = _____

$6\sigma = \dfrac{6}{d_2}\bar{R} =$ _____

MODIFIED CONTROL LIMITS FOR AVERAGES

BASED ON SPECIFICATION LIMITS AND PROCESS CAPABILITY.
APPLICABLE ONLY IF: US − LS > 6σ.

US = _____   LS = _____

$A_M\bar{R} =$ ____ x ____ = _____ $A_M\bar{R} =$ _____ = _____

$URL_{\bar{X}} = US - A_M\bar{R} =$ _____ $LRL_{\bar{X}} = LS + A_M\bar{R} =$ _____

FACTORS FOR CONTROL LIMITS

n	A_2	D_4	d_2	$\dfrac{3}{d_2}$	A_M
2	1.880	3.268	1.128	2.659	0.779
3	1.023	2.574	1.693	1.772	0.749
4	0.729	2.282	2.059	1.457	0.728
5	0.577	2.114	2.326	1.290	0.713
6	0.483	2.004	2.534	1.184	0.701

VARIABLES CONTROL CHART (X̄ & R)

PART NAME (PRODUCT)	OPERATION (PROCESS)		PART NO. 999776	CHART NO. 1
MOTOR SHAFT	OUTSIDE DIAMETER		SPECIFICATION LIMITS .910" – .930"	
OPERATOR S. SMITH	MACHINE #0823 SHAFT GRINDER	GAGE AIR GAGE	UNIT OF MEASURE .0001"	ZERO EQUALS N/A

TIME	S1	S2	S3	S4	S5	SUM	AVERAGE X̄	RANGE R
12/1								
7:00	.920	.921	.922	.921		3.694	.921	.002
8:10	.918	.919	.920	.919		3.676	.919	.002
9:20	.918	.920	.922	.920		3.680	.920	.004
10:30	.924	.921	.919	.920		3.684	.921	.005
11:40	.919	.920	.919	.918		3.676	.919	.002
12:50	.920	.921	.921	.922		3.684	.921	.002
1:00	.920	.922	.920	.918		3.680	.920	.004
2:10	.924	.920	.921	.922		3.687	.922	.004
12/2								
7:10	.915	.920	.918	.920				
8:20	.912	.915	.913	.914				
9:30	.920	.919	.923	.916				
10:40	.919	.912	.913	.915				
11:50	.918	.920	.913	.916				
12:00	.915	.913	.910	.912				
1:10	.919	.920	.915	.911				
2:20	.915	.916	.926	.921				
12/3								
7:20	.915	.925	.926	.928				
8:30	.917	.918	.920	.921				
9:40	.925	.920	.919	.915				
10:50	.927	.924	.922	.920				
11:00	.923	.922	.922	.925				
12:10	.920	.923	.921	.923				
1:20	.914	.910	.915	.920				
2:30	.918	.918	.926	.930				
12/4								
7:30	.926	.224	.913	.918				

NOTES:

AVERAGES: .930 .925 .920 .915 .910

RANGES: .015 .010 .005

CALCULATION WORK SHEET

CONTROL LIMITS

SUBGROUPS
INCLUDED _____   _____

$\bar{R} = \dfrac{\Sigma R}{k} =$ _____ = _____   _____ = _____

$\bar{\bar{X}} = \dfrac{\Sigma \bar{X}}{k} =$ _____ = _____   _____ = _____

OR

$\bar{X}'$ (MIDSPEC. OR STD.) = _____   = _____

$A_2\bar{R} =$ _____ x _____ = _____   x _____ = _____

$UCL_{\bar{X}} = \bar{\bar{X}} + A_2\bar{R} =$ _____   = _____

$LCL_{\bar{X}} = \bar{\bar{X}} - A_2\bar{R} =$ _____   = _____

$UCL_R = D_4\bar{R} =$ _____ x _____ = _____   x _____ = _____

LIMITS FOR INDIVIDUALS

COMPARE WITH SPECIFICATION OR
TOLERANCE LIMITS

$\bar{\bar{X}}$ = _____

$\dfrac{3}{d_2}\bar{R} =$ _____ x _____ = _____

$UL_x = \bar{\bar{X}} + \dfrac{3}{d_2}\bar{R} =$ _____

$LL_x = \bar{\bar{X}} - \dfrac{3}{d_2}\bar{R} =$ _____

US = _____

LS = _____

$US - LS$ = _____

$6\sigma = \dfrac{6}{d_2}\bar{R} =$ _____

MODIFIED CONTROL LIMITS FOR AVERAGES

BASED ON SPECIFICATION LIMITS AND PROCESS CAPABILITY.
APPLICABLE ONLY IF: $US - LS > 6\sigma$.

US = _____ LS = _____

$A_M\bar{R} =$ _____ x _____ = _____ $A_M\bar{R}$ = _____

$URL_{\bar{X}} = US - A_M\bar{R} =$ _____ $LRL_{\bar{X}} = LS + A_M\bar{R} =$ _____

FACTORS FOR CONTROL LIMITS

n	A_2	D_4	d_2	$\dfrac{3}{d_2}$	A_M
2	1.880	3.268	1.128	2.659	0.779
3	1.023	2.574	1.693	1.772	0.749
4	0.729	2.282	2.059	1.457	0.728
5	0.577	2.114	2.326	1.290	0.713
6	0.483	2.004	2.534	1.184	0.701

Index